How Border Peripheries are Changing
the Nature of Arab States

Maha Yahya
Editor

How Border Peripheries are Changing the Nature of Arab States

palgrave
macmillan

Editor
Maha Yahya
Malcolm H. Kerr Carnegie Middle East Center
Beirut, Lebanon

ISBN 978-3-031-09186-5   ISBN 978-3-031-09187-2 (eBook)
https://doi.org/10.1007/978-3-031-09187-2

© The Editor(s) (if applicable) and The Author(s), under exclusive licence to Springer Nature Switzerland AG 2023
This work is subject to copyright. All rights are solely and exclusively licensed by the Publisher, whether the whole or part of the material is concerned, specifically the rights of translation, reprinting, reuse of illustrations, recitation, broadcasting, reproduction on microfilms or in any other physical way, and transmission or information storage and retrieval, electronic adaptation, computer software, or by similar or dissimilar methodology now known or hereafter developed.
The use of general descriptive names, registered names, trademarks, service marks, etc. in this publication does not imply, even in the absence of a specific statement, that such names are exempt from the relevant protective laws and regulations and therefore free for general use.
The publisher, the authors, and the editors are safe to assume that the advice and information in this book are believed to be true and accurate at the date of publication. Neither the publisher nor the authors or the editors give a warranty, expressed or implied, with respect to the material contained herein or for any errors or omissions that may have been made. The publisher remains neutral with regard to jurisdictional claims in published maps and institutional affiliations.

This Palgrave Macmillan imprint is published by the registered company Springer Nature Switzerland AG.
The registered company address is: Gewerbestrasse 11, 6330 Cham, Switzerland

To those living in the peripheries who aspire to a better future.

ACKNOWLEDGMENTS

This book has been in the making for the past two years in the most challenging of circumstances. It is a product of work undertaken by scholars of the Malcolm H. Kerr Carnegie Middle East Center, who had to contend with questions of safety and security in the context of regional conflicts as well as a global pandemic that brought the world to a standstill. While initial fieldwork was conducted physically, we had to adjust to new realities as travel on field visits as well as in-person meetings and interviews, usually the precondition of any fieldwork, became impossible. As our lives became virtual, researchers devised innovative approaches to gaining access to the information needed for their analysis. In-person interviews took place online, while field research was facilitated through a network of local researchers based in the areas under study, without whom this book would not have been possible. Jameel Barakat supported the work on Iraq, while the rest of the local researchers in Algeria, Tunisia, Syria, and Yemen have asked to remain anonymous out of concern for their own safety.

The writing of this book would not have been possible without generous funding from the Carnegie Corporation of New York (CCNY) and the unwavering support of Hillary Wiesner and Nehal Amer. The initial idea for the book came from a project that the Malcolm H. Kerr Carnegie Middle East Center is undertaking on cross-border conflicts in the Middle East and North Africa, Asia, and Africa, in partnership with the Asia Foundation and the Rift Valley Institute, and with the support of the United Kingdom Foreign, Commonwealth and Development Office (UKFCDO).

vii

viii ACKNOWLEDGMENTS

I also owe an enormous debt of gratitude to my colleagues at the Malcolm H. Kerr Carnegie Middle East Center, beginning with fellow scholars who carried out fieldwork in extremely difficult environments and who came together consistently to discuss research challenges and findings. Senior Editor Michael Young did invaluable work on the chapters and steered us brilliantly to this final product. Editorial Consultant Rayyan Al-Shawaf also provided significant support in the process. Mohanad Hage Ali, Senior Fellow and Communications Director, and Marianne Sarkis, our Program Manager, supported the process and helped keep the book on track. Issam Kayssi, Nada Ahmed, Lina Dernaika, and Mustapha Al-Aweek were indispensable to us all in our research.

Most importantly, I would like to thank the many people who agreed to be interviewed, including local officials, activists, and residents of the peripheries discussed in the book, many of whom asked to remain anonymous for fear of reprisals. To them we own an incalculable debt of gratitude.

CONTENTS

1   Introduction   1
Maha Yahya

2   Smuggling and State Formation: A Match Made in Algeria   17
Dalia Ghanem

3   Cronies and Contraband: Why Integrating Tunisia's
Informal Economic Elite Has Become Necessary   39
Hamza Meddeb

4   North Pacific: Why Lebanon's Akkar Region Weathered
the Syrian Conflict   63
Maha Yahya and Mohanad Hage Ali

5   Transnationalization of a Borderland: Center, Periphery,
and Identity in Western Iraq   85
Harith Hasan

6   How Syria's War Extended Border Policies to Much of the
Country   105
Kheder Khaddour and Kevin Mazur

x CONTENTS

7 Hadramawt's Emergence as a Center: A Confluence of
Yemeni Circumstances and Hadrami Resourcefulness   131
Ahmed Nagi

8 The Center Gives: Southern Syria and the Rise of New
Peripheral Powerbrokers   159
Armenak Tokmajyan

9 On the Edge: How Risks from Iraq Have Helped Form
Kuwaiti Identity   185
Bader Al-Saif

Index   213

Notes on Contributors

Mohanad Hage Ali is a senior fellow and the director of communications at the Malcolm H. Kerr Carnegie Middle East Center. At Carnegie, his work focuses mainly on militant Islam and the emerging regional powers in the Levant. He has published a book titled *Nationalism, Transnationalism and Political Islam: Hizbullah's Institutional Identity* (Palgrave, 2017), and co-edited *A Restless Revival: Political Islam After the 2011 Uprisings* (2021).

Bader Al-Saif is Assistant Professor of History at Kuwait University, where his research focuses on the Gulf and Arabian Peninsula. Al-Saif is also a nonresident fellow at the Arab Gulf States Institute in Washington and a former nonresident fellow at the Malcolm H. Kerr Carnegie Middle East Center in Beirut. His most recent publications include *Along the Kuwaiti-Saudi Border, Stability Is Built on Flexibility* (2021).

Dalia Ghanem is a former resident scholar at the Malcolm H. Kerr Carnegie Middle East Center in Beirut. Her research focuses on Algeria's political, economic, social, and security developments as well as radicalization, civil-military relationships, and gender. Ghanem is the author of an upcoming book entitled *Understanding the Persistence of Competitive Authoritarianism in Algeria*. Ghanem is now a senior analyst in charge of the Middle East and North Africa portfolio at the European Union Institute for Security Studies (EUISS) in Paris.

Harith Hasan is a nonresident senior fellow at the Malcolm H. Kerr Carnegie Middle East Center, where his research focuses on Iraq,

xi

sectarianism, identity politics, religious actors, and state-society relations. He is the author of *Eden Denied: Environmental Decay, Illicit Activities, and Instability in Iraq's Southern Border Area* (2022) and *The Making of the Kurdish Frontier: Power, Conflict, and Governance in the Iraqi-Syrian Borderlands* (2021, with Kheder Khaddour).

Kheder Khaddour is a nonresident scholar at the Malcolm H. Kerr Carnegie Middle East Center in Beirut. His research centers on civil-military relations and local identities in the Levant, with a focus on Syria. He is the author of *Border Nation: The Reshaping of the Syrian-Turkish Borderlands* (2022 with Armenak Tokmajyan) and *The Making of the Kurdish Frontier: Power, Conflict, and Governance in the Iraqi-Syrian Borderlands* (2021, with Harith Hassan).

Kevin Mazur Kevin Mazur is a lecturer at Northwestern University. He is the author of *Revolution in Syria: Identity, Networks, and Repression* (2021).

Hamza Meddeb is a nonresident scholar at the Malcolm H. Kerr Carnegie Middle East Center, where his research focuses on economic reform, political economy of conflicts, and border insecurity across the Middle East and North Africa. He is the author of *The Hidden Face of Informal Cross-border Trade in Tunisia After 2011* (2021) and *The Volatile Tunisia-Libya Border: Between Tunisia's Security Policy and Libya's Militia Factions* (2020).

Ahmed Nagi is a nonresident scholar at the Malcolm H. Kerr Carnegie Middle East Center in Beirut, where his research centers on Yemen and the Gulf states. Nagi is also a country coordinator on Yemen at Varieties of Democracy Institute (V-Dem), Sweden, and co-founder of Insight Source Center for Research and Consulting, Yemen. He is the author of numerous publications on Yemen, the most recent of which are *The Barriers to Southern Yemeni Political Aspirations Are Mainly in the South* (2022) and *Yemeni Border Markets: From Economic Incubator to Military Frontline* (2021).

Armenak Tokmajyan is a nonresident scholar at the Malcolm H. Kerr Carnegie Middle East Center in Beirut. His research focuses on borders and conflict, Syrian refugees, and state-society relations in Syria. Before joining Carnegie, Tokmajyan worked as a research fellow at International Crisis Group, focusing mainly on Syrian refugees in Lebanon and patterns of displacement inside Syria. His most recent publications include *Border Nation: The Reshaping of the Syrian-Turkish Borderlands* (with Kheder Khaddour, 2022) and *How Southern Syria Has Been Transformed into a Regional Powder Keg* (2020).

Maha Yahya is the director of the Malcolm H. Kerr Carnegie Middle East Center, where her work focuses broadly on regional polarization and power struggles, political violence and identity politics, pluralism, social justice, and the political and socio-economic implications of the migration/refugee crisis. She has numerous publications the most recent of which are three co-edited volumes: *A Restless Revival: Political Islam After the 2011 Uprisings* (2021); *Contentious Politics in the Syrian Conflict: Opposition, Representation, and Resistance* (2020); and *Unheard Voices: What Syrian Refugees Need to Return Home* (2018).

ABBREVIATIONS

AQAP	Al-Qaeda in the Arabian Peninsula
AQIM	Al Qaeda in the Islamic Maghreb
ERC Equipose (ERCE)	Energy Resource Consultants Ltd (ERC) and Equipoise Solutions Ltd (Equipoise)
FLN	National Liberation Front
GCC	Gulf Cooperation Council
GSPC	Salafi Group for Preaching and Combat
HEF	Hadrami Elite Forces
HTA	Hadramawt Tribes Alliance
IMF	International Monetary Fund
IRGC	Islamic Revolutionary Guard Corps
KDP	Kurdistan Democratic Party
KRG	Kurdistan Regional Government
MOC	Military Operations Center
MOU	Memorandum of Understanding
NDC	National Dialogue Conference
NDF	National Defense Forces
NLF	National Liberation Front
OPEC	Organization of the Petroleum Exporting Countries
PDRY	People's Democratic Republic of Yemen
PFLOAG	Popular Front for the Liberation of the Arabian Gulf
PKK	Kurdistan Workers' Party
PMF	Popular Mobilization Forces
SDF	Syrian Democratic Forces
SSNP	Syrian Social Nationalist Party

STC Southern Transitional Council
UAE United Arab Emirates
UN   United Nations
YBS Sinjar Resistance Units

LIST OF MAPS

Map 2.1	Points of discharge along the Algerian-Tunisian border	25
Map 3.1	The Tunisian-Libyan border	47
Map 4.1	Lebanon's northern border region	65
Map 5.1	General overview of the Iraqi-Syrian border	88
Map 6.1	General map of Syria	108
Map 6.2	Damascus and its environs	111
Map 7.1	NDC map of a proposed federal Yemen	134
Map 7.2	Hadramawt governorate map	141
Map 9.1	Kuwait and Iraq's shared waterway	191

CHAPTER 1

Introduction

Maha Yahya

In 2014, Islamic State fighters stationed at a border crossing between Iraq and Syria declared the end of the Sykes-Picot agreement of 1916, which had defined spheres of influence in the Levant, primarily between Britain and France.[1] It was lost on the fighters that the agreement never drew specific borders. In popular Arab and international interpretations of Sykes-Picot, the agreement divided the Arab world, and the Muslim community, into multiple, unnatural entities.[2] By declaring the end of Sykes-Picot, the Islamic State was positioning itself as a force that was reuniting the region under the banner of Islam—symbolism that could resonate with many across the Arab world.

What was as interesting was where the declaration took place, namely, on a boundary that had once been among the most policed in the region. That both Syria and Iraq had lost control of their border regions only illustrated the seismic transformations that the region has undergone in the last two decades, especially after the invasion of Iraq in 2003 and the Arab uprisings starting in 2011. And while the Islamic State was ultimately repelled, the governance and socioeconomic challenges of the centralized

---

M. Yahya (✉)
Malcolm H. Kerr Carnegie Middle East Center, Beirut, Lebanon
e-mail: myahya@carnegie-mec.org

© The Author(s), under exclusive license to Springer Nature Switzerland AG 2023
M. Yahya (ed.), *How Border Peripheries are Changing the Nature of Arab States*, https://doi.org/10.1007/978-3-031-09187-2_1

1

states of the Middle East and North Africa persist and are often best revealed in their border areas.

To understand where many of these countries stand today, one has only to look at their peripheries. These are places where the sovereignty and authority of states is being transformed, the political legitimacy of their ruling elites are being questioned, and economic orders are being reshaped. However, alongside the elements of change, there is also continuity across the region, which include the durability of states, and even of regimes, and their borders. As Louise Fawcett has written, while state sovereignty is being contested at multiple levels throughout the region, "continuity-state (even regime) survival and border preservation—is likely to prevail over major change."[3]

Consolidating the Center

As elsewhere, Middle Eastern and North African states are the product of multiple dynamics at the subnational, national, regional, and global levels. The impact of colonialism, for example, has varied among countries in quite significant ways. However, colonialism did contribute to creating "incomplete, distorted versions of European modern states," which were then "shaped and reshaped by indigenous elites as they sought to transform and control the societies they came to govern."[4]

After independence, most states in the Middle East and North Africa tended to focus on developing their capitals and surrounding areas as the locus of state power. Whether it is Lebanon, Tunisia, Syria, Kuwait, Yemen, or Iraq, the consolidation of authority in the new states was accompanied by the subordination of peripheral regions to the interests of the center and its political and economic elites.[5] Regions that had once been well integrated into regional networks of trade and exchange suddenly found themselves on the margins of modern states, their communications lines cut off by new national borders.

As Arab states developed, their leaders came to govern through increasingly despotic methods. As Robert Springborg has argued, republics, and to a lesser degree monarchies, put in place "deep states" that undermined governmental institutions upon which effective governance and rule of law rested. Instead, they expanded their security apparatus and revamped educational systems in keeping with their respective ideologies and privileged repression and patronage at the expense of inclusive economic development.[6]

In parallel, they also developed what institutional economists led by Douglass North have termed "limited access orders," in which political and economic elites appropriated for themselves privileged control over their economies, and the rents accruing from them, barring access to outsiders.[7] The political and economic repercussions of such orders included the curtailing of citizens' rights and the increasing dependence of the elites on protection by institutions of the deep states—militaries, security services, and sometimes judicial systems.

Over time, independent Arab states came to be characterized by what the Egyptian scholar Nazih N. Ayubi has called the qualities of a "fierce state," combining an ability to provide services and employment with the coercive capacities to protect themselves.[8] Simultaneously, such states were relatively weak in lacking both the ideological means to impose their legitimacy and the capacity to penetrate society through taxation, which would have ultimately led to demands for representation.[9] This made for states that were overdeveloped in some areas and underdeveloped in others.

The way these "fierce" states engaged with their border peripheries has varied across the Arab world. Newly independent states often sought to extend their reach to all their citizens and integrate their territories by expanding infrastructure, legislation, and development projects to national peripheries. Across much of the region, borders became tools in state centralization campaigns, allowing regimes to better control societies.[10] Border functions, whether economic, military, or even societal, came under the strict authority of central and highly securitized states. The inability or unwillingness of states to sustain such a process, or to apply this approach uniformly to all border areas, resulted in imbalances. While some border areas thrived, others suffered from systematic neglect, stagnation, and impoverishment. Consequently, certain border regions became unmoored from the center, with their inhabitants, if or when possible, seeking goods and services in neighboring countries. Many inhabitants of Lebanon's northern Akkar region, for instance, maintained crossborder ties with Syria prior to the conflict there, where they took advantage of education and health services and from where they purchased cheaper Syrian goods. Similar dynamics have been evident on the Algerian-Tunisian border.[11]

These "fierce states" were also highly opportunistic, in the sense that some of them tolerated informal and illicit economic activities by border populations as a means of reducing the financial burden on the center. These activities were often closely monitored by the security forces and indeed became sources of rent for these forces. In turn, such rents also helped guarantee their loyalty to the regimes in place.

This inconsistency in the treatment of border areas was often shaped by the center's perceptions of threat. Borders considered vulnerable could be highly securitized, with a concomitant negative impact on social and economic development. Notable examples of this are the Arabization policies of Saddam Hussein of Iraq and Hafez al-Assad of Syria. Both worked to depopulate and Arabize parts of their borders inhabited by their Kurdish populations, in order to stymie projects aimed at unifying the Kurds. Similarly, Egypt adopted a highly securitized approach to Nubian inhabitants of border areas with Sudan, who were displaced and closely monitored by the security apparatus. Other countries, in contrast, came to regard the development of border regions as a dimension of enhanced border security. Kuwait adopted such an approach after the Iraqi invasion, during which it initiated housing and other projects as a means of asserting its authority in these regions.

Governance Failures and Alternate Centers of Authority

The onset of the Arab uprisings in 2011 complicated many of these preexisting dynamics. The popular demonstrations, which began as domestic expressions of discontent that in several countries led to the toppling of longstanding autocrats, unleashed regional and international dynamics that are still being felt today. Armed conflicts that erupted in several Arab states, among them Syria, Libya, and Yemen, provoked regional and international foreign interventions and have drawn in a broad range of nonstate and transnational actors. Yet the fundamental socioeconomic and political triggers of discontent that led to the uprisings have not been addressed. In fact, bad governance, polarization, and conflict, followed by the ripple effects of containment measures related to the COVID-19 pandemic, have made conditions worse throughout the region. This has been accompanied by a drastic rollback in development gains—education, health, and so on—in addition to mass population displacements and new refugee flows in the region, to Europe and beyond. The situation has been exacerbated most recently by the impact of the Ukraine conflict on economies and food security. The impact of these dynamics will likely last for generations with significant implications for state authority and local governance capacities.

Today, across the region, state authority is being challenged in multiple border areas, to the detriment of the central state. New self-governing entities have emerged beyond the purview of capitals, such as Rojava, the de facto autonomous Kurdish-controlled region in northern Syria. More fragmented makeups have also come into being, as in Libya, where one government nominally controls the west of the country, another the east, and individual cities retain significant autonomy, even controlling border crossings. A similar process is also unfolding in Yemen. At the same time, despite periods of increased securitization, border areas in other Arab states have become more porous, such as the borders between Syria and Iraq or Algeria and Tunisia, with increasing crossborder movements of goods and people.

The jury is still out on the impact of the erosion of central state structures throughout the Arab world. While such changes are transforming governance modalities across the region, it remains to be seen whether they will lead to a reconfiguration of states and borders. Such dynamics could further embolden ethnic groups in their search for autonomy or independence. They could generate more robust local governance mechanisms away from the reach of the central state. And they could invite even greater regional or international intervention to fill the vacuums that are being created. For now, what is evident is that states have been seriously weakened by internal challenges and external interventions and remain unable to exert full control over their territory and borders. External interventions have put much greater pressure on border areas, further eating away at the ability of states to control all their territory. However, it is noticeable that this has not resulted in significant changes to national boundaries, even in countries where conflicts continue.

The limited reach, or breakdown, of central authority in the border regions of many states has led to recurring outcomes. These include the emergence or expansion of illicit networks of exchange; the rise of new nonstate actors in border regions, including paramilitary or jihadi groups; political voids that have led to foreign intervention; the growth of transnational networks; and greater border porosity allowing for an easier circulation of migrants, combatants, arms, and trafficked goods. These developments point to an increasing disconnect between what Robert Jackson and Carl Rosberg have termed juridical and empirical statehood. The former refers to the internationally recognized legal sovereignty of the state, while the latter references a state's ability to monopolize the use of force and exert sovereignty over its territory.[12] Even as international recognition of states in the Middle East and North Africa within their juridical boundaries has not really changed, empirically the capacity of many of these states to assert their authority at home has been greatly diminished.

More critically, these dynamics suggest that borders do not alone define or demarcate a state's sovereignty. Domestic sovereignty, which relates to social, economic, and security realities in border regions, often fluctuates based on political conditions at given moments of time, as well as on historical trajectories of specific areas. The rise of the Islamic State in Iraq's western border regions, which was mainly a consequence of the marginalization of these regions by successive Iraqi governments after the US invasion in 2003, itself a result of sectarian rivalries and the collapse of the neighboring Syrian state starting in 2011, is one example of this. History, geography, and politics all affect the extent to which states exert control over their territories and the various degrees of border porosity.

Challenges to empirical sovereignty also mean that various border functions of the state are becoming systematically delinked. Once closely connected, functions such as maintaining territorial sovereignty and controlling the flow of goods and people across national boundaries have become subject to a changing array of nonstate actors in these areas, many of them tied to foreign countries, rather than to the policies of their central government. Basically, subnational and transnational spaces that have often existed in border regions of the Middle East and North Africa are now being impacted to a greater degree by dynamics unrelated to center-periphery relations in these states. They are also leading to the emergence of new modalities of border control and management.

Collectively, the essays in this volume examine the multiple dimensions of such processes. They address both continuity and change which have been observable in conflict-stricken countries, such as Syria, Iraq, and Yemen, or in fragile political or economic contexts, such as in Lebanon, Tunisia, and Algeria, as well as stable monarchies like Kuwait. The chapters seek to transcend the preoccupation of modernization theory with the impact of the center on peripheries while ignoring the impact of peripheries on the center. Rather, what we posit here is that transformations at the center can often be understood by looking at power struggles and the organization of society on the peripheries of nations. The book also presents an alternate perspective on how societies in peripheral zones are coping with, and adjusting to, the momentous changes affecting state systems. Their coping mechanisms include the emergence of political, regulatory, and economic practices that are reconstituting the Arab state today as an entity characterized by increasing hybridity between state and nonstate actors, legal and illegal activity, and an inordinate mix of order and disorder.

Unpacking these realities is critical for our understanding of how governance systems and societal dynamics are changing. First, it raises questions as to whether the current instrumentalization of borders across much of the Middle East and North Africa, represents a complete turning point for the region or is simply a critical juncture in changing conceptualizations of statehood and of sovereignty. In the case of the latter, it is clear that while distinct aspects of sovereignty are being challenged (such as domestic sovereignty), the sovereignty of all states in question continues to be recognized internationally.

Second, it questions whether the state should be the primary analytical entry point for the study of governance. Or rather, should we consider the persistence and expansion of informality in the hybrid political orders that are emerging as a far more definitive feature of future governance in the region and for understanding the relational dynamics between centers and their peripheries? If so, this creates problems for interpretations of the state that are focused on the center and calls into question dominant approaches in international relations that tend to consider the Middle East and North Africa mainly from the perspective of functional or failed states. From this perspective, the relationship of the state to nonstate actors is presumed to be quite nuanced, in that the state has often coopted such actors and outsourced a variety of functions to them, whether for social or security-related reasons.

And third, when it comes to the socioeconomic repercussions, the chapters in this volume raise implicit questions as to whether what we are witnessing today in terms of the transformation of border areas will lead to greater fragmentation and dislocation or whether they are passing phenomena characteristic of current challenges.

These questions have not been fully addressed in the literature on border studies in the region. The field of border studies is characterized by multiple disciplines and frameworks that seek to capture specific aspects of border dynamics and their broader political or socioeconomic relevance.[13] The range of perspectives cover securitization and territorial demarcation, the historical and sociocultural contexts of border areas, the emergence of

8   M. YAHYA

separatist movements, and connections between territory, boundaries, and identity. Some have also focused on the shifting perceptions of borders and their institutionalization in a context of nation building. For countries of the Middle East and North Africa, the volume on Contentious borders by Rafaella A. Del Sarto, Louise Fawcett, and Asli A. Okyay represents the first attempt at exploring challenges to borders in the Middle East and North Africa following the 2011 uprisings. Articles in this edition challenge assumptions about the artificiality of MENA country borders and attempt to situate changes in the context of wide-ranging political and socioeconomic transformations.

The case studies covered in this volume present a broad spectrum of border challenges evident in the region today and go somewhat beyond the issues raised in previous works on borders. Relying on primary field work in their respective areas, the authors in this collection attempt to assess the implications of border dynamics for the state and the means through which the state has accommodated them. The chapters highlight the complexity of borders, showing them to be realities that transcend mere "lines in the sand." They also examine the multifaceted nature of political contestation and territoriality across the region, as well as the disparate nature and origin of the challenges in border areas, including the historic trajectory of state-society relations. What is also made clear is that while borders have lost some of their functions, they continue to play a critical role in defining local, national, and regional dynamics. Here the concept of limited statehood is useful for assessing the modalities through which restrictions on statehood are addressed and the mechanisms through which hybrid political orders emerge.[14]

WHAT CAN THE STATE ACHIEVE?

In several of the countries covered in this volume, central authorities, whether for reasons of social stability, economic necessity, or political expediency, have accommodated themselves to the realities in border areas, going as far as to accept, and even integrate, illicit networks into governance mechanisms. By allowing their peripheries to detach themselves from the authority of the center, through the involvement of local actors in the crossborder informal economy or smuggling, many states have effectively helped to consolidate new forms of center-periphery relations. These have redefined an understanding of state power and its limits.

At the heart of this redefinition lies a changing concept of what the state can achieve. In their inability or even unwillingness to provide equitable regional development, many Arab states have effectively been unable to fulfill the unwritten social contract that has prevailed domestically since independence. This social contract holds that societies will obey those in power in exchange for an adequate standard of living. But the inability of states to fulfill their end of the bargain has led to a degree of tolerance for informal economic actors and smugglers in border areas, who have come to play valuable social and economic roles that are beyond the state's reach. In short, states have willingly ceded essential functions of statehood to a range of nonstate actors, including service delivery and border management.

Algeria is a case in point. Otherwise characterized by strong central authority, the state has consented to surrendering a measure of its sovereignty by giving wider latitude to informal traders and smugglers on the country's border with Tunisia. As Dalia Ghanem argues in her chapter, the Algerian state has done so because it is aware of its own limitations in preventing such activities from taking place. It also realizes that the revenues generated help underprivileged local communities, thus maintaining social peace. And the Algerian state has normalized this in some ways by enrolling smugglers in its border security efforts.

Such dynamics are also apparent in the power struggles that exist between peripheries and centers, as well as between an older elite embedded in pre-2011 economic structures and a new elite emerging in the context of economic and societal transformations in peripheral areas. In Tunisia, as Hamza Meddeb argues in his chapter, the authorities have also looked the other way on illicit crossborder activity, even as they have hardened their approach to border security. Today Tunisian merchants in marginalized southeastern Tunisia on the border with Libya are suffering from a combination of factors. Their government has reinforced border security, hindering illicit crossborder trafficking that had brought money and cheap products to an impoverished region. At the same time, the rivalries and conflicts among militias on the Libyan side of the border have disrupted Tunisian merchants' trade networks inside Libya. This has raised social tensions in southeastern Tunisia, with the potential for generating more instability. However, even when there has been an opportunity to integrate entrepreneurs of the informal economy into the formal economy, powerful interest groups in the capital blocked the process. This has prevented the renegotiation of center-periphery relations that are more equitable.

In Lebanon's northern region of Akkar, crossborder networks, including smuggling networks, have also affected stability and reactions in the country's capital, Beirut, but in less expected ways. As Mohanad Hage Ali and I show in our chapter, family, tribal, and smuggling networks between Akkar and Syria, combined with a tradition of sectarian coexistence in the region, were major factors contributing to sparing Akkar the sectarian blowback from the Syrian conflict. The pragmatism that such networks engendered helped to neutralize sectarian animosities, even when this was not the case in other parts of Lebanon.

This is not simply about state failure or the incapacity of the state to project its power and assert is authority over its territory. As Robert Rotberg cautions in the context of failed African countries and their consequences for a post-Cold War era, one must consider how states are failing and in what ways. As he argues, geography, history, and politics all affect where and how states fail or their degree of weakness and vulnerability.[15] The case studies in this volume highlight the multiple dynamics affecting states in the region, the integrity of its institutions, and capacities, from the perspective of their peripheries. They emphasize the need to distinguish the de jure characteristics of the state from the de facto characteristics, especially in light of the generalized fragmentation of authority and governance across multiple borders in the region.[16]

As peripheral and border regions have slipped out of the grasp of central state authority, hybrid political, economic, and security arrangements have emerged to fill resulting power vacuums in border areas.[17] Such arrangements have involved local, regional, and international political actors and most often consist of local tribal leaders, militias, smugglers, religious networks, civil society figures, or organizations agreeing with state representatives to provide services and engage in or facilitate economic or security activities. However, hybridity, or the assumption and involvement of nonstate actors in these roles, has entailed a loss of sovereignty—including a monopoly of the instruments of violence and control over the movement of goods and people across national boundaries.

A good example of such hybridity is Iraq's relations with Iran along their common border, particularly its southern portion. In assisting Iraq to recapture territory from the Islamic State group starting in 2014, Iran supported militias belonging to the Popular Mobilization Forces (PMF). These forces helped reimpose the writ of the Iraqi authorities in those parts of its western border controlled by the Islamic State. However, powerful pro-Iranian PMF militias also resisted the Iraqi government's efforts to assert greater state control over the militias' activities, as well as over the eastern border with Iran. This has undermined Baghdad's authority while favoring Tehran's regional political agenda.

In his chapter, Harith Hasan zeroes in on Iraq's western border with Syria. In the past two decades, the strong centralizing policies of the former Iraqi Baath regime, which had shaped social, economic, and cultural identities in that border area, have been replaced by frequent political voids that successive nonstate actors have tried to fill, often by connecting the border regions with alternative centers. Among the actors that have tried doing so are the Kurdistan Workers Party, the Islamic State, and Iraqi paramilitary groups closely allied with Tehran. In time, this has transformed the Iraq-Syria border into an Iranian zone of influence whose future trajectory will be determined by geopolitical and regional dynamics rather than developments inside Iraq.

Such changes have highlighted another dimension of state breakdown in Arab border areas, namely, the integration of these areas into regional political calculations. Throughout the Levant and North Africa, border zones have been instrumentalized and are playing a salient role in regional rivalries. States are exploiting the fragmentation in border areas either to neutralize what they regard as threats to their interests or because they see opportunities to integrate those areas into their political agendas. Iraq's border with Syria has been a key passage point for combatants and weapons that have allowed Iran to consolidate its influence in Syria and Lebanon. Iran and Hezbollah have also tried to use Syria's borderland with Jordan and the boundary with the occupied Golan Heights to put pressure on Israel and Amman. And Turkey's border with Syria has become a vast zone of multinational confrontation in which Turkish, Syrian, Russian, Iranian, and US political and military objectives are playing out.

The hybrid arrangements in these regions also create a paradox. By reflecting state disaggregation and atrophy, such mechanisms also reaffirm the importance of centralized states in holding things together. They highlight the continuity of state institutions and in some cases of regime survival. But even where hybrid orders are not present, the marginalization of border communities may give rise to situations in which border areas are profoundly affected by the policies of neighboring and regional countries.

In states that no longer control their border territories, local communities have come to abide by alternate interpretations of statehood, where what the state may consider objectionable is embraced by locals as necessary for their survival or wellbeing. At the same time, border dynamics, because of their implications for neighboring or regional states, are having a powerful impact on central governments. That is why many borders have ceased to be simply national boundaries, instead becoming demarcation lines between regional and international powers, encompassing wider conflicts. This loss of control over border zones is altering the fundamental characteristics of state authority.

REDEFINING SOVEREIGNTY FROM THE PERIPHERY

The transformation of the concept of sovereignty due to the collapse in state capacity is addressed by several authors in the book, as is its impact on governance. What is clear is that a desire to maintain the integrity of borders remains in place, even as the nature of the state continues to be contested. Kheder Khaddour and Kevin Mazur show how the conflict in Syria has led the Assad regime to double down on efforts to reassert its control over the territories it has lost and the key role of longstanding border policies in this process. This was done by managing former opposition-held areas recaptured by regime forces in much the same way as it used to manage sensitive border areas, through security-focused measures. Governance in Syria is now dominated by the security organs, even in mundane matters, and the recourse to this method of operating owes a great deal to how the regime administered border regions in the past.

Changes in notions of sovereignty have also impacted concepts of centers and peripheries, as well as power dynamics within and between localities. In his chapter, Ahmed Nagi looks at how the conflict in Yemen has modified the perception of state sovereignty in the region of Hadramawt. There, the strong appeal of autonomy within a Yemeni state underlines the extent to which the people of Hadramawt have tended to regard the governorate as a center rather than a periphery. This is based, primarily, on two realities: the fact that Hadramawt enjoyed a semi-independent status for centuries prior to the creation of the state of South Yemen in 1967, into which it was incorporated, and the region's legacy of having long served as a center for surrounding areas.

Similarly, Armenak Tokmajyan, in his chapter on Syria, describes how the Syrian regime's momentary loss of sovereignty over southern Syria has had a major impact on center-periphery relations there. Younger power-brokers who arose during the conflict have replaced the traditional power-brokers who had previously acted as intermediaries with Damascus. Unlike their elders, however, the new powerbrokers are strongly influenced by the politics of regional and international players, many of whom have intervened at various stages in the Syrian crisis. The central authorities have had to adapt their approach to peripheral areas in response to these changing realities, all the while seeking to ultimately reverse the erosion of its power on the ground when it can.

The outliers when it comes to these dynamics are the Gulf states, which are neither fragile nor conflict ridden, and for whom border dynamics have played a central role in defining the nature and identity of their states. Bader Al-Saif, in his chapter, focuses on how the border conflict with Iraq has affected the nature of governance in Kuwait, shaping the country's national identity. After the Iraqi invasion and occupation between August 1990 and February 1991, Kuwait adopted policies to better integrate border regions with Iraq into the Kuwaiti state and guard against what had happened. The country's 2035 national development plan serves as a framework to do so. The ultimate aim, Saif believes, should be to turn the border into a shared zone of opportunity for the two countries.

BACK TO THE FUTURE?

The impact of disarray in the governance of both fragile and conflict-ridden countries of the Middle East and North Africa, especially their border areas, is not transient. Many countries undergoing change are unlikely to soon, if ever, revert to the status quo ante. Greater national fragmentation, significant social and economic dislocation, and the incorporation of local conflicts into regional rivalries mean that onetime peripheries are becoming new centers, as in parts of Syria and Yemen, while some former centers may become regional peripheries. In the latter case, the subordination of Baghdad and Damascus to Iran and its regional ambitions, for example, is already taking place. The reasons why such situations could become permanent are many. They include the weakness of central state institutions throughout the Arab world, which are no longer capable of reintegrating peripheral border regions, given these institutions' dramatically diminished financial and institutional capabilities, the erosion in political legitimacy, and the lack of an effective regional stabilizer to check outside interventions in states of the region. Where this will lead is uncertain, as we are witnessing the birth of a new order still in the making.

Borders are an important new element providing an alternative path to understanding state formation and reformation in the Middle East and North Africa. Today, borders are being continually reconstituted, both as ideas and as physical entities. In that way, they may represent a foretelling of the region's future as the rules of the past are being rewritten.

NOTES

1. Sykes-Picot refers to a secret agreement between Britain and France (as well as Russia) in 1916 to define their zones of influence following the dissolution of the Ottoman Empire after World War I. It was named for its key interlocuters, Mark Sykes and François Georges-Picot. The actual borders were eventually determined by the League of Nations in 1932, following a series of conferences and treaties including the Paris Peace Conference of 1919, the San Remo agreement of 1920, and the Treaty of Sèvres, among others.
2. See, for example, Robin Wright, "Imagining a Remapped Middle East," *New York Times*, September 28, 2013.
3. Louise Fawcett, "States and Sovereignty in the Middle East: myths and realities" in *International Affairs*, 93:4, July 2017, 780–807. See also I. William Zartman, "States Boundaries and Sovereignty in the Middle East: unsteady but unchanging" in *International Affairs* 93:4, July 2017, 973–948.
4. Miguel Angel Centeno, Atul Kohli and Deborah J. Yashar, "Unpacking States in the Developing World: Capacity, Performance and Politics," in *States in the Developing World*, 1–34.
5. Roger Owen, *State, Power and Politics in the Making of the Modern Middle East*, 3rd ed (New York and London: Routledge, 2004)
6. Robert Springborg, *Political Economics of the Middle East and North Africa*, (Cambridge: Polity Press, 2020).
7. Douglass C. North, John Joseph Wallis, Steven B. Webb, and Barry R. Weingast, In the Shadow of Violence: Politics, Economics, and the Problems of Development (Cambridge: Cambridge University Press, 2013)
8. Nazih N. Ayubi, *Over-Stating the Arab State, Politics and Society in the Middle East*, (London: I.B. Tauris, 1995), 447-459
9. Michael Mann, "The Autonomous Power of the State: Its Origins, Mechanisms and Results," *European Journal of Sociology*, vol. 25, Issue 2, November 1984, 185–213.

1 INTRODUCTION   15

10. This is notwithstanding some experimentation of unity between Egypt and Syria 1958–1961 and between Baathist Iraq and Syria, for example, in 1978–1979. The latter attempt was never implemented.
11. Dalia Ghanem, *Algeria's Borderlands: A Country Unto Themselves* (Malcom H. Kerr Carnegie Middle East Center, 27 May 2022 found on https://carnegie-mec.org/2020/05/27/algeria-s-borderlands-country-unto-themselves-pub-81881
12. See Robert Jackson and Carl Rosberg, "Why Africa's Weak States Persist: The Empirical and Juridical in Statehood," *World Politics*, 35 no. 1, October 1982, 1–24.
13. Vladimir Kolossov, Border Studies: Changing Perspectives and theorterical approaches, in Geopolitics, 2005, 10 (4), 606-632; Harout Akedian and Harith Hassan, State Atrophy and the reconfiguration of borderlands in Syria and Iraq: Post 2011 dynamics, in Political Geography, June 2020, Vol 80 available on https://www.sciencedirect.com/science/article/pii/S096262981930109X
14. Abel Polese and Ruth Hanau Santini, "Limited Statehood and its Security Implications on the Fragmentation Political Order in The Middle East and North Africa," *Small Wars and Insurgencies*, 2018, Vol 29, no 3, 379–390.
15. Robert I Rotberg, "Failed States in the world of terror" in *Foreign Affairs* 81:4 July-August 2002, p. 127.
16. Fawcette, Ibid.
17. The concept of hybrid governance has a long pedigree in African studies, but has only recently been applied to the Middle Eastern context, especially in the wake of post-2011 challenges to formal governing structures. For background, see Volker Boege, Anne Brown, Kevin Clements and Anna Nolan, "On Hybrid Political Orders and Emerging States: State Formation in the Context of 'Fragility,'" Berghof Research Center for Constructive Conflict Management, 2008.

CHAPTER 2

Smuggling and State Formation: A Match Made in Algeria

Dalia Ghanem

INTRODUCTION

In Algeria, state formation is a work-in-progress. As demonstrated by cross-border smuggling between Algeria and its northeastern neighbor Tunisia, smugglers and state officials are engaged in a continuous effort to strike a balance between a centralized state and a *de facto* semiautonomous periphery. In this part of the country, the formal and the documented function alongside the informal and the undocumented. Everyday mechanisms connect the two theoretically incompatible modes of existence.[1] The formal component is represented by state institutions, border police, customs, and territorial markers such as trenches, checkpoints, and crossings. The informal element is represented by marginal actors such as smuggling kingpins, small-time smugglers, lookouts, drivers, and sellers of smuggled goods, all of whom lack legal standing but have a significant direct and indirect impact on the borderland economy. These

---

D. Ghanem (✉)
European Union Institute for Security Studies (EUISS), Paris, France
e-mail: dalia.ghanem@iss.europa.eu

© The Author(s), under exclusive license to Springer Nature Switzerland AG 2023
M. Yahya (ed.), *How Border Peripheries are Changing the Nature of Arab States*, https://doi.org/10.1007/978-3-031-09187-2_2

17

marginal-cum-significant actors are not granted free rein by the state, yet neither are they shackled by stringent restrictions. Their leeway, which alternately widens and narrows, is subject to continuous negotiation and renegotiation with local authorities.[2]

Such give-and-take between representatives of the formal and informal spheres serves to attenuate the sovereignty of the state, albeit with the latter's acquiescence. What in most situations the state would monopolize is in Algeria's northeast a matter of shared responsibility: determining how to deal with a law-breaking activity, providing social welfare, and achieving security. The state consents to an arrangement that encroaches on its sovereignty because it is aware of its limitations and because the result is demonstrably beneficial, what with smugglers sustaining underprivileged communities economically and even helping to maintain security.

Smuggling's storied history, which includes a prominent role in the Algerian War of Independence (1954–1962) waged against French occupying forces, helped to lay the groundwork for the current situation. Cross-border relations between Algeria and Tunisia date to the early colonial era. In 1830, France wrested control of Algeria from the Ottoman Empire through a successful military campaign. The French then began expropriating land and repressing the local population. The northeastern regions of the country were not spared. As a result, many inhabitants of Algeria's northeast left for Tunis, which was at the time a *Beylik*, an autonomous district of the Ottoman Empire. Tunisian border regions such as Al-Kef, Nefta, and Thala became home to thousands of Algerian migrants. Some of these migrants conducted cross-border raids to avenge the loss of their land, while others colluded with local tribes to establish smuggling networks. Despite major efforts on the part of France's military forces to stamp out such activities, particularly after the establishment of the French protectorate of Tunisia in 1881, the phenomenon persisted.[3]

The smuggling networks were indispensable to the success of Algerian rebels in the Algerian War of Independence. Following Tunisia's independence from France in 1956, President Habib Bourguiba allowed the National Liberation Front (FLN), the main Algerian nationalist political party, to establish its headquarters in the country's capital, Tunis. The FLN's military wing, the National Liberation Army (ALN), set up military training camps in Ghardimaou, Sakiet Sidi Youssef, Gafsa, and Kasserine, among other Tunisian areas near the border.[4] The men who underwent training in these camps would subsequently infiltrate Algeria and launch attacks on the French. Cross-border smuggling of munitions and other supplies was also widespread.

In 1962, Algeria gained independence from France.[5] However, the emergence of a centralized and unitary Algerian state alongside an independent Tunisia did little to weaken social, cultural, and economic connections between Algerian and Tunisian communities along the 1010-kilometer border between the two countries.[6] Moreover, the state would eventually reach an accommodation-of-sorts with the smugglers, one that is very much in evidence today. Though the authorities condemn the illegal trade, sometimes even portraying it as an infringement on Algerian sovereignty, they seldom crack down on its purveyors and instead generally maintain a studied *laissez-faire* policy.[7]

WHY SMUGGLING IS ECONOMICALLY ATTRACTIVE

In Algeria, the long-lasting profitability of smuggling has been bound up with the country's policy of subsidizing gasoline, which in turn is made possible by the country's oil reserves. Oil was discovered in Algeria in 1956—in Edjeleh followed by Hassi Messaoud—and production began two years later. In 1969, seven years after the country gained independence, Algeria joined the Organization of the Petroleum Exporting Countries (OPEC), and in 1971, the authorities nationalized the oil and gas industry.[8] Sonatrach, created in 1963 as Algeria's national oil and gas company, was allowed to dominate the hydrocarbon sector, taking charge of no less than 80 percent of all hydrocarbon production.

Hydrocarbons quickly become the country's economic backbone—with Sonatrach, and the Algerian state behind it, reaping the benefits.[9] This has remained the case. According to the latest estimates from the International Monetary Fund (IMF), revenue generated from the hydrocarbon sector constitutes approximately one-third of total national revenue.[10] Since independence, and largely due to Algeria's socialist orientation, the country's economic energy-consumption model has been based on the provision of major subsidies for everyday items—gasoline, fuel, foodstuffs, medicine—at well below their market cost. Even housing has traditionally been subsidized. In 2016, energy subsidies represented 50 percent of total subsidies, which amounted to approximately $28 billion, absorbing 30 percent of the state budget and more than 10 percent of the GDP.[11] In any given year, the price of gasoline in Algeria is three to nine times cheaper than in Western countries. For instance, in August 2021, a liter of gasoline in Algeria cost $0.34,[12] whereas in France the price was $1.82.[13]

In the late 1990s, Algeria experienced a significant economic upturn. The cost of a barrel of oil went from $10 in 1998 to more than $100 in 2008—and did not change significantly over the next half decade. As a result, Algeria's foreign exchange reserves rose considerably, going from $12 billion at the end of 2000 to an annual average of $127 billion from 2013 until 2020, with an all-time high of $194 billion in the first quarter of 2014.[14] This enabled the regime to buy social peace and weather the Arab Spring, which began in 2011. For example, that year, in an effort to contain rising food prices and alleviate severe social unrest, the government extended food subsidies while simultaneously lowering customs duties on imported food products. Wheat, sugar, and milk were among the key consumer items to be generously subsidized. Indeed, the milk subsidy rose to 50 percent. The government also provided significant pay raises to state officials, monetary assistance to farmers, interest-free loans to unemployed youth, and massive infusions of funds into infrastructure and housing projects.[15]

However, following the drop in oil prices in June 2014 and the historical collapse of March 2020 due to tensions between Russia and Saudi Arabia and OPEC member states' failure to reach an agreement, prices fell to their lowest level since 1991. The Algerian regime found itself unable to continue with its cost-heavy subsidies. The same was true of neighboring countries such as Morocco[16] and Tunisia,[17] which removed or dramatically reduced almost all their subsidies between 2012 and 2017. In Tunisia, for instance, prices of gasoline products Super Unleaded, Super Diesel, and regular Diesel increased by 41, 67, and 41 percent, respectively, between December 2010 and June 2018.[18] Even with Algeria increasing the price of gasoline, however, prices remained very low compared to other countries. For instance, in 2016, the government raised the price of gasoline by 34 percent. Yet, at $0.28 per gallon, Algerian gasoline still compared favorably with an average world value, based on 165 countries, of $0.98.[19] In September 2021, Algerian gasoline remained the fifth cheapest globally out of 167 countries, standing at $0.33.[20] In Tunisia, the price stood at $0.75, and in Morocco it was $1.17.[21]

While it is true that the smuggling of Algerian subsidized products, especially gasoline and fuel, to Tunisia and Morocco is hardly a new phenomenon, it has grown in scope since these two countries reduced their subsidies this past decade. Indeed, since the subsidy reforms in Tunisia and

Morocco, the volume of smuggled gasoline and fuel between Algeria and the two countries has increased tenfold.[22] According to interviews conducted with customs agents, the gendarmerie, smugglers, and wholesalers in Algeria's M'Daourouche, Al-Ouenza, and Bir El Ater in March and April 2019, as well as Tunisia's Kasserine during the same period, the smuggling of fuel and gasoline accounts for 70 to 75 percent of the jobs in the region.[23] It is also a lucrative activity, with several smugglers revealing that they earned between $150 and $300 per day.

An estimated 5 million tons of fuel of all kinds (including gasoline), or 25 percent of the total generated annually, is smuggled from Algeria to Tunisia, Morocco, Mali, and Niger every year.[24] According to research conducted by Hocine Hamdani, professor at the National Superior School of Statistics and Applied Economics, fuel smuggling has increased by 5–6 percent every year since 2006. The smuggled gasoline, specifically, supplies no fewer than 600,000 cars beyond Algeria's borders every year.[25] According to the same source, this constitutes an estimated loss of 1.5 billion liters per year, the equivalent of some $2 billion for Algeria.

Clearly, Algeria's subsidization policy has strained the state's budget; led to overconsumption and waste; reduced crude exports; increased cross-border smuggling; reduced investment in the transportation, biodiversity, and renewable energy sectors; and even reinforced the social inequalities it was supposed to fix. In 2011, with the start of the Arab Spring and the war in Libya, entire northeastern towns in Algeria experienced shortages because the gasoline they were supposed to have on hand was instead smuggled to Libya via Tunisia.[26] In a bid to reduce the squandering of oil products, the authorities imposed a limit on sales at gas stations situated in border regions.[27] Commercial vehicles were allowed no more than $5 a day at the gas station, and trucks were capped at $25.[28] However, this strategy did not work for two reasons: to begin with, controls were not strict, and the limitation was hard to enforce, especially since the state is not as present in these border regions as in big cities; secondly, because gas station owners benefit from illegal traffic, their connivance with smugglers remained very strong.

In November 2020, the government increased the price of diesel from $0.19 to $0.23[29] and that of gasoline from $0.35 to $0.37.[30] This came following a five-year period (2014 to 2019) during which subsidies increased by 12 percent, a trend Algerian economists warned could no longer continue.[31] Yet even with the increase in prices, both Algerian diesel and gasoline remained among the cheapest in the world. Perhaps with this in mind, the government also introduced, by way of the 2021 finance bill, a gasoline tax on all vehicles exiting the country via border crossing.[32] The rates of this tax were $18 for tourist vehicles, $21 for utility vehicles and trucks lighter than ten tons, and $72 for trucks over ten tons as well as buses. The tax was subsequently modified to $3 for tourist vehicles, $25 for utility vehicles and trucks lighter than ten tons, and $87 for trucks over ten tons as well as buses.[33] Former Energy Minister Abdelmadjid Attar explained that this tax would not eliminate smuggling but would limit the losses it caused.[34]

That may be so, but it stands to reason that reducing or even lifting subsidies and letting the market regulate itself would virtually eliminate smuggling and waste. Such an approach would appear to be all the more pressing because, by most accounts, the country can no longer sustain its subsidization policy. Algeria's real GDP shrank by 5.5 percent in 2020, while the hydrocarbon sector shrank by 8.5 percent.[35] Yet the Algerian authorities have long feared that doing away with subsidies would spark a revolution. This fear is not unfounded. In October 1988, the government did lift subsidies, only to face an outbreak of mass social unrest that threatened its grip on power. Black October, as it was called, spooked the authorities to such a degree that no subsequent government seriously considered lifting subsidies.

Until the fall of 2021. In October of that year, driven to action by Algeria's floundering economy, the authorities began preparations for a progressive and gradual approach to restructuring, and even eliminating, generalized subsidies. Indeed, the government announced, via the official newspaper *El Moudjahid*, draft finance law 2022. This law includes a provision, Article 187, intended to ensure that the most vulnerable sectors of society would continue to receive state aid. Article 187 stipulates "the introduction of a new provision of the finance law for the establishment of a targeting device for state subsidies, for the benefit of low- and middle-income households."[36]

In other words, the government has adopted a policy of targeted subsidies, whereby it reduces or even gradually eliminates subsidies for high-income households even as it increases subsidies for low-income families. This would provide for a more equitable allocation of subsidy resources. Whether the government proceeds with such a plan, and whether its definition of low- and middle-income families is broad enough to include all Algerians in need of state support, remains to be seen. Lifting subsidies wholesale without creating any kind of social safety net would bring about

2 SMUGGLING AND STATE FORMATION: A MATCH MADE IN ALGERIA

the very social explosion successive Algerian governments have feared since 1988, the specter of which may have receded of late owing to a narrowly focused concern with macrolevel economics.

THE SMUGGLERS' RATIONALE

Whether Algerian or Tunisian, male or female, practitioners of the trade bristle at the designation "smuggling" (*tahrib*). For them, the activity is business (*tijara*) or work (*khedma*).[37] When pressed as to why they break the law for a living, smugglers generally cite two justifications. The first is that cross-border trade is one of the few sources of income in a region characterized by perpetual economic underdevelopment. The second is that the choice of such a livelihood is a natural outcome of cross-border kinship.

Crucially, smugglers enjoy the backing of their communities, which stand to benefit from the continuation of their unlawful trade in gasoline, foodstuffs, and sundry other products. Like the smugglers themselves, most members of borderland communities consider the activity to be morally legitimate, even if technically illegal. For the people of Tébessa, Al-Ouenza, and Bir El Ater in Algeria, as well as Gafsa, Kasserine, and Haydra in Tunisia, smuggling is a means of making ends meet by exploiting cross-border differences in prices and exchange rates. Without the modest profits the smugglers generate, the already underprivileged people of Algeria's northeastern and Tunisia's western borderlands would face financial ruin.

Indeed, the crux of the matter is that smuggling is driven by economic necessity. In both northeastern Algeria and western Tunisia, the borderland economy suffers from several structural deficits. These include a weak labor market, high rates of unemployment, and scant tourism despite the presence of Roman and Byzantine ruins.[38] Such a state-of-affairs is hardly new. Indeed, investment in borderland development projects on the part of both Algiers and Tunis has long fallen short. Even when investment was earmarked for the borderlands, incompetence and corruption ensured that it had a very limited impact.

For example, Algeria's efforts since the 1970s to bridge the economic gap between the prosperous coastal north and the impoverished interior have been met with little success. Localities situated along or near the country's northeastern border, such as Bir El Ater, El Kouif, and Bakkaria, continue to suffer from severe socioeconomic underdevelopment.[39]

24   D. GHANEM

Similarly, in Tunisia, the state has failed to integrate into the national economy remote and long-deprived western areas such as Kasserine, Feriana, and Foussana. The farther away the capital, the greater the inequalities. One Algerian smuggler explained the situation in particularly blunt terms:

> There is nothing else to do in the region. The governor will tell you that unemployment is at 7 percent and that we want easy money. Well, look around you and tell me, what else do we have? Everyone smuggles here, even women. [...] People think this way: I will wake up today and smuggle some 70 containers of gas, and then my family will have dinner tonight and the day after and sometimes for the rest of the month. Simple as that. It is a matter of survival.[40]

In short, whether in northeastern Algeria or western Tunisia, the atrophied formal economy leaves locals with virtually no alternative to participating in a time-tested parallel economy undergirded by smuggling. The need to sustain and even bolster this parallel economy becomes more pressing with the massive annual influx of young people into a stagnant job market. In such an unforgiving environment, smuggling is a means of surviving. To borrow a description of a similar situation in another part of the world, the border has become a "corridor of opportunity."[41]

Then there is the crucial matter of kinship. Kinship exerts an integrative influence across a national dividing line between Algeria and Tunisia. The border is dismissed by those who live in its vicinity as an arbitrary colonial demarcation—even if it is maintained by independent Algeria and Tunisia—that splits families.[42] Without the trust and goodwill born of blood ties, circumventing official channels to forge economic links across the two countries would almost certainly have proven more difficult. Smuggling may be driven by economic necessity, but it is facilitated in no small part by cross-border family relationships.[43]

Consider the case of Abdelhamid, a Tunisian who, with two of his brothers, is in the business of smuggling gasoline from Algeria into Tunisia. In Algeria, an oil-producing country, gasoline is subsidized, and the price of a liter is up to three times lower than in Tunisia. The two brothers' role is to enter Algeria, purchase the gasoline at any one of several movable points just across the border, and smuggle it into Tunisia. Abdelhamid sells it at the family shop in Kasserine. Abdelhamid's Algerian cousins, who live in Al-Ouenza, help with the all-important

2 SMUGGLING AND STATE FORMATION: A MATCH MADE IN ALGERIA

matter of navigation. They apprise Abdelhamid's brothers of how to evade Algerian border security on any given day as well as how best to reach that day's pre-arranged point of exchange with the Algerian gasoline seller. Recently, they have even provided Abdelhamid and brothers with advice on how they might expand their business to include other products (Map 2.1).[44]

Kinship also facilitates ties between smugglers on the one hand and border security and customs agents on the other. Many smugglers have relatives, friends, or acquaintances within the security forces or customs departments. As such, they can build on existing relationships. An Algerian former customs agent in Bir El Ater had this to say about how and why he helped a smuggler with his trade:

> My brother-in-law worked as a smuggler. What was I supposed to do? I helped him: I gave him tips, arranged phone calls, and did my best to keep him untouched on both sides of the borders. [...] After all, he's family.[45]

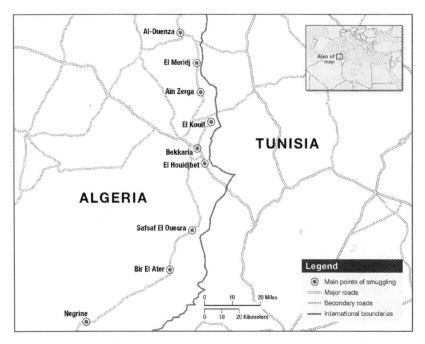

Map 2.1   Points of discharge along the Algerian-Tunisian border

26   D. GHANEM

Indeed, in both Algeria and Tunisia, lower-level security officials tasked with patrolling the border are usually locals, as are customs agents entrusted with conducting searches of travelers' possessions. Security officials on one or another side of the border frequently "open the stretch" for smugglers, enabling them to pass unhindered.[46] Customs agents often turn a blind eye to the transportation of large quantities of goods clearly intended for commercial sale and for which the transporter may lack proof of legal purchase. This level of cooperation is difficult if not impossible to secure through bribes alone.

Sharing Sovereignty

The smuggling dynamic at play in Algeria's northeastern borderlands calls into question several assumptions concerning the unitary nation state. Algeria is a unified, centralized, and quasi-authoritarian entity, yet it has found itself obliged to come to terms with one of the most disadvantaged sectors of its population in a far-flung region. In this respect, the periphery's leverage over the center is akin to the tail that wags the dog. Nevertheless, while the state has admittedly ceded a degree of power to non-state actors—and peripheral ones at that—it is not in retreat. Shared sovereignty is the order of the day. Broadly speaking, such shared sovereignty extends across three distinct realms, all of which are normally the exclusive preserve of the state: the law, social welfare, and security.

When it comes to the law, there is no question that the sort of cross-border trade described here is illegal. Yet there is a category of illegal activities that is of little concern to the authorities. Smuggling gasoline and a host of other products across the border falls into this category. Drugs and weapons do not. Smugglers, it turns out, are perceived by the state as existing across a spectrum. At one end are those whose ambitions are such that they take up the lucrative trade of drugs and arms and even enter into partnerships with jihadis, all without regard for the authorities' concerns. At the other end are those who, though keen to earn much-needed money for their families, refrain from crossing such red lines. In trying to stamp out one kind of smuggling even as they allow another kind to flourish, the authorities have for all intents and purposes adopted the smugglers' position that what is illegal in the technical sense may remain licit in the larger moral reckoning. Smugglers of gasoline, an illegal-yet-licit activity, have to contend with the occasional crackdown, but this is more often than not a perfunctory and short-lived demonstration of state power.[47]

Social welfare constitutes the second arena over which sovereignty is shared. Smuggling is at the heart of an economic network that provides the people of the borderlands with varying degrees of social welfare. The Algerian state has proven itself incapable of creating enough jobs for the young men and women with whom the job market is inundated every year. This problem is especially acute in the borderlands. The authorities realize that, in border areas, smuggling offers a homegrown solution to the problem. Smuggling directly creates jobs, as the smugglers require people to fill ancillary roles such as lookouts, drivers, and porters. Additionally, smugglers have a hand in stimulating the larger economy by making goods available at prices cheaper than the market rate, purchasing sports utility vehicles for their trade, and supplementing the meager income of border security officials and customs agents through bribes. In absorbing the unemployed and the underemployed, smuggling defuses social discontent and compensates for the central government's enduring neglect of a peripheral region.

By far the most significant example of the Algerian state and smugglers sharing sovereignty is that of border security. The Algerian authorities have correctly determined that granting smugglers a measure of latitude better enables the state to manipulate them. "In a way, they help us protect the borders" is how one Algerian customs agent summed up a situation in which the state shares certain duties with some of the very people it is meant to pursue.[48] Algeria's canny stratagem has succeeded in turning smugglers, who are technically a criminal element, into an instrument that serves state security and ensured that the strategically important borderlands do not slip out of the state's grasp. To understand how this arrangement came about, it is important to take a close look at the dilemma with which Algiers was faced following the Arab Spring uprisings in neighboring countries.

From the perspective of Algiers, border security is a perennial issue, albeit a protean one. In the early 1990s, the threat was deemed to be spillover of the Tuareg rebellion in Mali and Niger. Beginning in 2011, when the Arab Spring uprisings broke out, the Algerian authorities worried about what might come their way through the border with Tunisia. The concern was not simply that the security vacuum that followed the uprisings in Tunisia and Libya, and the accompanying weakening of the two countries' border controls, would lead to a surge in smuggling. It was only

28   D. GHANEM

a matter of time, or so the thinking went, before at least some Algerian smugglers of gasoline and other products turned their attention to arms and drugs.[49]

Algiers' assessment was correct. Certain smugglers took advantage of the newly lax security on the Tunisian side to change their business model from smuggling gasoline and food staples into Tunisia to smuggling drugs (mainly *zatla*, or cannabis resin) and weapons into Algeria. Some even took things a step further, entering into a marriage of convenience with Tunisian or Tunisia-based jihadis.[50] The jihadis had money to spare and were the principal buyers of arms and drugs. They also retained the services of the smugglers to help them evade capture when crossing the border in either direction and navigating the borderlands of both countries.

In Algiers, fears began to grow that the new jihadis increasingly making their way into the country via Tunisia were linking up with isolated yet hardened jihadis in Algeria's interior. This combination of new blood and veteran groups would create favorable conditions for the resurgence of full-blown jihadism in a country still suffering from what the authorities called "residual terrorism" dating to the 1990s civil war, which pitted the state against various Islamist groups.[51] Of particular concern to the authorities was the Salafi Group for Preaching and Combat (GSPC), which had joined Al Qaeda in 2007 to become Al Qaeda in the Islamic Maghreb (AQIM). Traditionally, the GSPC's activities were confined to parts of Algiers and the Berber hinterland of Kabylia. Adopting Al Qaida's brand endowed it with greater regional allure. This became readily apparent following the Arab Spring, when Tunisians and Libyans began streaming across Tunisia's newly porous border with Algeria in order to join the group. AQIM absorbed them and also proved able to expand the scope of its activities. For example, it launched recruitment drives in southern Algeria, where it sought to tap into the frustrations of marginalized communities in Ghardaïa, Ouargla, and In Salah.[52]

Yet the Algerian security services had difficulty clamping down on smuggling and infiltration because of a decline in the effectiveness of their Tunisian counterparts. From the perspective of Algeria's policymakers, the border with Tunisia had become a sieve (*colander*).[53] The Tunisians were aware of the problem; by their own admission, they were struggling to secure Tunisia's borders and combat smuggling networks.[54] Algeria initiated a round of bilateral meetings between the two countries' border security agencies for the purpose of exchanging information and better coordinating anti-smuggling operations. Official figures show that this made a difference. In 2012, 441 smuggling operations were stopped by the Tunisian National Guard at the Tunisian-Algerian border, as opposed to 91 in 2011.[55] Borderland clashes between Algerian law enforcement and AQIM as well as other groups began to occur. Several terrorists, smugglers, and law enforcement officials were killed during these clashes. When jihadis were captured on or near the border, it often emerged that they were Tunisians and others either trying to enter Algeria or, having undergone training by Algerian jihadi veterans, on their way to Tunisia or elsewhere to carry out operations. This confirmed the Algerian government's suspicions of growing cross-border collusion between disparate jihadi elements.

However, Algerian intelligence agencies estimated that only a fraction of smuggling and infiltration operations were being thwarted.[56] Thus, Algerian-Tunisian cooperation in matters of border security clearly was not enough. Given the prevailing logic in Algiers, however, this realization did not at first translate into a qualitative shift in approach on the part of the authorities. Despite periodic changes in its composition, the Algerian government is essentially a long-lasting and military-backed regime. As such, it tends to gravitate to security solutions for most problems and often pays scant attention to economic and social factors. Sure enough, when it came to the latest threat, the government decided that if Algerian-Tunisian security cooperation was not achieving the desired results, a unilateral Algerian security drive would succeed. To that end, the defense budget was increased dramatically, going from 3.5 percent of the GDP in 2010 to 4.3 in 2011 and 6.2 percent in 2015, with the government purchasing new equipment and investing in counter-terrorism training for its personnel.[57] The authorities also dispatched military units to the country's borders, tightened the rules governing crossing to and from Tunisia, and shut border crossings with other neighboring countries.

Militarization took place on the troublesome border with Tunisia and areas in its vicinity, but also elsewhere. By late 2011, Algeria had positioned 7000 Gendarmerie Border Guards on the border with Libya and 20,000 men in the fourth and sixth military regions (Ouargla and Tamanrasset, respectively). In 2012, following an attack on the headquarters of the gendarmerie in Ouargla, the government assigned units to protect that border province's Hassi Messaoud oil fields. The same year, Algiers established 30 new gendarmerie bases at various points on the country's borders with Libya, Mali, and Niger. In addition, 3000 men

30   D. GHANEM

were dispatched to air bases to serve as rapid response forces transportable by helicopter or military aircraft.[58]

However, despite these efforts, Algeria had only middling success when it came to stemming the tide of smuggling and jihadi infiltration. Worse yet, in 2013, a major terrorist attack targeted the Tiguentourine gas facility in the country's southeast, with the jihadi perpetrators having infiltrated Algeria from Libya.[59] The Algerian authorities, whether on the local level or in Algiers itself, began to come to grips with a sobering realization. Even if long stretches of the border were closely monitored, the country would remain exposed to infiltration. The sheer size of Algeria hampered the state's efforts to secure its borders, as did the mountainous terrain in part of the country's northeast, near Tunisia. The already overstretched security forces could not maintain a presence all along Algeria's borders, and launching repeated and sustained campaigns against smugglers would further strain their limited resources.

Following the Tiguentourine attack, a perceptible shift in local authorities' thinking began to take place when it came to the matter of security: since jihadis were a far greater threat than the likes of gasoline smugglers, perhaps the latter could be used against the former. Over the next few years, this became a reality. Algerian local authorities across the (mostly northeastern) borderlands struck deals with Algerian smugglers.[60] The deal was simple and always the same. The smugglers undertook to steer clear of drugs, weapons, and jihadis and to inform on those of their peers who broke this cardinal rule. Such smugglers thus became the eyes and ears of border security. In return for their services, and so long as they bribed the right border officials, the smugglers could expect to go about their business without significant hindrance. Indeed, the authorities indicated to smugglers that they would refrain from cracking down on the smuggling of gasoline, foodstuffs, and other innocuous items.[61]

The arrangement worked for three reasons. The first was the resourcefulness of local authorities in the borderlands. Without their setting things in motion, such an unorthodox arrangement would have had little chance of being broached, let alone going into effect. Indeed, it is almost inconceivable that the politico-military establishment in Algiers would have proposed collusion between some of its own elements and smugglers as the solution to the problem it faced.

The second reason was the amenability of the majority of the smugglers themselves. Living up to their end of the bargain proved relatively easy, as most smugglers were not part of jihadi networks and were only too eager to jettison rogue elements that might imperil an advantageous relationship with border officials.[62] Moreover, once involved, they were disinclined to renege on their commitments, given the severe consequences. Recalling his time in the military, a recently retired officer who was posted to the border with Tunisia explained that, through the arrangement, the security services put the smugglers in a bind. "If they worked against us, we worked against them," he said. "If one guy was involved in bad business, we cracked down on the entire network, and this could affect an entire locality, as they were all involved in smuggling."[63]

The third reason is arguably the most interesting. Algiers may not have initiated collusion between border security and smugglers, but it proved flexible enough to live with such a scheme. This was critical to the scheme's success, as it was inevitable that, in a quasi-authoritarian and tightly run state, the government would sooner or later learn of what was going on at the border. That Algiers did not subsequently move to end the collusion made all the difference to its continuation.

Perhaps the chief factor accounting for both the local authorities' entering into an agreement with smugglers and Algiers' noninterference in the matter was a historical precedent of sorts, and a relatively recent one at that. During the civil war of the 1990s, the Algerian security forces managed to turn some jihadis into informants. In exchange for renouncing their ideology and aiding Algerian security services' domestic intelligence and counter-terrorism operations, former jihadis escaped prosecution and near-certain conviction.[64] In other words, the Algerian state coupled its hard security approach with a softer one that included conciliatory measures such as truces, amnesties, and rehabilitation programs.[65] Jihadists willing to abandon their militant ways and return to civilian life often called on their former comrades to surrender. Others, such as the former leader of the GSPC, Hassan Hattab, not only spoke out against jihadi violence but cooperated with the security forces in intelligence gathering and helped to foil attacks.[66]

The deal struck between the Algerian state and smugglers appears to have enjoyed similar success. A high-ranking army officer with knowledge of the situation put it thus:

Our method proved its worth. We did our best to secure the borders and we dispatched men and military materiel, but this cannot work without the help of locals. [...] You have youth here, most of them are unemployed and marginalized. They do their business—okay, it's an economic loss for the

32   D. GHANEM

country, but it's a security gain. They directly or indirectly help us keep the border safe. We deal with the devil that we know. [...] Simply put, you cannot fight terrorism without the help of the communities from which terrorist groups recruit. You recruit them first and you ensure that things go smoothly with them. There is trust between us even if the headlines of the newspapers say the opposite. [...] We incorporate, if I may put it this way, the influencers among the smugglers into our strategy. They are not formal leaders, but they are listened to in the smuggling world.[67]

Indeed, over the past several years, jihadi attacks on Algerian soil have declined in frequency. The Global Terrorism Index classified the impact of terrorist attacks on Algerian soil in 2020 as "low."[68] Strictly speaking, it is impossible to establish a causal correlation between the Algerian state's deal with smugglers and the diminishing jihadi threat. It also seems likely that militarization has played a role in the phenomenon; since May 2013, the government has installed 80 checkpoints along the 1010-kilometer border between Algeria and Tunisia, established 20 closed military zones, and deployed 60,000 military personnel.[69] Yet it is almost certainly the case that, had jihadi activity increased, the arrangement between local authorities and smugglers would not have lasted this long. And the arrangement seems destined to remain in effect, thanks to a conviction among local authorities in the borderlands and policymakers in Algiers that it is effective. As such, the Algerian state appears to have enhanced its security not in spite of ceding a degree of sovereignty to non-state actors but precisely because it has taken this unusual step.

CONCLUSION

Since the inception of the modern Algerian state in 1962, the Algerian authorities have devised, renewed, and refined a host of strategies to retain their grip on power. The situation in the country's northeastern borderlands proves as much. That a state should voluntarily share sovereignty with non-state actors will strike many as counterintuitive, even more so if the state in question is quasi-authoritarian and the non-state actors are petty smugglers. Viewed in context, however, Algeria's peculiar approach to its northeastern borderlands reveals itself to be an exercise in adaptive policymaking vis-à-vis a complex and potentially combustible situation. Recognizing their inability to alleviate the plight of the borderlands' inhabitants in a direct manner, the authorities in Algiers have opted for a *laissez-faire* approach to local initiatives meant to do precisely that. This approach, however, is not indicative of an "anything goes" attitude. On the contrary, irrespective of the advantages to the people of the borderlands, the Algerian authorities are *laissez-faire* in a decidedly selective and ultimately self-serving manner.

In fact, although there is no official or written concord between the Algerian state and smugglers, the latter's activity has for all intents and purposes been institutionalized. This institutionalization is no less significant for being informal in nature. It includes, as a sort of governing framework, the understanding between the two sides over what sort of smuggling is permissible. As such, the informal institutionalization of smuggling has not simply created a gray zone in which a pursuit can be illegal yet licit but has served to establish parameters for the activity, reduce the risk of misunderstanding, and lay out the expected benefits that the state and the smugglers can separately expect to accrue. The state has coopted the smugglers, and the smugglers have become part of the state.

NOTES

1. Michel de Certeau, *The Practice of Everyday Life* (Berkeley: University of California Press, 1984), 35.
2. The empirical basis of this article is multi-site fieldwork in Algeria (Tébessa, Al-Ouenza, Bir El Ater, M'Daourouche) and in Tunisia (Kasserine Governorate). I interviewed ordinary citizens, smugglers, and state officials (customs and gendarmerie). To protect interviewees, I have changed their names. Place names remain unchanged.
3. Julia A. Clancy-Smith, *Rebel and Saint: Muslim Notables, Populist Protest, Colonial Encounters (Algeria and Tunisia, 1800-1904)* (Berkeley: University of California Press, 1997), 13.
4. Jacques Valette, "1956 : le FLN porte la guerre d'Algérie en Tunisie" [1956: The FLN Takes the War from Algeria to Tunisia], *Guerres mondiales et conflits contemporains* 224, no. 6 (2006): 65-79.
5. For more on the creation of borders in the MENA region, see Raffaella A. Del Sarto, "Contentious Borders in the Middle East and North Africa: Context and Concepts," *International Affairs* 93, no. 4 (July 2017): 767–787.
6. On how smuggling is a historically customary practice, see Hamza Meddeb, *Courir ou mourir. Course à el Khobza et domination au quotidien dans la Tunisie de Ben Ali* [Run or Die. The Race to Bread and Daily Domination in Ben Ali's Tunisia] (Paris: Institut d'Études Politiques, 2012).

7. Dalia Ghanem, "Algeria's Borderlands: A Country Unto Themselves," Malcolm H. Kerr Carnegie Middle East Center, May 27, 2020, https://carnegie-mec.org/2020/05/27/algeria-s-borderlands-country-unto-themselves-pub-81881.
8. Hocine Malti, "Algeria and OPEC," Algeria Watch, February 2018, https://algeria-watch.org/?p=3064.
9. OPEC, "Algeria Facts and Figures," https://www.opec.org/opec_web/en/about_us/146.htm.
10. U.S. EIA, "Algeria Analysis," March 25, 2019, https://www.eia.gov/international/analysis/country/DZA.
11. Nadjia Bouaricha, "Le case-tête des subventions" [The Subsidy Puzzle], *El Watan*, July 27, 2017, https://algeria-watch.org/?p=12761.
12. Combien coute.net, "Le prix de l'essence en Algérie en 2021" [The Price of Gasoline in Algeria in 2021], https://www.combien-coute.net/essence/algerie/alger/.
13. Turbo, "Carburants : les prix de l'essence et du Diesel toujours aussi hauts" [Fuel: Gasoline and Diesel Prices Still Very High], August 23, 2021, https://bit.ly/3BZGR9z'essence%20toujours%20aussi%20ch%C3%A8re%20!&text=Ainsi%2C%20le%20prix%20de%20vente,euro%20en%20d%C3%A9but%20d'ann%C3%A9e.
14. Trading Economics, "Algeria Foreign Exchange Reserves" (2021 data), https://tradingeconomics.com/algeria/foreign-exchange-reserves.
15. Lahcen Achy, "The Price of Stability in Algeria," Carnegie Middle East Center, April 2013, https://carnegieendowment.org/files/price_stability_algeria.pdf.
16. Laura El-Katiri, "Morocco's Green Energy Opportunity," OCP Policy Center, October 2016, https://media.africaportal.org/documents/OCPPC-PP1614v1.pdf.
17. "La Tunisie se soumet au FMI et suspend ses subventions au carburant" [Tunisia Submits to IMF, Suspends Fuel Subsidies], *Algérie Eco*, July 4, 2017, https://www.algerie-eco.com/2017/07/04/tunisie-se-soumet-fmi-suspend-subventions-carburant/.
18. Hamza, "Evolution des prix de l'essence et du gasoil : Plus de 40% d'augmentation depuis 2010" [Evolution of Gasoline and Diesel Prices: An Increase of More than 40 Percent since 2010], June 25, 2018, https://www.webmanagercenter.com/2018/06/25/421457/evolution-des-prix-de-lessence-et-du-gasoil-plus-de-40-daugmentation-depuis-2010/.
19. The Global Economy.com, "Algeria," https://www.theglobaleconomy.com/Algeria/gasoline_prices/.

20. GlobalPetrolPrices, "Gasoline Prices, Litre," November 8, 2021, https://www.globalpetrolprices.com/gasoline_prices/.
21. GlobalPetrolPrices, ibid.
22. Hocine Hamdani, "Impact De La Malediction Des Subventions Des Carburants En Algerie Sur La Longevite Des Reserves Petrolieres" [Impact of the Curse of Fuel Subsidies in Algeria on the Longevity of Petroleum Reserves], *Revue d'économie et de statistique appliquée* 11, no. 2: 364-379, https://www.asjp.cerist.dz/en/article/57654.
23. Author's interviews with several smugglers, wholesalers, and customs agents on the Algerian-Tunisian border, March-April 2019 and March 2020.
24. Hocine Hamdani, "Impact De La Malediction Des Subventions Des Carburants En Algerie Sur La Longevite Des Reserves Petrolieres," op cit.
25. Hocine Hamdani, ibid.
26. France 24, "La contrebande vers la Libye assèche les pompes à essence dans l'Est algérien" [Smuggling to Libya Dries up Petrol Pumps in Eastern Algeria], August 11, 2011, https://observers.france24.com/fr/20110810-contrebande-vers-libye-asseche-pompes-essence-est-algerien-tebessa-penurie-essence-tunisie.
27. France 24, ibid.
28. Nadjib Touaibia, "Contrebande en Algérie: 1,5 milliards de litres de carburant détournés chaque année vers l'étranger" [Contraband in Algeria: 1.5 billion Liters of Fuel Diverted Abroad Each Year], *MediaTerranee*, December 22, 2013, https://www.mediaterranee.com/2212013-contrebande-en-algerie-15-milliards-de-litres-de-carburant-par-detourne-vers-letranger.html.
29. Arezki Benali, "Carburants : L'Algérie classée 5ème pour les plus bas prix de l'essence et le diesel, et première pour le GPL-c" [Algeria Ranked 5th in Lowest Gasoline and Diesel Prices, and First in LPG-C], *Algerie Eco*, January 6, 2019, https://bit.ly/3qF5nsv.
30. "Al-Jaza'ir Tutabbiq Ziyadat Jadida 'ala 'Asaar al-Wuqood" [Algeria Imposes New Increases on the Price of Fuel], *Al-Quds Al-Arabi*, June 6, 2020, https://bit.ly/327mvNi.
31. Abderrahmi Bessaha, "La question des subventions en Algérie situation actuelle et pistes de réformes" [The Question of Subsidies in Algeria, Current Situation and Avenues for Reform], *El Watan*, January 27, 2020, https://www.elwatan.com/pages-hebdo/sup-eco/la-question-des-subventions-en-algerie-situation-actuelle-et-pistes-de-reformes-27-01-2020.
32. APS, "PLF 2021: la taxe sur la consommation des carburants limitera les pertes issues de la contrebande" [PLF 2021: The Tax on Fuel Consumption Will Limit Losses from Smuggling], November 3, 2020, https://www.

aps.dz/economie/112271-plf-2021-la-taxe-sur-la-consommation-des-carburants-limitera-les-pertes-issues-de-la-contrebande.

33. "Ibtida'an min al-Ghad..Dariba Jadida 'ala Dukhool al-'Arabat min al-Jaza'ir ila Tunis" [Starting from Tomorrow...A New Tax on the Entry of Vehicles from Algeria to Tunisia], Nessma TV, December 31, 2020, https://bit.ly/31VyywW.

34. APS, "PLF 2021: la taxe sur la consommation des carburants limitera les pertes issues de la contrebande," op cit.

35. The World Bank, "Algeria Economic Update—April 2021," April 2, 2021, https://thedocs.worldbank.org/en/doc/bb7f0f274cf7427a06bac-e51771c863d-0280012021/original/1-mpo-sm21-algeria-dza-kcm.pdf.

36. Farida Larbi, "Révision du système des subventions : Une cartographie des revenus des citoyens en phase d'élaboration" [Revision of the Subsidy System: A Mapping of Citizens' Income Under Development], *El Moudjahid*, October, 31, 2021, https://www.elmoudjahid.dz/fr/economie/revision-du-systeme-des-subventions-une-cartographie-des-revenus-des-citoyens-en-phase-d-elaboration-174065.

37. These are the terms used by the smugglers themselves. In general, their activity falls within what is broadly regarded as the informal economy.

38. Dalia Ghanem, "Photo Essay: Algeria's Forgotten Borderlands," *Diwan*, Malcolm H. Kerr Carnegie Middle East Center, February 24, 2020, https://carnegie-mec.org/diwan/81064.

39. The state launched an industrialization drive around two main axes: a littoral axis from Annaba to Skikda and a southern axis consisting of Guelma, Sétif, Constantine, and Batna. In Annaba, a steel manufacturing complex was built, and in Constantine, a mechanical and textile complex was established.

40. Author interview with an Algerian smuggler, M'Daourouch, March 27, 2019.

41. Donna K. Flynn, " 'We Are the Border': Identity, Exchange, and the State along the Bénin-Nigeria Border," *American Ethnologist* 24, no. 2 (May 1997): 311-330.

42. In places such as Bakkaria and Umm Ali, among others, the border passes through localities that kept the same name on both sides. In Ghardimaou, the front door of a school is on the Tunisian side, while the back door opens onto the Algerian side. Also, families from the same tribe, like Awlad Abid, have been separated by the border and hence live on either side of it.

43. This is not unique to Algeria and Tunisia. See, for example, Thomas Hüsken, "The Practice and Culture of Smuggling in the Borderland of Egypt and Libya," *International Affairs* 93, no. 4 (2017): 899.

2 SMUGGLING AND STATE FORMATION: A MATCH MADE IN ALGERIA   37

44. Author interviews with "Abdelhamid," a Tunisian smuggler, Kasserine, March 2-3, 2019.
45. Author interview with an Algerian former customs agent, Bir El Ater, March 27, 2019.
46. *Yefethou al-batha* ("opening the stretch") is the term used by many smugglers to describe the opening of the road by security forces and customs every night between Algeria and Tunisia. To read more about the connivence of the security forces with smugglers and the bargaining that precedes agreements, see Dalia Ghanem, "Algeria's Borderlands: A Country Unto Themselves," op. cit.
47. Author observation.
48. Author interview with an Algerian customs agent, Algerian-Tunisian border, March 27, 2019. For more, see Dalia Ghanem, "Algeria's Borderlands: A Country Unto Themselves," op. cit.
49. Author interview with an Algerian army intelligence officer (via phone), February 12, 2021.
50. Author interview, ibid.
51. Author interview, ibid.
52. International Crisis Group, "Algeria's South: Trouble's Bellwether," Report No. 171, November 21, 2016, https://www.crisisgroup.org/middle-east-north-africa/north-africa/algeria/algeria-s-south-trouble-s-bellwether.
53. Author interview with a former army officer who worked in the Algerian military's intelligence branch (via phone), February 10, 2021.
54. Benjamin Roger, "Tunisie – Algérie : la frontière de tous les trafics" [Tunisia—Algeria: The Border of All Traffic], *Jeune Afrique*, February 4, 2013, https://www.jeuneafrique.com/138476/politique/tunisie-algrie-la-fronti-re-de-tous-les-trafics/.
55. Benjamin Roger, ibid.
56. Benjamin Roger, ibid.
57. World Bank, "Military Expenditures (% of GDP)—Algeria," https://data.worldbank.org/indicator/MS.MIL.XPND.GD.ZS?locations=DZ.
58. Laurence Aïda Ammour, "La stratégie algérienne de lutte anti-terroriste : entre impératifs de sécurité intérieure et recherche de stabilité régionale" [The Algerian Anti-Terrorism Strategy: Between Internal Security Imperatives and the Search for Regional Stability], Centre Français de Recherche sur le Renseignement, bulletin de documentation no. 22, October 2019, https://cf2r.org/documentation/la-strategie-algerienne-de-lutte-anti-terroriste-entre-imperatifs-de-securite-interieure-et-recherche-de-stabilite-regionale/.
59. L.M., "Sud de la Libye: guerre d'influence à la frontière algérienne" [Southern Libya: War of Influence on the Algerian Border],

38   D. GHANEM

Liberté, April 7, 2015, https://www.liberte-algerie.com/actualite/sud-de-la-libye-guerre-dinfluence-a-la-frontiere-algerienne-223424.

60. The localities in question include Bir El Ater, Negrine, El Kouif, Bekkaria, Al-Ouenza, Umm Ali, Aïn Zerga, El-Meridj, El Houidjbet, Safsaf El Ouesra, Aïn Ben Khelil, Sfissifa, Djenienne Bourezg, Kasdir. Farther south, in Al-Oued, localities include Taleb Larbi, Douar Al-Maa, and Ben Guecha.

61. Author interview with an Algerian army intelligence officer (via phone), February 12, 2021, op. cit.

62. Interviewees involved in the smuggling of products and goods (mainly gasoline and food items) did not refer to themselves as "smugglers." Notably, however, they did use the term when describing individuals involved in the trafficking of drugs and arms.

63. Author interview with a former colonel in the Algerian military (via phone), February 18, 2021.

64. Author interview, ibid.

65. Dalia Ghanem, "A Life After Jihadism," *Diwan*, Malcolm H. Kerr Carnegie Middle East Center, November 17, 2017, https://carnegie-mec.org/diwan/74708.

66. Farid Alilat, "Algérie: Hassan Hattab et la raison d'État" [Algeria: Hassan Hattab and the National Interest], *Jeune Afrique*, October 23, 2017, https://www.jeuneafrique.com/mag/483553/politique/algerie-hassan-hattab-et-la-raison-detat/.

67. Author interview with a serving army officer who was previously assigned to the fifth military region (RM V: Constantine), via Signal, April 29, 2021.

68. Institute for Economics & Peace, "Global Terrorism Index 2020: Measuring The Impact Of Terrorism," 2020, https://visionofhumanity.org/wp-content/uploads/2020/11/GTI-2020-web-1.pdf.

69. Laurence Aïda Ammour, "La stratégie algérienne de lutte anti-terroriste : entre impératifs de sécurité intérieure et recherche de stabilité régionale," op. cit.

CHAPTER 3

Cronies and Contraband: Why Integrating Tunisia's Informal Economic Elite Has Become Necessary

Hamza Meddeb

INTRODUCTION

A decade after the uprising of 2010–2011, Tunisia's peripheral regions continue to suffer from high unemployment, an underdeveloped private sector, and the existence of a significant informal economy—in which economic actors avoid paying taxes and their activities are neither licensed nor included in national accounts. However, government efforts since that time to improve security along the borders with Libya and Algeria have created obstacles to informal cross-border economic exchanges and

---

Hamza Meddeb is a nonresident scholar at the Malcolm H. Kerr Carnegie Middle East Center, where his research focuses on economic reform, the political economy of conflicts, and border insecurity across the Middle East and North Africa.

H. Meddeb (✉)
Malcolm H. Kerr Carnegie Middle East Center, Beirut, Lebanon
e-mail: hamza.meddeb@carnegie-mec.org

© The Author(s), under exclusive license to Springer Nature Switzerland AG 2023
M. Yahya (ed.), *How Border Peripheries are Changing the Nature of Arab States*, https://doi.org/10.1007/978-3-031-09187-2_3

39

smuggling that the local population had relied upon for its livelihood. This has further aggravated social and economic difficulties in these already neglected areas of the country.[1]

The absence of a formal private sector that could drive development in peripheral regions reflects official neglect, but it is also very much related to the existence of contending economic elites.[2] Those elites that benefit from state support have defended an economic order that has given emerging social forces limited access to the market and to economic opportunities.[3] The Tunisian business community is suffering from deep polarization between well-established, politically connected economic elites of the formal economy on the one hand and entrepreneurs of the informal economy and those involved in smuggling on the other. The established elites are made up of influential business people from the eastern coastal regions and large urban centers who, since independence in 1956, have enjoyed government favoritism and profited from rent-seeking positions.[4] The entrepreneurs of the informal economy come mainly from Tunisia's marginalized periphery and emerged under the late president Zine al-Abedin ben Ali.[5] For decades they have been engaged in, and confined to, the border trade.

Since 2011, however, the peripheral elite has aspired to carve out a place for itself in Tunisia's established economic elite and gain access to the same advantages.[6] This reflects how the country, even as it has evolved politically, has also seen an ongoing transformation of its economic order through a renegotiation of center-periphery relations. For now, integration of the peripheral elite has progressed little, largely because it is opposed by powerful interest groups in Tunis. Yet this issue is being actively considered by President Qaïs Saied, who augmented his power through an effective coup in July 2021.[7] Tunisian leaders understand that such integration is needed because of the financial losses caused by the informal economy, which Tunisia can no longer afford. Moreover, the prosperity of this peripheral elite is tied to social stability in the border regions and beyond that to Tunisian political stability and, ultimately, the authority and integrity of the state.

THE EMERGENCE OF TWO ECONOMIC ELITES

Regional inequalities can be a potent source of nationwide tension. Nothing has underlined this more than the fact that Tunisia's interior and border regions were the hotbed of the 2010–2011 uprising and since then have been a major source of political contestation.[8] Yet this phenomenon is hardly new. Conscious policy decisions since Tunisians independence have resulted in a substantial development gap between the eastern coastal areas and the periphery.

After a decade of socialism during the 1960s, in the 1970s Tunisia liberalized its economy.[9] The country opened up its markets and promoted private entrepreneurship, as the Bourguiba regime at the time encouraged Tunisians to establish companies. Many civil servants entered into business activities, as did young entrepreneurs from the coastal regions of Tunis, the Sahel, and Sfax. They benefited from state support in their access to credit under advantageous terms, licenses, and other incentives.[10] The aim was to create a class of industrialists and entrepreneurs connected to the regime that could promote government-sponsored industrialization and drive economic growth, without eroding the authoritarian powers of the state and its control of society. These new economic actors were regarded as the backbone of Tunisia's private sector.

Such efforts put in place a dual economy.[11] This was based on an off-shore, export-oriented sector functioning in parallel to a local market that was protected from outside competition, in which regime cronies played an important part. The export-orientated economy was focused on tourism and low-cost outsourcing, and led to an increase in infrastructure investment in coastal regions, near large cities, ports, and airports. Investment incentives were oriented toward maintaining competitiveness and access to international markets by keeping domestic wages low, at the expense of agricultural and rural areas. Progressively, this reduced Tunisia's peripheries to reservoirs of cheap labor, agricultural products, and raw materials for the more developed industries and services sector activities operating in the coastal regions, while private and infrastructural investment in peripheral part of the country remained limited.[12]

By the end of 1990, however, there was a shift in the way the economy was being run. Coming from the social margins and initially involved in the informal economy, the Ben Ali clan—members of the president's family and those of his wife's Trabelsi family—became a prominent economic actor in the formal economy. It built alliances with certain economic elites through its domination of the main business association, L'Union Tunisienne de l'Industrie, du Commerce et de l'Artisanat.[13] Companies sought to establish links with the president's circle of well-entrenched insiders and cronies to increase their own market share and protect themselves against the predation of Tunisian law enforcement bodies. This system allowed connected entrepreneurs to obtain licenses, evade paying taxes and import tariffs, avoid tighter controls, and gain access to banking credit at advantageous conditions.[14] Business alliances, but also alliances through marriage, cemented relations between the Ben Ali clan and the rest of the influential business elites. This created bonds of interdependency that lasted until Ben Ali's downfall in January 2011.[15]

The activities of the politically connected elites impacted the Tunisian state's financial position negatively. The nonpayment of taxes and tariffs led to considerable fiscal losses, but also resulted in substantial inequalities.[16] Favored entrepreneurs enjoyed a cost advantage over their counterparts who respected the rules—one based neither on efficiency nor performance. According to conservative estimates, underreporting of unit prices alone enabled connected firms to evade import tariffs worth at least $1.2 billion between 2002 and 2009.[17]

Protection against law enforcement led to the spread of corruption and allowed opportunistic elites to enrich themselves. This enabled Ben Ali's regime to maintain a broad cooptation strategy aimed at securing the loyalty of cronies involved in the transnational trade. A World Bank working paper from 2015 analyzed evasion gaps during Ben Ali's time in office. These gaps were defined as the difference between the value of exports to Tunisia reported by the exporting countries and the value of imports reported by Tunisian customs and were correlated with imports by politically connected firms.[18] The prices that these connected firms reported to customs officials were lower than those declared by other firms. The association was especially strong for commodities subject to high tariffs whose prices were underreported, such as electronic appliances, automobile equipment, or tobacco products. In 2018, the United Nations Economic and Social Commission for Western Asia estimated that illicit financial flows from the faulty invoicing of foreign trade represented 16 percent of Tunisia's foreign non-oil trade between 2008 and 2015—the highest amount in the Arab world.[19]

Tunisia's trade restrictions, whether based on tariff or nontariff barriers, were not simply procedural. The World Bank working paper cited earlier found evidence that the regulation of imports from many sectors was to some extent dictated by the Ben Ali clan's private business interests.[20] For the regime, these arbitrary restrictions served a vital political function in giving brokerage power to families connected to Ben Ali. By providing protection from the customs authorities and law enforcement agencies in exchange for a fee, the president's entourage also helped create an environment in which bribes and kickbacks accompanying cross-border trade flourished. This served as an incentive for entrepreneurs to rely on brokerage services to pay fewer taxes, avoid tighter controls, and under-report goods.

The Ben Ali clan itself profited handsomely from this situation. Enterprises with direct ownership links to the clan confiscated in the aftermath of the Tunisian uprising accounted for 3 percent of all private-sector output and appropriated approximately 20 percent of all private-sector profits.[21] This capture of the state went hand in hand with a deeper geographical asymmetry in the business community. At the time of Ben Ali's downfall, 85 percent of enterprises that provided 92 percent of private-sector jobs were clustered in the coastal regions.[22] Ninety-two percent of all industrial firms were located within an hour's drive of Tunisia's three largest cities—Tunis, Sfax, and Sousse—with forty-four percent located in the area of Greater Tunis alone.[23] Economic activity in the three coastal cities accounted for 85 percent of Tunisia's GDP. In contrast, enterprises operating in the inland districts of Tunisia provided only 8 percent of private-sector jobs.[24]

This pattern of marginalization was aggravated by the Ben Ali regime's spending choices, as two-thirds of public investment was allocated to coastal regions.[25] However, the absence of state-led development in areas bordering Algeria and Libya also pushed the state to rely increasingly on informal trade as a substitute for this.[26] This led to the emergence of two forms of cross-border exchanges: one channel that made use of official border crossings for fraudulent transactions in which the value of goods was underestimated, or not registered at all, in exchange for bribes and smuggling. Tunisia's border economy was tightly controlled by the country's security and administrative services—the police, the National Guard, border guards, and customs officials—which, in exchange for bribes, protected smugglers and currency dealers. Permission to conduct their trade was tied up with the acceptance of an informal system that was characterized by clientelistic relations between smugglers and currency dealers on the one hand and security and border officials on the other.[27]

Tunisia's pursuit of informal cross-border exchanges with its neighbors enabled the country to maintain its coastal-centric development model. Ben Ali's regime built a delicate authoritarian bargain with communities living in the peripheries. In exchange for quiescence, the regime tolerated smuggling and cross-border informal trade, providing a source of income for the countless inhabitants of economically deprived regions in southeastern and western Tunisia.[28] This allowed for economic growth that the state was unable to generate itself without a massive public investment program. Such a program was not an option for a regime eager to control the country's debt and budget deficit.[29] At the same time, bribes collected by the security and administrative services gave them an incentive to remain loyal to the regime, which received kickbacks as part of the arrangement.[30]

From a social and economic perspective, smuggling turned into a boon for a select group of smugglers and currency dealers who succeeded in developing their businesses using their close relations with the customs services and security bodies. An elite emerged at the end of 1990s and grew in the first decade of the new century.[31] It was active in smuggling consumer goods, tobacco, and alcohol, as well as engaging in foreign currency transfers and exchanges. Border economies in the peripheries saw the rise of large operators who played an important role in connecting Tunisia with Turkey and Asian markets through importation networks in Libya and Algeria. At the end of the Ben Ali regime, informal cross-border trade represented a significant part of Tunisia's bilateral trade with its neighbors, accounting for more than half of the official trade with Libya and more than the total of official trade with Algeria.[32]

According to reports issued by the World Bank between 2013 and 2015, Tunisia's informal economy accounted for between 39 and 50 percent of its GDP.[33] Bilateral informal trade was significant, especially with Libya. In 2015, the World Bank estimated trade with Libya at around $498 million, with cigarettes accounting for $200 million, fuel for $148 million, and other goods for $150 million.[34] The loss of public revenues for the state has been significant. In 2013, it was estimated to be at least 1.2 billion Tunisian dinars, equivalent to $500 million, of which around 500 million Tunisian dinars ($200 million) were in customs duties, or more than one-sixth of total customs duties.[35] Given the size of the losses and the importance of informal economic actors, the state has no choice but to adopt a new approach.

THE POST-2011 ECONOMY AND THE FAILURE TO INTEGRATE PERIPHERAL ELITES

Ben Ali's downfall brought crucial changes to Tunisia's formal and informal economies. In the years following the uprising, the country faced major economic challenges. This had the effect of increasing the size of the informal economy as entrepreneurs sought to remain competitive. The new situation also created an incentive for the government to bring entrepreneurs of the informal economy and smugglers into the formal economy, in order to cut the financial losses to the state from their activities. However, the failure of that effort until now, due primarily to the resistance of powerful interest groups, has created a situation that may only lead to a worsening of social and economic conditions.

In the aftermath of the uprising, companies that had been controlled by the former president and his Trabelsi in-laws were confiscated by the state, with many of them being resold to entrepreneurs who had been connected to the Ben Ali regime.[36] At the same time, powerful family-owned holding companies sought to consolidate their position by involving themselves in politics, either by funding political parties or through the efforts of their owners to establish parties of their own or enter parliament themselves. In the 2019 parliament, for instance, 14 percent of representatives were business people.[37]

In Tunisia's peripheral areas, the uprising unleashed dynamics that brought about major changes that increased the pressure on the central authorities to revise their previous policies. The war in Libya was a major blow to eastern border communities, aggravating their social predicament. The removal of Moammar al-Qaddafi's regime and the deterioration in Libya's security environment forced some 40,000 Tunisian workers to leave the country.[38] For over four decades Libya had been a major destination for seasonal workers, mostly from Tunisia's marginalized regions. The loss of income increased poverty among large swathes of the population, with 10,000–15,000 Tunisian families having received no income since 2011 because of the Libyan crisis.[39]

Meanwhile, shifts in the border economies and in government security policy transformed the environment along the borders with Libya and Algeria. After Ben Ali's downfall, the border economies became much more unpredictable, as security in Libya deteriorated and as new actors emerged seeking to exploit the vacuum along Tunisia's borders.[40] This included organized crime networks that wanted to turn Tunisia into a staging post for the trafficking of arms and drugs between Algeria and Libya. It also included ambitious smugglers who were willing to challenge the smuggling networks in place that had been coopted by the customs authorities and the security services.[41] The absence of measures to address economic and regulatory differences between Tunisia and its oil-producing neighbors—whether involving tariffs, tax levels, or subsidies—increased price gaps. This created a strong impetus for smuggling while also increasing corruption among the agents of the state. Consequently, smugglers had to compete among themselves to be protected by such agents in order to secure profits as best as they could. The main loser was the state, which after Ben Ali's removal had an opening to modify cross-border economic relations to its advantage but could not dislodge the networks in place.

While the entrepreneurs of the informal economy and smugglers faced a more volatile environment, they also realized that the new situation presented potential advantages. They hoped to benefit from an amnesty giving them a chance to legalize their activities and integrate into the formal economy. As one currency dealer puts it, "2011 was an opportunity to open a new page. There was hope for change and a feeling that with new elites there will be a new start for these [peripheral] regions. But nothing changed. The momentum was lost and a crisis of confidence took place between people and the new elites."[42]

This crisis of confidence was aggravated by a new emphasis on security that emerged in 2015, following two terrorist attacks that profoundly altered the situation in Tunisia. In March, gunmen affiliated with the Islamic State group attacked the Bardo National Museum in Tunis, killing 22 people. Three months later, Islamic extremists were responsible for a mass shooting at a tourist resort in Port El Kantaoui, near Sousse, in which 38 people were killed.[43] In response, the authorities, conflating jihadism and smuggling, tightened border restrictions; increased police, army, and customs controls; and cracked down on smuggling networks operating through Libya and Algeria, hindering cross-border trade.[44] This drastically limited the flow of goods supplying the Tunisian market.[45] Such measures also excluded many of the informal economic actors active along the border. More damagingly, the security measures benefited maritime networks operating through Tunisia's ports. Large-scale entrepreneurs imported commodities by sea directly from Turkey and Asia, undermining the smaller-scale, land-based border networks that could not compete with them (Map 3.1).

By 2019, Tunisia's economy could no longer put up with the losses due to the informal economy. The expansionary fiscal policy adopted after the uprising, characterized by elevated levels of public spending, was unsustainable.[46] Between 2011 and 2018, public expenditures rose from 24 to 30 percent of GDP, while tax revenues rose more modestly, from 23 to 25 percent of GDP, over the same period.[47] The public debt rose from 40 percent of GDP in 2010 to 73 percent in 2019. The COVID-19

3 CRONIES AND CONTRABAND: WHY INTEGRATING TUNISIA'S INFORMAL... 47

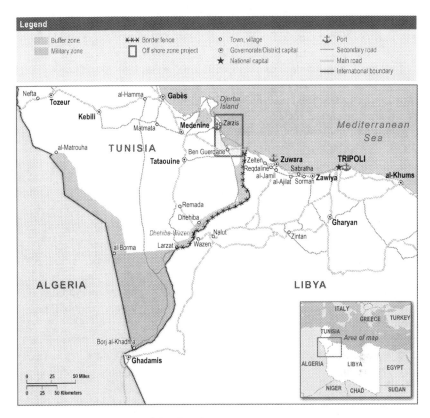

Map 3.1 The Tunisian-Libyan border

pandemic exacerbated these imbalances, contributing to an 8.8 percent decline in GDP in 2020.[48] The fiscal deficit rose to more than 12 percent of GDP, and the public debt expanded to more than 90 percent of GDP.[49]

The worsening fiscal crisis made it urgent for the state to secure new sources of revenue. This is what led officials to consider granting a fiscal amnesty to smugglers and currency dealers in Tunisia's peripheral regions, who would pay a fine before pursuing economic opportunities legally.[50] Providing a mechanism for the inclusion and cooptation of these elites and compensating them for the losses they incurred by surrendering their cross-border trade was seen as the only way of stabilizing Tunisia's unpredictable peripheries. At the same time, without such a mechanism, there

48 H. MEDDEB

was a risk of seeing these elites turned into spoilers. Tunisia's economy needed to be transformed, and one crucial aspect of this transformation was the inclusion of the peripheral elites into the formal economy.

However, there were major impediments to such a process. Not only did the integration of smugglers and entrepreneurs of the informal economy hit up against the interests of powerful interest groups, it also brought out the ambiguities of the informal sector itself, making a consensus over policy difficult. The obstacles were particularly visible in February–June 2020, when the government of then prime minister Elyes Fakhfakh presented a draft stimulus package to generate revenues at a time when the COVID-19 pandemic had hit Tunisia's public finances hard.[51] The package was initially formulated around three objectives—economic recovery, the integration of the informal sector, and the regularization of past foreign currency exchange violations. However, once it was introduced in parliament, debated by its financial committee, and approved by the committee in September 2020 after the government's dismissal, it had been stripped of two-thirds of its content and didn't include any mention of the integration of informal economic actors or the regularization of currency violations. This had led the Fakhfakh government, before it left office, to decide that it would not immediately bring the package before the full parliament for a vote.[52] In a legislature known to bend to interest groups, this was intriguing. Why had formalization of the informal sector failed?

One reason was that the state bureaucracy, represented mainly by the customs administration and security agencies, opposed it.[53] These institutions were acting on behalf of politically connected business interests to block the emergence of a competing business elite from the periphery. At the same time, they were also enhancing their own role as gatekeepers of the economy, through their ability to protect the privileges of certain economic actors while barring others.

There was another facet to their calculations. The entrepreneurs of the informal economy and smugglers provided rents to the security agencies and customs authorities, in exchange for receiving protection. If the activities of informal actors were regularized, those rents would disappear. This situation continued after Ben Ali's fall, with the circle of beneficiaries having perhaps even expanded.[54] A former trade minister confirmed the involvement of security and customs agencies in shielding informal cross-border activities, explaining how they would notify smugglers beforehand of raids. "There are 70 wholesalers involved in smuggling in Ben Guerdane," the former minister recalled. "When Tunis ordered the security and customs services to raid warehouses, by the time officers arrived, the goods had been cleared out. High level officers kept warning smugglers ahead of time. This happens time and time again."[55]

Even a decade after the uprising, the Ministry of Interior has remained a black box governed by networks of officers that have resisted meaningful reform and political oversight.[56] Decades of informal economic activities and deepening illegality have created an incentive for the security agencies to collude with smuggling networks. The failure to implement security-sector reform after the fall of the dictatorship reinforced this trend, turning the police and security agencies into so-called entrepreneurs of insecurity, who don't enforce the law so much as employ it as a negotiating instrument, often through the sale of protection.

In view of this collusion, some political leaders have called for the creation of an anti-smuggling agency.[57] However, adding a new government body might be insufficient unless all the concerned parties take an active part in combating illegal economic practices, namely, the Ministry of Finance, the Tunisian Customs Service, the Ministry of Trade, and the Ministry of Interior's police forces and National Guard. Rather than requiring new government bodies, the present fragmentation of efforts mandates greater coordination among existing ones.

Resistance to the Fakhfakh government's package was also led by business elites who regarded the integration of informal entrepreneurs as a case of legalizing the illegal. Their assumption was that an implicit tradeoff was taking place, in which political parties and parliamentary blocs issued an amnesty to smugglers and illegal money changers in exchange for political funding. In their view, tax-paying entrepreneurs would bear the costs of such an amnesty. The leader of a major Tunisian manufacturing group expressed this thinking best: "I have worked and created jobs and tax-paying businesses for the last 30 years. Granting smugglers an amnesty would send the wrong signal and turn us, the businessmen, into a laughingstock. Making money illegally and paying a fine of 10–15 percent in exchange for an amnesty and a clean slate is just unacceptable."[58]

Besides the question of fairness, some businessmen have justified their opposition to the integration of smugglers and informal economic actors by the fact that an amnesty would be perceived as tolerance for the expanded informalization of the Tunisian economy that has taken place since 2011.[59] Indeed, faced with greater competition and an uncertain economic climate, many entrepreneurs have sought to lower their costs by looking for ways to dodge taxation and circumvent regulations. To those opposing this drift, the Fakhfakh government's proposal risked downplaying unfair competitive practices, especially in manufacturing sectors directly threatened by the informal importation of automobiles, household goods, and electrical appliances. As the businessmen quoted earlier put it, "The issue at stake is not so much the formalization of the informal sector as the informalization of the formal. Informality has become massive."[60]

Complicity between part of the political class and business elites also played a role in undermining the government's proposal. Political parties afraid of antagonizing the business elites by approving the plan instead blocked it.[61] While a small number of individuals linked to the informal sector and smuggling were members of parliament in 2019, having been elected in border constituencies, they appeared more interested in self-preservation than in advocating for the integration of their peers into the formal economy. Nor was Tunisia's political leadership strong enough to push the Fakhfakh package through, amid the conflicting agendas of interest groups in the country.

The integration of informal entrepreneurs also hit up against the ambiguities of their situation, preventing a consensus that would facilitate the formulation of clear policies. Behind the idea of formalization there is a notion that economies are divided into clear categories. In reality, there are many connections between formal and informal economies. Tunisia's informal entrepreneurs supplied shops, regional markets, and businesses, and were part of supply chains, even though they operated partly or totally in an informal context. Some did not pay taxes, others did not have import licenses even though they paid taxes, and most did not comply with the rules of registered firms and currency legislation. While figures are hard to come by, according to Joussour, a Tunis-based think tank, the loss of revenues for the state because of informal activities increased from 1.2 billion Tunisian dinars ($500 million) in 2013 to 1.5 billion Tunisian dinars ($625 million) in 2016.[62] By operating in a gray zone between the legal and the illegal, informal economic actors made it much more difficult for the government to pass legislation sharply separating the formal and the informal and in that way curb their activities.

More broadly, the Fakhfakh government's plan rubbed against the way the central authorities tend to view Tunisia's geographical peripheries. For them, border regions represent buffer zones, so their focus is on security rather than development. Contraband is often perceived as a security problem, not a problem caused by the discrepancies between fiscal and subsidy regimes in Tunisia and in oil-producing neighboring countries. The unconsidered and often irrelevant link made between jihadism and smuggling stigmatizes peripheries as hotbeds of religious extremism. This makes the idea of integrating informal economic actors and smugglers into the formal economy that much more difficult.

The failure of the Fakhfakh government's economic package only echoed what had happened to earlier efforts to integrate informal entrepreneurs into the formal economy. In 2012, the Tunisian government sought to establish a logistics and free-trade zone in the country's southeast, near the city of Ben Guerdane on the border with Libya.[63] This would have allowed peripheral entrepreneurs operating on the border to register their businesses and gain import licenses, regularizing cross-border trade, developing Ben Guerdane, and increasing state revenues. However, eight years later the project remains in limbo. Disputes over land ownership delayed implementation of the project until 2017. More profound issues related to the lack of investment in border districts were a principal problem.[64] In the initial vision, Ben Guerdane was to provide services as well as warehouse facilities, shops, transportation, and assemblage plants for the Tunisian manufacturing sector, geared toward exports.[65] The plan was built on existing duty-free zones around the port of Zarzis, which serves Ben Guerdane, and they were themselves in urgent need of infrastructural investment. For Ben Guerdane to become a regional trade hub, Zarzis port has to be modernized, while an ambitious and attractive business model must be devised to entice enterprises. This includes granting tax incentives to Tunisian and Libyan businessmen, whether they are involved in the formal or informal sector. This did not take place, however, suggesting a lack of commitment to the project.

Complicating matters further was that the Tunisian central bank opposed granting a special fiscal status to tax-free zones inside Tunisia.[66] This attitude was replicated among members of the political class. The politicians' ideological divergences effectively blocked a project that could have helped address the dire need for regional development in a marginalized border area, forcing the Fakhfakh government to temporarily shelve the Ben Guerdane plan in 2020.[67] And yet, persuading entrepreneurs of the informal economy to legalize their activities remains a necessity if Tunisia is to benefit from the revenues of cross-border trade and if peripheral parts of the country are to become stable.

The Costs of Failing to Integrate the Elites of the Informal Economy

In a highly unpredictable regional context because of tensions in Libya, and given the ensuing fragility of the security situation along Tunisia's borders, the failure to integrate peripheral elites into the formal economy will have negative repercussions. That is why the Tunisian state today must think strategically. Rather than falling into a simplistic dichotomy that peripheral economic elites are either victims or a threat to the established order, the state has to examine ways to come to terms with them in a changing environment. Since the effective coup by President Qaïs Saied in July 2021, anticipated outside funding for Tunisia has either failed to materialize or may take time to come. This has obliged the government to once again consider an amnesty for entrepreneurs of the informal economy and smugglers, in order to collect fines and replenish the state's coffers.

The first consequence of nonintegration would be a reshuffling of illicit networks. Because of heightened border security and the crackdown on Tunisian-Libyan smuggling, some of the networks that had operated through land borders have redirected their activities to maritime routes, particularly through the Sfax and Sousse ports. The importance of such routes was already evident during the first decade of the century, when they were developed by Ben Ali's friends and family, especially in the central coastal region of the Sahel. Today, the impetus to circumvent land routes is even more pressing because of the poor security situation in Libya and delays in establishing a logistics and free-trade zone in Ben Guerdane, which would breathe life into the Tunisian-Libyan land trade.

More importantly, unless peripheral elites are integrated into the formal economy, the militarization of the Tunisian-Libyan border will reinforce these elites' marginalization and dependency on trade with Libya. This, in turn, will make it more likely that they become pawns of armed Libyan groups on the other side, which are pursuing their own commercial and military objectives. If the balance of power in Libya shifts, the economic repercussions will be felt in Tunisia and could aggravate the already explosive social situation in marginalized areas.[68] Given the stalemate in Libya, armed factions there are using the border to put pressure on Tunisian traders through border closures, harassment, and extortion. Their control of border areas is a valuable asset in negotiations with the Tunisian

3 CRONIES AND CONTRABAND: WHY INTEGRATING TUNISIA'S INFORMAL... 53

authorities over the opening of border posts or in the factions' efforts to be accepted as legitimate interlocutors by Tunisia.

Without a comprehensive strategy to integrate informal economic actors or smugglers, Tunisia's financial situation will remain precarious. This will be exacerbated by the rise of maritime trade networks in which the volume of trade is routinely underreported,[69] as well as the fact that, amid rising competition and the interruption of cross-border trade because of heightened border security procedures, entrepreneurs are increasingly resorting to informal measures to remain in the market.[70] This trend has been reinforced as foreign competitors who desire a greater share of North African trade, namely, Turkish and Asian trading partners, particularly the Chinese, have also sought to sidestep local restrictions and regulations to reduce their costs and gain market share. Far from being a negligible part of regional trade flows, the entwining of formal and informal supply chains appears to be a critical part of the geoeconomic landscape in the Mediterranean, and the Tunisian state is paying heavily for this.

The failure to integrate smugglers and entrepreneurs of the informal economy will also further fragment Tunisia's economic elites. This may lead to destabilization in the context of a trade war between nations that use informal means to expand their market share, such as Turkey and East Asian countries, and those that do not, such as the European countries. This will have repercussions in Tunisia, where well-established economic elites that operate in the export sector and are connected to Europe are now competing against emerging elites tied to Asian and Turkish suppliers that have adopted informal trade strategies.[71] The situation echoes a historical episode from the nineteenth century, when colonial powers were fighting for control of North African markets. The British used their outpost in Malta as a base from which to convey smuggled British goods into Tunisia against the will of the French colonial government.[72]

Regardless of the larger geoeconomic dynamics, informal trade continues to pose problems for Tunisia's domestic constituencies. Unlike Ben Ali's regime, which used the border economy as a social safety valve, Tunisia's post-2011 governments have destabilized border communities by adopting a security-focused approach to borders. In 2020–2021, the combination of a military escalation in Libya and the COVID-19 pandemic brought the border economy to a near standstill. In Ben Guerdane and beyond, thousands of cross-border traders, small retailers, shopkeepers, informal fuel vendors, and currency exchange dealers suspended their activities, making an already dire economic situation in border areas worse.

On the Tunisian-Algerian border, the Algerian authorities blocked all passage between March and September 2020, in order to contain the spread of COVID-19.[73] Along with the developments along the border with Libya, this helped fuel social tensions, particularly in the marginalized region of Tataouine, where protestors in 2017, and again in 2020, demanded greater regional development and a more equitable distribution of the region's oil and gas revenues, which have not benefited the inhabitants in any way.[74] The Tataouine protests were highly significant in that they were multiyear affairs that profoundly damaged the credibility of the Tunisian government. Protesters hindered oil production for months, leading foreign oil companies to threaten to withdraw from their concessions.[75] The protests underlined the inhabitants' resilience in securing their demands, as well as the state's vulnerabilities in dealing with manifestations of social dissent. This only reaffirmed the need to find innovative solutions to the sharp decline in the border economy. The integration of the elites of the informal economy is one way of generating economic activity in border areas that would benefit not only the inhabitants of these regions but also the state itself, which would be in a better position to address discontent.

CONCLUSION

Since seizing power on July 25, 2021, President Qaïs Saied has become the strongman in Tunisia. However, paradoxically, he has also appeared to be weak because of his inability to resolve the country's social and economic ills, let alone offer a clear direction to do so. Instead, Saied has focused his rhetoric on fighting corruption. Tunisia's economic difficulties have obliged the authorities to again consider integrating informal elites into the formal economy. If this goes forward it would signal a transformative opening of Tunisia's economy to new social forces.

For now, however, Saied appears to be caught in a dilemma. His principal challenge is to consolidate his rule, which requires rewriting the constitution and establishing a presidential system. However, his prioritization of political affairs over addressing people's economic needs, especially in interior and peripheral regions, is bound to provoke a backlash. Moreover, it is likely to mean that he will pursue the securitization strategy adopted by previous governments in border regions. This will feed discontent as Tunisians are facing the harsh social and economic repercussions of the

COVID-19 pandemic. The result could well be rising instability and anger along the border, undermining Saied's popularity.

Instead, Tunisia needs to adopt a calculated approach to its border areas and structurally alter the framework of trade there. Tunisia would benefit from improving its relations with Algeria, in order to explore the possibility of concluding a free-trade agreement. Such an approach, by creating a basis to legalize informal trade between the two countries and by expanding trade relations overall, would be a game changer for Tunisia's western border regions.

The situation with Libya is more problematical. The political situation there remains far from stable, and uncertainty in Libya has often had a direct impact on Tunisian border areas. Tunisia can address this by accelerating implementation of the Special Economic Zone plan for Ben Guerdane. This would help strengthen the resilience of border communities by encouraging companies to settle there and transform the region into a trade hub. Smugglers would be tempted to register and become transporters, while traders would pay minimal taxes, and Libya's business class would be attracted to do business with southeastern Tunisia. Such a plan would offer the inhabitants of the region with a long-term direction that protects them from the unstable security environment across the border. Only by engaging in new thinking and redirecting Tunisia's economy toward widening the number of stakeholders in the formal economy can the country decisively address the mounting economic difficulties that have affected it in the past decade.

Notes

1. Olfa Lamloum, "Marginalization, Insecurity and Uncertainty on the Tunisian-Libyan Border: Ben Guerdane and Dhehiba from the Perspective of Their Inhabitants," International Alert, December 2016, http://international-alert.org/sites/default/files/TunisiaLibya_MarginalisationInsecurityUncertaintyBorder_EN_2016.pdf.
2. Hamza Meddeb, "Peripheral Vision. How Europe Can Help Preserve Tunisia's Fragile Democracy," European Council on Foreign Relations, January 13, 2017, https://ecfr.eu/publication/peripheral_vision_how_europe_can_preserve_tunisias_democracy_7215/
3. Douglass C. North, John Joseph Wallis, Steven B. Webb, and Barry R. Weingast, *In the Shadow of Violence: Politics, Economics, and the Problems of Development* (Cambridge: Cambridge University Press, 2013), 1–23.

4. Eva Bellin, *Stalled Democracy: Capital, Labor, and the Paradox of State-Sponsored Development* (Ithaca: Cornell University Press, 2002), 11–45.
5. Lotfi Ayadi, Nancy Benjamin, Sami Bensassi, and Gaël Raballand, "Estimating Informal Trade Across Tunisia's Land Borders," Policy Research Working Paper 6731, World Bank 2013, http://documents.worldbank.org/curated/en/856231468173645854/pdf/WPS6731.pdf.
6. International Crisis Group, "La Transition Bloquée : Corruption et Régionalisme en Tunisie" [Blocked Transition : Corruption and Regionalism in Tunisia], Rapport Moyen-Orient/Afrique du Nord, 177, (Brussels : International Crisis Group, 2017), https://www.crisisgroup.org/fr/middle-east-north-africa/north-africa/tunisia/177-blocked-transition-corruption-and-regionalism-tunisia
7. Mathieu Galtier, "Tunisie: Kais Saied Dispose de 100 Jours Pour Trouver 2,4 milliards de Dinars" [Tunisia: Kais Saied Has 100 Days to Find 2.4 Billion Dinars], *Jeune Afrique*, September 22, 2021, https://www.jeuneafrique.com/1237479/economie/kais-saied-dispose-de-100-jours-pour-trouver-24-milliards-deuros/
8. Hamza Meddeb, "Life on the Edge: How Protests in Tataouine Forced Tunis to Back Down," Malcolm H. Kerr Carnegie Middle East Center, February 1, 2021, https://carnegie-mec.org/2021/02/01/life-on-edge-how-protests-in-tataouine-forced-tunis-to-back-down-pub-83768
9. Eva Bellin, *Stalled Democracy*, 23.
10. Eva Bellin, "The Politics of Profit in Tunisia: Utility of the Rentier Paradigm?" *World Development* 22, No. 3, 1994, 427–436.
11. African Development Bank, "Tunisia: Economic and Social Challenges Beyond the Revolution" (Tunisia: African Development Bank, 2012), https://www.afdb.org/sites/default/files/documents/projects-and-operations/tunisia_economic_and_social_challenges.pdf
12. Béatrice Hibou, "La Formation Asymétrique de l'État en Tunisie. Les Territoires de l'Injustice" [The Asymmetric Formation of the State in Tunisia. The Territories of Injustice], in L'État d'Injustice au Maghreb: Maroc et Tunisie [The State of Injustice in the Maghreb: Morocco and Tunisia], edited by Irene Bono, Béatrice Hibou, Hamza Meddeb, and Mohamed Tozy (Paris: Karthala, 2015), 99–150.
13. Hassen Arouri, Leila Baghdadi, and Bob Rijkers, "How Do Dictators Get Rich? State Capture in Ben Ali's Tunisia." In *Crony Capitalism in the Middle East: Business and Politics from Liberalization to the Arab Spring*, edited by Ishac Diwan, Adeel Malik, and Izak Atiyas, (Oxford, New York: Oxford University Press, 2019), 173–204.
14. Béatrice Hibou, *The Force of Obedience: The Political Economy of Repression in Tunisia* (Cambridge: Polity Press, 2011), 31–58.

3 CRONIES AND CONTRABAND: WHY INTEGRATING TUNISIA'S INFORMAL... 57

15. Bob Rijkers, Caroline Freund, and Antonio Nucifora, "All in the Family: State Capture in Tunisia," Policy Research Working Paper 6810, World Bank, March 2014, http://documents1.worldbank.org/curated/en/440461468173649062/pdf/WPS6810.pdf.
16. Bob Rijkers, Leila Baghdadi, and Gael Raballand, "Political Connections and Tariff Evasion: Evidence from Tunisia," Policy Research Working Paper 7336, World Bank, 2015, http://documents1.worldbank.org/curated/en/828841468179081001/pdf/WPS7336.pdf.
17. *Ibid.*
18. *Ibid.*
19. United Nations Economic and Social Commission for Western Asia, "Illicit Financial Flows in the Arab Region" (Beirut: United Nations Economic and Social Commission for Western Asia, January 2018), https://www.unescwa.org/publications/illicit-financial-flows-arab-region; See also, Chafik Ben Rouine, "Tunisie: Premier Pays Arabe en Termes de Flux Financiers Illicites" [Tunisia: The Number One Arab Country in Terms of Illicit Financial Flows], Data Analysis 19 (Tunis: Observatoire Tunisien de l'Economie, 2019), https://www.economie-tunisie.org/sites/default/files/20190121-datanalysis-19-en-bap_0.pdf.
20. Bob Rijkers, Leila Baghdadi, and Gael Raballand, "Political Connections and Tariff Evasion."
21. Bob Rijkers, Caroline Freund, and Antonio Nucifora, "All in the Family."
22. World Bank, "The Unfinished Revolution: Bringing Opportunity, Good Jobs and Greater Wealth to All Tunisians," (Washington, DC: World Bank, 2014), http://documents.worldbank.org/curated/en/658461468312323813/pdf/861790DPR0P12800Box385314B00PUBLIC0.pdf.
23. Fayçal Zidi, *Politiques Économiques et Disparités Régionales en Tunisie: Une Analyse en Équilibre Général Micro-Stimulé* [Economic Policies and Regional Disparities in Tunisia. A General Equilibrium Analysis], Sorbonne Nouvelle University Paris III, (Paris: Ph.D. Thesis, 2013), https://halshs.archives-ouvertes.fr/tel-00965133/document.
24. *Ibid.*
25. Livre Blanc du Développement Régional. Une Nouvelle Vision du Développement Régional [White Book on Regional Development. A New Vision of Regional Development] (Tunis: Ministry of Regional Development, 2011).
26. Lotfi Ayadi, Nancy Benjamin, Sami Bensassi, and Gaël Raballand, "Estimating Informal Trade."
27. Hamza Meddeb, "The Volatile Tunisia-Libya Border: Between Tunisia's Security Policy and Libya's Militia Factions," Malcolm H. Kerr Carnegie Middle East Center, September 3, 2020, https://carnegie-mec.

58 H. MEDDEB

org/2020/09/03/volatile-tunisia-libya-border-between-tunisia-s-security-policy-and-libya-s-militia-factions-pub-82647

28. For an overview of the Tunisian-Libyan border economy from historical and ethnographic perspectives, see Hamza Meddeb, "Courir ou Mourir. Course à El Khobza et Domination au Quotidien dans la Tunisie de Ben Ali" [Run or Die: The Race to El Khobza and Daily Domination in Ben Ali's Tunisia] (Ph.D. thesis, Institut d'Études Politiques de Paris, 2012), https://www.academia.edu/43570339/Courir_ou_mourir._Course_à_el_khobza_et_domination_au_quotidien_dans_la_Tunisie_de_Ben_Ali

29. Béatrice Hibou, *The Force of Obedience.*

30. Max Gallien, "Informal Institutions and the Regulation of Smuggling in North Africa," *Perspectives on Politics* 18, No. 2 (2019): 1–17

31. International Crisis Group, "La Transition Bloquée: Corruption et Régionalisme en Tunisie."

32. World Bank, "The Unfinished Revolution."

33. Lotfi Ayadi, Nancy Benjamin, Sami Bensassi, and Gaël Raballand, "Estimating Informal Trade."

34. Katherine Pollock and Frederic Wehrey, "The Tunisian-Libyan Border: Security Aspirations and Socioeconomic Realities," Carnegie Endowment for International Peace, August 21, 2018, https://carnegieendowment.org/2018/08/21/tunisian-libyan-border-security-aspirations-and-socioeconomic-realities-pub-77087.

35. Lotfi Ayadi, Nancy Benjamin, Sami Bensassi, and Gaël Raballand, "Estimating Informal Trade."

36. Mohamed Oubnal and Houda Ben Hammouda, "The Political Economy of Business Elites in Tunisia. Actors, Strategies and Identities," Economic Research Forum Working Paper Series No. 1273, December 2018, https://erf.org.eg/publications/the-political-economy-of-business-elites-in-tunisia-actors-strategies-and-identities/

37. "Rijal al-Aaamal fil-barlaman attounsi: Dawafaa' attarachuh' wa asrar al-fawz" [Businesspeople in the Tunisian Parliament: Motivations for Running and the Secrets of Their Victories], *Erem News*, October 9, 2019, https://www.eremnews.com/news/maghreb-news/1998438

38. World Bank Group, "Impact of the Libyan Crisis on the Tunisian Economy," February 2017, http://documents.worldbank.org/curated/en/517981490766125612/pdf/ACS16340-WP-P158090-PUBLIC-Impact-of-Libya-Crisis-on-the-Tunisian-Economy-Long-Version.pdf

39. United Nations Economic and Social Council for Western Asia, "Situation Brief: The Libyan Conflict and its Impact on Egypt and Tunisia," (New York: United Nations, August 12, 2014), https://www.unescwa.org/sites/www.unescwa.org/files/page_attachments/the_libyan_conflict_and_its_impact_on_egypt_and_tunisia_0.pdf.

3 CRONIES AND CONTRABAND: WHY INTEGRATING TUNISIA'S INFORMAL... 59

40. Hamza Meddeb, "Rente Frontalière et Injustice Sociale en Tunisie" [Border Rent and Social Injustice in Tunisia], in Irene Bono, Béatrice Hibou, Hamza Meddeb, and Mohamed Tozy (Eds.), L'État d'Injustice au Maghreb: Maroc et Tunisie [The State of Injustice in the Maghreb: Morocco and Tunisia] (Paris: Karthala, 2015), 63–98.
41. Hamza Meddeb, "Smugglers, Tribes and Militias: The Rise of Local Forces in the Tunisian-Libyan Border Region," in *Inside Wars: Local Dynamics of Conflicts in Syria and Libya*, edited by Luigi Narbone, Agnès Favier, and Virginie Collombier (Florence: European University Institute, 2016), 38–43, http://cadmus.eui.eu/bitstream/handle/1814/41644/Inside%20wars_2016.pdf.
42. Interview with the currency dealer who requested not to be identified by name, Dhehiba, Tataouine, August 2020
43. Katherine Pollock and Frederic Wehrey, "The Tunisian-Libyan Border: Security Aspirations and Socioeconomic Realities."
44. World Bank Group, "Impact of the Libyan Crisis on the Tunisian Economy."
45. Katherine Pollock and Frederic Wehrey, "The Tunisian-Libyan Border: Security Aspirations and Socioeconomic Realities."
46. Ishac Diwan, "Tunisia's Upcoming Challenge: Fixing the Economy Before It's Too Late," Arab Reform Initiative, September 23, 2019, https://www.arab-reform.net/publication/tunisias-upcoming-challenge-fixing-the-economy-before-its-too-late/
47. *Ibid.*
48. Tarek Megerisi, "Back From the Brink: A Better Way for Europe to Support Tunisia's Democratic Transition," European Council on Foreign Relations Policy Brief, June 30, 2021, https://ecfr.eu/publication/back-from-the-brink-a-better-way-for-europe-to-support-tunisias-democratic-transition/
49. *Ibid.*
50. Interview with an adviser to former prime minister Elyes Fakhfakh who asked not to be identified by name, Tunis, December 2020.
51. "Fakhfakh: Examen du Projet de Loi sur l'Intégration de l'Économie Parallèle" [Fakhfakh: The Draft Law Related to the Integration of the Informal Economy Under Examination], *L'Économiste Maghrébin*, August 21, 2020. https://www.leconomistemaghrebin.com/2020/08/21/fakhfakh-vers-projet-loi-relatif-integration-economie-parallele/
52. Interview with a former Tunisian Minister of Trade who asked not to be identified by name, Tunis, October 2020.
53. *Ibid.*
54. International Crisis Group, "La Tunisie des Frontières: Jihad et Contrebande" [Tunisia's Borders: Jihad and Contraband], Rapport Moyen-Orient/Afrique

60   H. MEDDEB

du Nord 148 (Brussels: International Crisis Group, 2013), https://www.crisisgroup.org/middle-east-north-africa/north-africa/tunisia/tunisia-s-borders-jihadism-and-contraband.

55. Interview with a former Tunisian minister of trade who asked not to be identified by name, Tunis, October 2020.
56. Yezid Sayigh, "Missed Opportunity: The politics of Police Reform in Egypt and Tunisia," Malcolm H. Kerr Carnegie Middle East Center, March 17, 2015, https://carnegie-mec.org/2015/03/17/missed-opportunity-politics-of-police-reform-in-egypt-and-tunisia-pub-59391
57. Interview with Iyad Elloumi, Tunisian parliamentarian and member of the parliamentary Finance Committee, Tunis, October 2020.
58. Interview with Bassam Loukil, CEO of the Loukil Group, Tunis, October 2020.
59. Hamza Meddeb, "The Hidden Face of Informal Cross-Border trade in Tunisia After 2011," Malcolm H. Kerr Carnegie Middle East Center, May 27, 2021, https://carnegie-mec.org/2021/05/27/hidden-face-of-informal-cross-border-trade-in-tunisia-after-2011-pub-84621
60. Interview with Bassam Loukil, CEO Loukil Group, businessman, Tunis, October 2020.
61. Interview with Mabrouk Korchid, member of parliament from the region of Medenine, Tunis, October 2020.
62. Joussour, "Commencer par Cerner l'Informel pour Préparer son Cantonnement : Un Enjeu de Politique Publique" [Begin by Estimating the Informal Sector in Order to Prepare its Containment : A Public Policy Challenge], (Tunis : Joussour, 2016), https://www.think-joussour.org/wp-content/uploads/2020/10/2016-01-25-Le-secteur-informel-en-Tunisie.pdf
63. Interview with a former minister of trade who asked not to be identified by name, Tunis, October 2020.
64. Interview with Fethi Abaab, mayor of Ben Guerdane, Ben Guerdane, August 2020.
65. Instance Générale de Partenariat Public Privé, " Zone Logistique et de Libre Échange à Ben Guerdane" [Logistics and Free-Trade Zone in Ben Guerdane], (Tunis : Instance Générale de Partenariat Public Privé, 2018), http://www.igppp.tn/sites/default/files/Fiches_descriptives/06-Fiche-CT-ZALC-Ben-Guerdane-FR-003-VFC-KA.pdf
66. Interview with Moez Laabidi, former member of the Economic Analysis Council, an advisory body to the prime minister, Tunis, November 2020. The central bank wants to give priority to reforming currency legislation ("code de change") before granting a special currency status to tax-free zones.

3 CRONIES AND CONTRABAND: WHY INTEGRATING TUNISIA'S INFORMAL... 61

67. Mahmoud Anis Bettaieb, "Quid de la Loi de Relance : Regards Critique sur le Projet de Loi No. 104/2020" [What About the Law for Economic Recovery: Critical Insights on Draft Law No. 104/2020], *Leaders*, November 8, 2020, https://www.leaders.com.tn/article/30887-quid-de-la-loi-de-relance-regards-critiques-sur-le-projet-de-loi-n-104-2020
68. Frederic Wehrey, "Tunisia's Wake-up Call: How Security Challenges From Libya Are Shaping Defense Reform," Carnegie Endowment for International Peace, March 18, 2020, https://carnegieendowment.org/2020/03/18/tunisia-s-wake-up-call-how-security-challenges-from-libya-are-shaping-defense-reforms-pub-81312
69. United Nations Economic and Social Commission for Western Asia, "Illicit Financial Flows in the Arab Region," (Beirut: United Nations Economic and Social Commission for Western Asia, 2018), https://www.unescwa.org/publications/illicit-financial-flows-arab-region.
70. Majdi Saidi, "Tunis: Al-Istirad al-'Ashwa'i Yu'amiq al-Azma al-Iqtisaadiyyah wa Yufaqim al-'Ajz al-Tijari" [Tunisia: Anarchic Imports Aggravate the Economic Crisis and Exacerbate the Trade Deficit], Al-Jazeera, November 14, 2019, https://www.aljazeera.net/ebusiness/2019/11/14/تونس-الاستيراد-العشوائي-يعمق-الأزمة
71. Hamza Meddeb, "The Hidden Face of Informal Cross-Border trade in Tunisia After 2011."
72. Dalenda Largueche, *Pouvoir et Contrebande dans la Tunisie du 19ème Siècle* [Power and Smuggling in the Tunisia of the 19th Century] (Tunis: Céres Editions, 1999), 178–180.
73. "Covid-19: L'Algérie Maintient ses Frontières Fermées Jusqu'à Nouvel Ordre" [Covid-19: Algeria Keeps its Borders Closed Until Further Notice], *France 24*, June 30, 2020, https://www.france24.com/fr/20200630-covid-19-algerie-frontieres-fermees-confinement-cible-recrudescence-cas
74. Hamza Meddeb, "Life on the Edge: How Protests in Tataouine Forced Tunis to Back Down."
75. Author identified only as H. B.H., "Des Sociétés Pétrolières Informent Kais Saied de Leur Éventuel Départ de la Tunisie" [Oil Companies Inform Kais Saied of the Possibility That They May Leave Tunisia], *Réalités Online*, August 29, 2020, https://www.realites.com.tn/2020/08/des-societes-petrolieres-informent-kais-saied-de-leur-eventuel-depart-de-la-tunisie/

CHAPTER 4

North Pacific: Why Lebanon's Akkar Region Weathered the Syrian Conflict

Maha Yahya and Mohanad Hage Ali

INTRODUCTION

When the uprising in Syria broke out in 2011, many observers feared the knock-on effects in neighboring Lebanon. The violent turn the uprising took, with an Alawite-dominated regime fighting a mainly Sunni opposition, appeared to put one Lebanese region in particular at high risk, namely, the northern Lebanese region of Akkar, which borders Syria. Akkar's sectarian mix, with a majority of the population belonging to the Sunni community and the presence of an Alawite minority, as well as the region's widespread poverty and a population that might have benefited from taking up arms if this was funded by Syria's regional foes, were seen as elements that could facilitate its being drawn into the conflict next door.

Maha Yahya is the director of the Malcolm H. Kerr Carnegie Middle East Center in Beirut. Mohanad Hage Ali is a senior fellow at the center.

M. Yahya (✉) • M. H. Ali
Malcolm H. Kerr Carnegie Middle East Center, Beirut, Lebanon
e-mail: myahya@carnegie-mec.org

© The Author(s), under exclusive license to Springer Nature Switzerland AG 2023
M. Yahya (ed.), *How Border Peripheries are Changing the Nature of Arab States*, https://doi.org/10.1007/978-3-031-09187-2_4

63

In fact, the opposite occurred. Rather than becoming a place of sectarian confrontation, Akkar somehow helped to foster social peace in Lebanon at a difficult time, in contrast to the polarizing impact of the Syrian conflict in other parts of the country. More important, the northern border region was instrumental in shaping attitudes in Beirut, particularly responses by the central government and the military that, overall, served to defuse tensions nationally.

This situation was made possible by conditions specific to Akkar. Among them was a tradition of sectarian coexistence, socioeconomic marginalization that affected all religious communities equally, and a range of crossborder networks—family and tribal networks, as well as smuggling networks—that generated inherent pragmatism with regard to events in Syria. Equally significant was the fact that Akkar was, and remains, a major recruitment ground for the Lebanese armed forces; therefore, the military' goal of maintaining civil peace is one that many of the inhabitants share. All these factors helped to assuage the sectarian and ideological fault lines that had formed because of the conflict in Syria.

A TALE OF TWO COUNTRIES

If Akkar defied predictions that it would be engulfed by the deadly dynamics in Syria, this was partly because there had long been a disconnect between the peripheral region and the center. The conditions in Akkar, so unlike those in Beirut and its surrounding areas, led to outcomes that were different than expected thanks to the region's pluralism, relative neglect, social networks that facilitated contacts with Syria, and the influence of the Lebanese army.

Lebanon's borders with Syria are around 375 kilometers long, of which approximately 100 kilometers are located in Akkar. For the most part, the borders remain undemarcated, with nearly 37 areas in dispute.[1] Akkar is home to around 324,000 residents (or 6.7 percent of the total Lebanese population)[2] and includes both Christians and Muslims.[3] The region also hosts more than 106,000 Syrian refugees.[4] According to voter rolls from the 2018 elections, which give a fairly accurate impression of sectarian distribution, 62.4 percent of voters were Sunnis, 19.4 percent were Greek Orthodox Christians, 16.4 percent were Maronite Christians, and 1.7 percent were Alawites (Map 4.1).[5]

During the Lebanese civil war (1975–1990), Akkar was spared major violence, communal rifts, and the displacement that took place in Beirut,

4 NORTH PACIFIC: WHY LEBANON'S AKKAR REGION WEATHERED... 65

Map 4.1   Lebanon's northern border region

Mount Lebanon, South Lebanon, and the Beqaa Valley. This made for stronger communal coexistence, which a Sunni activist from the region described in this way: "There is no history of violence among Sunnis and Alawites in the region. While there may be no abundance of intermarriages between the two communities, strong business and tribal relations exist. Alawite businesses employ Sunnis and vice versa, and smugglers from both communities collaborate to maximize the usefulness of their respective networks."[6]

Others from Akkar have mentioned the presence of a large Greek Orthodox community as a significant factor in preserving intercommunal relations. The Greek Orthodox tended to join nonsectarian parties, such as the Syrian Social Nationalist Party (SSNP) and the Lebanese Communist Party, and in the post-2005 period, many supported the Free Patriotic Movement,[7] while Maronites have mainly supported more avowedly Christian political parties, such as the Kataeb, the Lebanese Forces, and the National Liberal Party.[8] The Orthodox community also maintained crossborder connections, having a large presence in Syria, whether in coastal areas or in the Wadi al-Nadara in Homs Governorate.[9]

Inter-sectarian relations have been reinforced by the fact that Akkar has long suffered from significant socioeconomic deprivation. This has affected all residents, irrespective of sectarian background creating a shared sense of oppression. What this has done is to stabilize communal relations, which allowed the inhabitants of Akkar to better address the sectarian rifts caused by war in Syria.

In 2021, two years after the beginning of Lebanon's economic collapse, the United Nations Economic and Social Council for West Asia reported that more than 92 percent of households living in Akkar were experiencing multidimensional poverty and 51.5 percent were facing extreme multidimensional poverty.[10] In 2018, Akkar was also where the highest illiteracy levels were recorded—11 percent of those above the age of ten were illiterate, compared to a national average of 7 percent.[11] Figures for the same year showed the region also had the highest age-dependency ratio nationally. This measures the number of under-age children or adults over 65 years old who are dependent on working family members. The ratio for Akkar was 87 percent, while the national average was 59 percent.[12]

Labor conditions are little better. In 2018, labor force participation in Akkar—the number of people in the labor force as a percentage of the total population—was one of the lowest in the country at 38 percent.[13] Sixty percent of those employed had informal jobs, while 42 percent worked in the informal sector.[14] This meant they were without access to any kind of legal social protection, exposing them to greater economic risks. Unemployment rates in Akkar are also high, at 54 percent for Lebanese and 65 percent for stateless individuals, in other words those who have been denied Lebanese citizenship.[15] This situation was compounded by the influx of more than 1 million Syrian refugees fleeing the Syrian conflict over the past decade.[16] Almost a third of refugees reside in North Lebanon, and the ratio of refugees to the local population stands at 28 percent.[17] This has created a race to the bottom between the poorest Lebanese and the vulnerable refugees.

Decades of political and social insecurity in Akkar have impeded investment, curtailed growth and job creation, and encouraged the out-migration of talent. This situation is reflected in the fact that economic life in the region revolves around four types of activity that are often typical of marginalized areas: agriculture, in which 11 percent of Akkar's population is active, compared to an average of 3 percent nationally; recruitment into the military;[18] small-scale retail services and businesses that employ less than five people;[19] and smuggling.[20]

Those employed formally have mainly joined the armed forces, as most households encourage a member to enlist in the military and take advantage of the benefits.[21] One of these is health insurance. In 2019, only 45 percent of Akkar's residents had health insurance, while 60 percent of those who did had received it through the army, compared to an average of 20 percent nationally.

Low levels of state investment in Akkar have contributed to the region's underdevelopment, and this is reflected in the poor condition of the region's services and infrastructure. Between 2011 and 2021, spending on education, health, and transportation in Akkar, measured as a percentage of total Lebanese state investment, was 8 percent, 10 percent, and 2 percent, respectively.[22] One indication of this is that public schools in Akkar are for the most part rented structures rather than buildings built and owned by the state as is the case elsewhere in the country. In addition, only 37 percent of homes are connected to drinking water.[23] These dismal conditions were such that in the past it was easier and more cost-effective for residents to obtain services in Syria.

Statelessness has been another, more insidious, form of marginalization. Most of those affected by this status in Akkar are Sunnis from the Wadi Khaled region, which comprises 22 towns. Since Lebanon's independence in 1943, the Lebanese state has denied a significant portion of its residents citizenship and the rights associated with this.[24] The problem was only partly addressed in 1994,[25] leaving 30,000–60,000 people without citizenship.[26] These individuals are denied the right to travel, work, and be educated, exacerbating their socioeconomic marginalization. The rationale behind denying them citizenship derives from Lebanon's sectarian system and fears that if they were to become citizens the demographic balance between Christians and Muslim would tilt even more toward Muslims.

A third factor that generated more pragmatic attitudes in Akkar toward the Syrian conflict, helping to shield the region from the conflict's political and sectarian ramifications, was the existence of multiple networks tying Akkar to Syria. These were, principally, tribal, familial, and smuggling networks.

Socially, Akkar is partially characterized by tribal and family networks that extend across the border into Syria.[27] For example, in Wadi Khaled, mainly a tribal region, families belonging to the same tribe reside on both sides of the border. The Khutbah tribe in Wadi Khaled includes the Asaad, Akkari, Sarhan, and Abdallah family branches. Relatives of the Asaad family reside on the Syrian side of the border town of Arida, while Syrian members of the Akkari, Sarhan, and Abdallah families live in Talkalakh, Mjameh, and Naoura in Syria, respectively. Other examples are the Yahya and Ali families in the Lebanese town of Akroum, who extend into the

68   M. YAHYA AND M. H. ALI

Syrian town of Hit. The Diab and Saadeddine families are split between Akroum and the Syrian town of Hawik.[28] Such family connections have facilitated crossborder marriages, but also trade relations and other economic activities, which include cooperation in smuggling networks.

One sign of the impact of sectarian coexistence and the value of pragmatism with regard to crossborder relations was the contrast that existed during the Syria conflict between Akkar and northern city of Tripoli. Armed clashes between Alawites in the Tripoli neighborhood of Jabal Mohsen and Sunnis in neighboring Bab al-Tabbaneh became a regular occurrence starting in June 2011.[29] The violence highlighted the strained relations between Sunnis and Alawites, and beyond that between Sunnis and Shia at the national level, as the Syrian conflict took a bloodier turn. However, the sectarian animosities in Tripoli did not translate into deep Sunni-Alawite discord in the border towns of Akkar.

In addition to tribal and familial ties, two other drivers enhancing crossborder networks were Syrian state policies and involvement in smuggling. For Syrian officials, Akkar has long been perceived as Syria's extension into Lebanon, given the existence of crossborder relationships.[30] More significantly, the region was also seen as vital for the Syrian regime's interests, given the potential impact of Akkar's Sunnis on those in Syria. The approach was present alongside the Lebanese state's marginalization of Akkar. This combination engendered a far more realistic view of relations with Syria than in other areas of Lebanon, which helped to absorb a certain level of discontent generated by the Syrian conflict.

There was nothing fortuitous in such a development. Lebanon's independence in 1943 marked a significant shift in the lives of the inhabitants of its northern peripheries. These areas were cut off from their traditional hinterland and trade hubs, with major cities such as Homs, Lataqiyya, Hama, and Aleppo now located in Syria.[31] Areas that had once been on transit routes toward the interior were suddenly on the margins of a new Lebanese state that was focused on developing Beirut and the adjacent Mount Lebanon region. This reality shaped the northern border area's view of politics at the center, as well as relations with Syria.

The start of the Lebanese civil war in 1975 took the process further, as Akkar became even more disconnected from the center and from adjoining Christian-majority districts such Bsharri, Zgharta, and Batroun. This allowed the region's pro-Syrian factions, notably the SSNP, which advocates for unity between Lebanon and Syria, to gain influence. Such trends led to a further solidification of ties between Akkar and Syria and were sustained by the fact that until 2011 the Syrian authorities allowed residents of Lebanese border areas to receive free medical treatment and education in Syria, as well as access to food and goods.[32] Syria's subsidy regime meant that prices were more affordable than in Lebanon for residents of Akkar's border towns, many of whom profited from the situation. At the same time, Syria's direct influence over Akkar in postwar Lebanon, when the country was under effective Syrian tutelage, meant that political parties with an interest in building up patronage networks in the area through development initiatives were unable to do so, as this might have hit up against Syrian control.

The Syrian uprising in 2011 triggered dramatic shifts in the lives and livelihoods of most Lebanese, and this was especially true of the residents of Akkar. The conflict changed the Syrian state's policies toward its border zones. Because the Syrian authorities were concerned about the possibility that combatants or weapons would be sent across the Lebanese-Syrian border illegally, they closed official crossing points on occasion and planted landmines along parts of the border to limit the movement of people and goods.[33] This situation was catastrophic for border communities. Farmers with farmlands inside Syria could no longer reach them. Lebanese fishermen were prevented from approaching Syria's coastline.[34] And the inhabitants of Akkar were denied access to cheaper Syrian goods and services, including education and health. Lebanese villages and towns were also shelled by the Syrian army under the pretext that they were harboring terrorists, leading to the loss of life and destruction of property.

Residents of the border area quickly adapted to the new reality through a greater reliance on smuggling and informal trade.[35] Smugglers found innovative ways to circumvent the measures taken by the Syrian authorities to disrupt the flow of goods between the two countries, including sending goods across the border on mules so as to avoid landmines.[36] Smuggling flourished through the three official border crossings as well as an estimated 136 informal crossings. This had been true even prior to the Syrian conflict and was facilitated by lax border controls, the relatively easy flow of goods and people between Lebanon and Syria, and tribal networks that spanned both sides of the frontier.

Two categories of smuggling could, and still can, be identified, and each played a role in allowing Akkar to avert the strong polarizing effect the violence in Syria provoked elsewhere in Lebanon. The first involved small-scale smuggling, conducted by families and individuals for limited profits. For residents of border towns, state neglect left them with few other options for making a living. In the words of one inhabitant, "[F]or us smuggling is a form of trade in a context where the state has forgotten about us and across borders that we do not recognize and believe to be artificial."[37] A local mayor went further in saying, "[W]ithout smuggling, many Akkaris would be begging on the streets of Tripoli."[38] These activities are usually carried out by local networks and take place at specified points of sale in border towns. For these smugglers, maintaining a flexible attitude toward relations with Syria during its conflict was a question of economic survival. This discouraged any actions that might have threatened such ties.

The second category of smuggling was far more organized and dominated by families with political links on both sides of the border. These individuals had established and sustained lucrative smuggling operations despite the momentous political and security changes in the region. Key figures in the business were also political representatives from Akkar and used their wealth as patronage to support local families and guarantee continued influence over the community.[39] This situation predated the Syria conflict and continues to this day.

The latter category of smugglers was the most significant in determining outlooks during the Syrian conflict. Because of their prominence, they had a voice in Beirut and were able to affect Lebanese policies.[40] Their approach was contradictory and mercenary, in many regards. These individuals profited from sending fighters and weapons into Syria for a fee, benefited from selling subsidized fuel to Syrians, and supported a policy of normalization with Damascus when the conflict ebbed after 2017, in order to reap the benefits of postwar reconstruction.[41]

Among the major smuggling families is the Ismail family. It belongs to the Ghannam tribe, a Bedouin tribe that spans Syria, Jordan, Iraq, and Saudi Arabia. Its involvement shows how crossborder tribal networks play a central role in smuggling and its associated politics. In the 2000 parliamentary elections, when Lebanon was still under Syrian domination, Jamal Ismail, who was known for his involvement in smuggling and for having relations with the Syrian security services, represented Akkar in parliament.[42] In the 2018 Lebanese elections, Ismail's nephew Mohammed Suleiman, also known for his ties with members of the Syrian security services, won a parliamentary seat, albeit this time as part of the Future Movement's bloc opposed to Syria!ized[43] The family has maintained its crossborder business, and prior to the Syrian withdrawal in 2005, Suleiman had already established a Syrian company with known regime links.[44] As he pursued a political career, the family business continued to operate inside Syria.

A distinguishing feature of the smuggling networks is that they were pluralistic in nature. They were led by individuals from a wide spectrum of sects and political loyalties and were characterized by a large degree of intercommunal relations that reflected the social and political mosaic of Akkar. The networks included Sunnis, Christians, and Alawites, and their political affiliations ranged from the Future Movement to Michel Aoun's Free Patriotic Movement to the pro-Syrian SSNP. According to northern politicians, the political class in Beirut was tolerant of the smuggling networks' connections with Syria after 2011, although these were often inconsistent with the political mood at the center, where hostility to the Syrian regime dominated in the Sunni sphere.[45]

Effectively, what existed in Akkar was an informal constituency of influential figures, whose self-interest dictated that they would not allow the political-sectarian situation there to spin out of control. This would have undermined their lucrative smuggling operations, which required partners on the Syrian side. Such opportunism and self-interest helped to allay sectarian tensions, and the fact that leading national politicians in Beirut went along with it showed they were shrewd enough to see the benefits of not clarifying Akkar's constructive ambiguities.

That is not to say, however, that the smuggling networks could not sometimes take measures that went against the interests of the Syrian authorities. When Arab Gulf states funded the Syrian opposition, these networks took part in supplying weapons and moving combatants into Syria.[46] The predominantly Sunni Future Movement, led by Saad al-Hariri, who was prime minister until 2011, backed Syrian opposition groups and was accused by Hezbollah and the Syrian regime of being an intermediary in supplying them with weapons and funds.[47] Some northern border villages also were located along supply lines to besieged opposition groups inside Syria.[48] However, the distinguishing feature of the networks' behavior in supporting the Syrian rebellion was monetary gain. It was business, nothing personal. A northern Lebanese Islamist activist involved in the Syrian uprising's support network summarized the smugglers' motivations:

> The smuggling was based not on ideological affinity, but on money. We knew the networks were useful because of their connections to the Syrian regime and their ability to bribe Syrian intelligence and military officers who

manned checkpoints on the other side of the border. Such usefulness does not come with ideological affiliation.[49]

A fourth factor that helped to stabilize Akkar was the high rate of conscription into the Lebanese armed forces and the relatively weak presence of Islamist militants or activity in the northern border region.[50] For a number of northern politicians and other officials, the two were related in that the population's dependency on recruitment into the military, therefore on the state, tended to deter youths from joining extremist groups.[51] Notable exceptions were the suicide bombers Mutassim Khaldoun al-Hassan and his brother Hassan, who carried out an attack against a Syrian military roadblock near Homs. Their actions received much coverage in Lebanese media outlets. However, the reality is that both young men were recruited and radicalized in Sweden, not in the Akkar, from where their family had emigrated.[52]

This seems to explain why public concerns by Lebanese officials that the Islamic State or the Al-Qaeda-affiliated Nusra Front would try to seize control of areas in Akkar never materialized.[53] Lebanese outlets continued to report on the potential threat of extremist networks in the region, but there was little evidence to back up these claims.[54] In contrast, extremist groups were able to take over parts of Lebanon's eastern border with Syria, near Arsal, until they were pushed out by the Lebanese armed forces in August 2017.[55] Akkar's tradition of intercommunal relations, the fact that cross-sectarian smuggling had created a more nuanced outlook with regard to Syria, as well as a need to maintain profitable relationships with Syrian officials, and the integration of local youths into the armed forces all served to reduce the impact of the Syria war on sectarian relations. This, in turn, would have significant and positive repercussions in Beirut.

Akkar's Impact on Beirut

The situation in Akkar had a multifaceted impact on decision-making in Beirut with regard to the Syrian conflict and its repercussions for Lebanon. This provoked equally multifaceted responses from the government of prime minister Najib Mikati (2011–2014) and later of Tammam Salam (2014–2016). While these responses may have reflected the government's constraints in a complex sectarian and political environment at the time, it proved effective in absorbing pressure at the right moments. The fact that Akkar remained calm encouraged the government to adapt to realities in the region, underlining that a laissez-faire attitude was preferable to taking steps that might have undermined the contradictions that somehow kept tensions under control.

Four major factors came to define the interaction between Akkar and the central government. First, the contentious political and sectarian environment made it all but impossible for the government to impose a unified, centralized policy with regard to the large numbers of Syrian refugees entering Lebanon. Second, in certain instances the situation in Akkar compelled the state to take a position on aggressive Syrian behavior, despite the fact that this angered Syria's Lebanese allies. Third, the complicated social relations in Akkar, in particular the sectarian and crossborder links due to smuggling operations, helped neutralize antagonisms there, which the government picked up on by allowing the region to resolve conflicts in its own way. And fourth, the presence of young recruits from Akkar in the armed forces gave the government an important lever to control developments on the ground.

First, for both humanitarian and political reasons, the Lebanese state was unable to take centralized steps to stem the flow of Syrian refugees. Initially, many of the refugees sought shelter with friends and family, and it would have been nearly impossible for the authorities to prevent this without provoking an angry local reaction. Moreover, until January 2015,[56] when border regulations changed, hundreds of thousands of Syrian refugees were allowed to enter Lebanon as there are no visa requirements between the countries.[57] Despite increasing xenophobia from some quarters, Sunnis were largely sympathetic to victims of the Syrian regime, and their parliamentarians shared this outlook. Moreover, state paralysis in the face of the enormity of the crisis meant local municipalities took the lead in shaping responses to the refugees' arrival.[58] In this context, there was also pressure on the government from Akkar parliamentarians to take advantage of international support and initiate development projects in the region.[59]

The practical outcome of this combination of factors cannot be understated. While the refugees would become a major demographic liability for Lebanon, the fact that the government was compelled to account for local dynamics on the periphery and continued allowing Syrians into the country helped to contain any sectarian backlash that might have accompanied a more restrictive policy. That municipalities near the border areas fronted responses to the refugees—not only in Akkar but also in the Beqaa Valley— meant that hitherto peripheral areas had much more of a say in policy decisions coming out of the capital. Indeed, the government, which was wracked by political rivalries and divisions, was pleased to devolve authority to the local level and push the burden of caring for refugees onto local councils, nongovernmental organizations, and ultimately international organizations. This was far from ideal, given the limited resources at the municipal level, but it did give wider latitude to those closest to the realities on the ground to say what was needed. A centralized refugee policy, in contrast, though perhaps better from an organizational perspective, would likely have been burdened by the political rifts then causing dysfunction within the government.

Second, spillover from the Syrian conflict affected Akkar in ways that forced the Lebanese authorities to take firm positions at times. In July 2012, the Syrian army shelled Lebanese border towns, mainly targeting the area of Wadi Khaled, while Syrian soldiers entered Lebanese villages and killed or injured a number of people including a cameraman from Al-Jadeed TV.[60] The attacks drew nationwide condemnation, augmented by concerns that the Syrian conflict would spread to the border area and draw in the Syrian army and their local allies, despite the efforts of the Lebanese armed forces to maintain order there.[61]

These incidents compelled then president Michel Suleiman to issue a strongly worded letter that was handed to the Syrian ambassador condemning the shelling and the civilian casualties.[62] In doing so, Suleiman bypassed the previously used communications channels with the Syrian government, including joint Syrian-Lebanese committees mandated with discussing security matters.[63] Despite criticism of the president from Syria's Lebanese allies, notably Hezbollah, his condemnation projected an image of national unity and decisiveness that reaffirmed the ability and willingness of the state to protect its citizens.

To explain the impact of the president's remarks, understanding the general context at the time is useful. For many Lebanese Sunnis, the repression in Syria came to be viewed in sectarian terms. As they saw it, the Alawite-dominated Syrian regime sought to retain its power against the majority of the population that was Sunni. Therefore, the repercussions of a Syrian military attack against a Sunni-majority region in Lebanon had the potential to sharpen sectarian divisions there, while the government's silence on what happened would have heightened Sunni indignation, disturbing the delicate sectarian balance that had prevailed until then in Akkar. That Suleiman took a determined stance, knowing full well that it would open him up to condemnation from the allies of Damascus, went a long way toward reassuring many Sunnis, helping to counterbalance the anger in Akkar that could have easily turned against a state perceived as weak.

Third, the crossborder links due to smuggling operations helped to create a more detached attitude with regard to Syria, one based on self-interest, which found its way back into decision-making in the capital. While the sectarian rhetoric in Akkar could have increased during different phases of the Syrian conflict, throughout that period the level of violence remained low. That the region stayed this way had a calming effect on Sunni attitudes in Beirut and other parts of Lebanon.

Viewed from the center, crossborder links with Syrian security and political officials seemed to contradict the Sunni resentment directed against the Syrian regime. However, opportunism justified it, so that self-interest, even if it existed alongside antagonism toward the leadership in Syria, dictated an attitude that diluted sectarian tensions. And this attitude was mainly visible in the smuggling networks operated by influential northern politicians and their clans, whose business interests were vital to defining attitudes in Beirut.[64] Lebanon's sectarian political system gave local parliamentarians a major say in appointing state officials in Akkar, including police and military officers who would contribute to shaping Beirut's response to events in the region.[65] The result was a hybrid system, one involving state officials on the one hand and tribal networks and local notables on the other. Even security or military appointees not affiliated with local politicians could gain financially from allowing smuggling operations to continue.[66] Therefore, when they would report back to the capital, these officials would often reiterate the positions of local notables in Akkar.

Effectively, what this meant is that the mood of local politicians had a hearing in the capital. Politicians from Akkar, rather than stoking public anger with what was going on in Syria, which perhaps would have allowed them to gain locally in sectarian terms, preferred to play this down in their statements and behavior in Beirut. A revealing example of this is Walid Baarini, the son of Wajih Baarini, a longstanding parliamentarian from Akkar who had developed a close relationship with key Syrian decision-makers. Walid was elected to parliament in 2018 as part of a list formed by Saad al-Hariri's Future Movement.[67] Hariri's antagonism toward the Syrian regime was driven by the fact that he accused it of involvement in his father's assassination in 2005. However, regardless of Walid Baarini's affiliation with Future, he never criticized or attacked the Syrian regime.

Instead, his public remarks were usually focused on denying involvement in smuggling or on issues pertaining to government services and local development in Akkar.

The needs of local communities in Akkar also impacted how officials in Beirut framed their changing attitudes toward Syria. After Hariri became prime minister in 2016, he and the Future Movement began promoting a line of argument that Lebanon, particularly the northern regions of Akkar and Tripoli, would benefit from Syria's reconstruction. This view helped to legitimize what should have been a controversial step, given Hariri's opposition to the Syrian leadership. As Hariri had put it at the time to residents of Akkar, "[G]iven your geographic location, the reconstruction of Syria, means that you will play a central role [in it]."[68] While not endorsing the Syrian regime, Hariri and other Sunnis envisaged a time when they would have to deal with Damascus. Akkar's politics, specifically the quest for economic development and trade with Syria, helped to realign the Future Movement's approach to that country after years of antagonism.

Finally, because many young people from Akkar are in the Lebanese army, military and political decision-makers in the capital were in tune with what was going on in the region and could better control it. Seeing that Akkar had preserved civil and sectarian peace, the army did not rock the boat. The reverse was also true. Young recruits from Akkar, a significant portion of the rank and file in the military, were a cornerstone of what is a leading institutional representative of a state whose priority is the containment of sectarian strife. This reinforced the mechanisms already in place to defuse sectarian polarization.[69] Moreover, conscripts from the region provided the army with eyes into local society, so that activities by extremists could be detected more easily.

Akkar acted as a buffer against the sectarian consequences of the war in Syria by presenting a contrast with the mood in Tripoli and Beirut. Ultimately, what the maintenance of social peace there expressed was an alternative affirming that coexistence could prevail in an area where the main religious communities involved in the Syrian fighting were present. More than that, Akkar never became a hotbed for extremism, as many had anticipated. In the end the region disproved many of the easy assumptions that had emanated primarily from Beirut. Having long been on the periphery of the modern Lebanese state, and of Lebanese minds, Akkar could take quiet satisfaction in the fact that after 2011 the central authorities in Beirut gained much from learning more about the region.

CONCLUSION

Lebanon's northern periphery has long personified the unbalanced nature of the state's investment in the country and beyond that the shortcomings of the Lebanese project of statehood. Since the establishment of Greater Lebanon in 1920 and independence in 1943, the focal point of national attention has been Beirut and Mount Lebanon. Yet in many regards, the neglected north, particularly Akkar, has embraced a vital attribute, sectarian coexistence, that has been central in Lebanon's portrayal of itself to the world. This positive contribution should reshape the center's attitude toward the northern periphery.

During the Syrian conflict, Akkar acted as a valuable ecosystem in which Lebanon's multiconfessional identity could sustain communal peace, despite violence and tensions elsewhere in the country. This achievement on its own should encourage the state to do more to preserve a region that has the possibility of so successfully bridging Lebanon's myriad differences. That means investing more in Akkar and its communities, rather than abandoning them so that they have to seek out the essentials of a decent life in neighboring Syria.

Akkar's deprivation, the fact that the central government was largely absent as the region welcomed tens of thousands of Syrian refugees, and the area's high reliance on smuggling have contributed to creating a new reality in the Lebanese state. Today, diverse authorities are defining critical aspects of particular regions in Lebanon. In Akkar two levels of domestic actors are shaping realities on the ground: the Lebanese state and local figures, including tribal representatives and those involved in the illicit trade who have political and economic influence. Such hybrid arrangements, whether in governing the periphery or impacting policy at the center, may constitute a microcosm of Lebanon's future politics, as its postwar elites have failed to put the state at the heart of initiatives to respond to Lebanon's many challenges. Such arrangements may have kept conflict at bay in Akkar, but in other areas of Lebanon the state's absence may mean the opposite is true.

NOTES

1. *Al-Nahar*, "Al-Maaber Ghayr al-Shariia wa Moukafahat al-Tahrib wa Mouktarahat lil Dabet: Al-Houdoud maa Souriya 357 km 36 Noukta Khilafya wa Ikfal 90%" [Illegal Crossings, Combating Smuggling, and

Proposals for Control: The Border With Syria is 357 kilometers, 36 Points of Contention, and 90 Percent is Closed], *Al-Nahar*, July 13, 2020, https://tinyurl.com/2mzy2f79.

2. "Labour Force and Household Living Conditions Survey 2018–2019 in Akkar," Central Administration of Statistics, 2020, 1–25, http://www.cas.gov.lb/images/Publications/Labour_Force_District_Statistics/AKKAR percent20FINAL.PDF.

3. Aicha Mouchref, "Forgotten Akkar: Socio-Economic Reality of the Akkar Region," Mada Association, January 2008, 3, https://fdocuments.in/document/socio-economic-assessmentforgotten-akkar.html.

4. According to data from the United Nations High Commissioner for Refugees, 106,121 Syrian refugees are registered in Akkar. See Operational Data Portal Refugee Situations, (United Nations High Commissioner for Refugees, November 4, 2020), https://data2.unhcr.org/en/documents/details/82685. See also, *Syrian Refugee Response*, (Beirut: United Nations High Commissioner for Refugees, 2020), https://data2.unhcr.org/en/documents/details/82685.

5. Kamal Feghali, "Tahlil intikhabat 2018: Dawaer wa Tawaef wa Ahzab wa Tahaloufat" [Analysis of the 2018 Elections: Constituencies, Sects, Parties and Alliances], *180 post.com*, December 21, 2021, https://180post.com/archives/24208

6. Interview with a Sunni activist from the border region in Akkar, who asked to remain anonymous due to his involvement in smuggling, January 15, 2022. He specifically mentioned an Alawite-owned bakery, belonging to parliamentarian Mustapha Hussein, which employs Sunni workers from neighboring towns.

7. Christina Jaber, "Al-Intikhabat al-Baladiyya al-Fariyya fi Shadra, Akkar: Tanafos Aaili wa Hizbi" [Municipal By-Elections in Shadra, Akkar: Family and Party Rivalries], *Al-Joumhouria*, October 5, 2019, https://tinyurl.com/2p93y7r6. See also, Najla Hammoud, "Akkar: Sibak Aaili wa Siyassi… wal Imtihan fi Rahba" [Akkar: A Political and Family Race… and the Test is in Rahba], *Greenarea*, April 19, 2016, https://tinyurl.com/5xzj6enj

8. Ghassan Saoud, "Al Qubayat Tousket Tayyar al Moustaqbal" [Qobayat Causes the Future Political Movement to Lose], originally published at *Al-Akhbar*, but reproduced by the Al-Manar website, March 4, 2013, https://archive.almanar.com.lb/article.php?id=434589

9. Sean Sprague, "Syria's Christian Valley: A Historically Christian Enclave Adapts and Thrives," Catholic Near East Welfare Association CNEWA, January, 2011, https://cnewa.org/magazine/syrias-christian-valley-33524/

10. Households are defined as multidimensionally poor if they are deprived in one or more dimensions under the index. They are considered to be suffering from extreme multidimensional poverty if they are deprived of two or more dimensions under the Global Multidimensional Poverty Index. See: "Multidimensional Poverty in Lebanon (2019–2021) Painful Reality and Uncertain prospects," United Nations Economic and Social Council for West Asia, Policy Brief 2, September 2021, 1–6, https://www.unescwa.org/publications/multidimensional-poverty-lebanon-2019-2021

11. "Labour Force and Household Living Conditions Survey 2018–2019 in Akkar," 1–25. Another report cites higher illiteracy figures for Akkar, compared to the national level. See, Mouchref, "Forgotten Akkar," 3.

12. See United Nations Development Program, "The Living Conditions Index According to Kadas," United Nations Development Program, http://www.undp.org.lb/programme/pro-poor/poverty/povertyinlebanon/molc/livingcondittion/E/Kadas.htm

13. Labor Force Participation rate by *qada*, or the small administrative circumscription, and by sex for 2018 are included in Table EA43 in Annex Tables of Labor Force and Household Living Conditions Survey 2018–2019, Lebanon. See also, "Labour Force and Household Living Conditions Survey (LFHLCS) 2018–2019 Lebanon," Central Administration of Statistics and International Labor Organization, 2019, https://tinyurl.com/2p9ewsb7

14. "Labour Force and Household Living Conditions Survey 2018–2019, Lebanon."

15. "Mapping and Understanding Statelessness in Akkar," United Nations High Commissioner for Refugees and Siren Associates, September 2021, https://sirenassociates.com/wp-content/uploads/2021/12/Mapping-and-understanding-statelessness-in-Akkar-2021.pdf

16. Sawsan Masri and Illina Srour, "Assessment of the Impact of Syrian Refugees in Lebanon and Their Employment Profile 2013," International Labor Organization, Regional Office for the Arab States, 2014, 42, https://www.ilo.org/wcmsp5/groups/public/%2D%2D-arabstates/%2D%2D-ro-beirut/documents/publication/wcms_240134.pdf

17. "Lebanon: North and Akkar Governorates Profile," United Nations Office for the Coordination of Humanitarian Affairs, Reliefweb, 2018, 1–2, https://reliefweb.int/report/lebanon/lebanon-north-akkar-governorates-profile-october-2018

18. While there is no official census of military conscripts from Akkar, the accepted figure among the politicians we interviewed is that nearly one third of the Lebanese Armed Forces are from Akkar. Interview with

80   M. YAHYA AND M. H. ALI

Mustafa Alloush, a Future Movement parliamentarian and the party's deputy secretary general, Beirut, February 8, 2022. A political advisor to Prime Minister Najib Mikati who asked not to be named confirmed this.

19. Tewodros Aragie Kebede, Svein Erik Stave, and Maha Kattaa, "Facing Multiple Crises: Rapid Assessment of the Impact of COVID-19 on Vulnerable Workers and Small-Scale Enterprises in Lebanon," International Labor Organization and Fafo Institute for Labor and Social Research, 2020, 28, https://www.ilo.org/wcmsp5/groups/public/%2D%2D-arabstates/%2D%2D-ro-beirut/documents/publication/wcms_747070.pdf

20. Alia Ibrahim, Mohammad Bsiki, and Ahmad Abid, "Smuggling from Lebanon to Syria: What, Why, and Where To?" *Daraj*, December 2, 2021, https://daraj.com/en/84699/. See also, "Report: Smuggling Line in Lebanon Stretches from Akkar to Bekaa," *Naharnet*, September 13, 2019, https://www.naharnet.com/stories/en/264739

21. See: Mouchref, "Forgotten Akkar," 1–28.

22. All signed and completed projects in Lebanon's different governorates are posted by the Council for Reconstruction and Development on its official website. Our researcher searched the site for projects in education, health, and transportation between 2011 and 2021 and calculated national average expenditures and regional average expenditures. All projects can be found at "Projects: Signed Contracts," Council for Development and Reconstruction, 2022, https://www.cdr.gov.lb/en-US/Projects.aspx

23. "Labour Force and Household Living Conditions Survey 2018–2019 in Akkar."

24. Nadia al-Faour, "How Lebanon's Antiquated Citizenship Laws Deny Stateless People and Their Children Basic Rights and Welfare," *Arab News*, January 14, 2022, https://www.arabnews.com/node/2003971/middle-east

25. Joudy El-Asmar, "Wadi Khaled Bordering Syria and Lebanon," *Mashalla News*, June 25, 2019, https://www.mashallahnews.com/wadi-khaled-bordering-syria-and-lebanon/#:~:text=Citizenship%2C%20no%20citizenship,1994%20that%20they%20became%20naturalised.

26. Nadia Al-Faour, "How Lebanon's Antiquated Citizenship Laws ..." https://www.arabnews.com/node/2003971/middle-east

27. Päivi Miettunen and Mohammed Shunnaq, "Tribal Networks and Informal Adaptive Mechanisms of Syrian Refugees: The Case of the Bani Khalid Tribe in Jordan, Syria, and Lebanon" (Beirut: Issam Fares Institute for Public Policy and International Affairs, American University of Beirut, 2020), 4–29, https://tinyurl.com/2p83mbdh

28. Youssef Diab, "Nouzouh Alaf al-Souriyin ila Loubnan Yakshef Oomok al-Tadakhol al-Dimoughrafi Bayna al-Baladayn" [The Displacement of

4 NORTH PACIFIC: WHY LEBANON'S AKKAR REGION WEATHERED... 81

Thousands of Syrians to Lebanon Reveals the Depth of the Demographic Overlap Between the Two Countries], *Al-Sharq al-Awsat*, May 21, 2011, https://archive.aawsat.com/details.asp?section=4&article=622661&issu eno=11862#.YjiLRerP1PY

29. Deutsche Welle, "Sadamat Damiya Bayna al-Aalawiyin wal Sunna fi Tarablos, Shamal Loubnan" [Bloody Clashes Between Alawites and Sunnis in Tripoli, North Lebanon], Deutsche Welle, June 17, 2011, https://tinyurl.com/288yshfh

30. International Crisis Group, "A Precarious Balancing Act: Lebanon and the Syrian Conflict," (Beirut: Crisis Group Middle East, 2012), 2.

31. Roger Owen, "The Political Economy of the Grand Liban, 1920-1970," in Roger Owen (Ed.), *Essays on the Crisis in Lebanon*, (London: Ithaca Press, 1976), 24.

32. Many localities in the border region lack public schools; therefore, to avoid a long commute to educate their children, families have resorted to educating their children in nearby Syrian towns, as well as to benefit from free medical services and cheap goods. See: Ghassan Saoud, "Wadi Khaled: Naamat al-Hawiya Nikma" [Wadi Khaled: The Blessing of Identity is a Curse], *Al-Akhbar*, April 7, 2017, https://al-akhbar.com/Politics/113568

33. Nouhad Topalian, "Aamaliyat al-Tahrib abr al-Maaber Ghayr al-Shariyya Toutih al-Qalak fi Loubnan" [Smuggling Through Illegal Crossings Raises Concerns in Lebanon], *Al-Mashareq*, July 4, 2017, https://almashareq.com/ar/articles/cnmi_am/features/2017/07/04/feature-01

34. *Lebanon Files*, "Maktal Ahad al-Sayyadin alathina Awkafathom Souriya fi al-Arida baad Itlak al-Nar ala Markabihim" [One of the Fishermen Arrested by Syria in Arida After Their Boats Were Fired Upon Has Died], *Lebanon Files*, January 15, 2012, https://www.lebanonfiles.com/news/329156/?mobile=no

35. *Sawt Beirut International*, "Army: Removing Pipes for Smuggling Mazout Into Syria," *Sawt Beirut International*, May 27, 2020, https://tinyurl.com/2p8u7nsw

36. Alia Ibrahim, Mohammad Bsiki, and Ahmad Abid, "Smuggling from Lebanon to Syria: What, Why, and Where To?"

37. Interview with Lebanese local official from northern Lebanon who requested that he remain anonymous, Wadi Khaled, January 23, 2022.

38. Interview with local mayor who requested to stay anonymous, Wadi Khaled, January 23, 2022.

39. *Ibid.*

40. Anne-Marie El-Hage, "The Fight Against Smuggling Between Lebanon and Syria: All Smoke and Mirrors," *L'Orient Today*, June 2, 2020, https://today.lorientlejour.com/article/1220202/the-fight-against-smuggling-between-lebanon-and-syria-all-smoke-and-mirrors.html

41. Michelle Nichols, "Weapons Being Smuggled Between Lebanon, Syria: U.N.," Reuters, May 9, 2012, https://tinyurl.com/2p8mk8hy.
42. *Al-Akhbar*, "Mohammed Suleiman: Rahlat Aashairia ila al-Barlamen" [Mohammed Suleiman: A Tribal Journey to Parliament], *Al-Akhbar*, May 24, 2018, https://tinyurl.com/ra4tfw9v
43. Lebanon Ministry of Interior and Municipalities, "North, District One," Website of the Lebanese Elections of 2018, https://tinyurl.com/2sv82c5d
44. *Al-Akhbar*, "Mohammed Suleiman: Rahlat Aashairiya ila al-Barlamen."
45. Interview with an advisor to Prime Minister Najib Mikati, Beirut, February 6, 2022
46. Light weapons purchased on the black market or shipped from other countries to the region, especially from Libya, are said to have been supplied to Syrian opposition militants by Lebanon's Sunni population. See, BBC, "Who is Supplying Weapons to the Warring Sides in Syria?" BBC, June 14, 2013, https://www.bbc.com/news/world-middle-east-22906965
47. *Al-Hurra*, "Saad al-Hariri Youwajeh Touhman bi Naql al-Asliha ila Souriya" [Saad Hariri Faces Accusations of Transferring Weapons to Syria], *Al-Hurra*, December 12, 2012, https://tinyurl.com/mry6ushh
48. Lebanon was central to the Syrian conflict, as the north acted as a supply line to the opposition in Homs and Syria's northern and eastern border regions, while Hezbollah played a crucial role in backing the Syrian regime, as its army became overstretched after two years of the conflict. See "Who is Supplying Weapons to the Warring Sides in Syria?" for weapons transferred from Lebanon to Syria. And for weapons entering Lebanon, see *Al-Arabiya News*, "Hezbollah's Control of Syrian Border Helps Transport Weapons Into Lebanon: Tlass," *Al-Arabiya News*, March 25, 2021, https://english.alarabiya.net/News/middle-east/2021/03/25/Hezbollah-Iran-s-control-of-Syrian-areas-helps-them-transport-weapons-Tlass
49. Interview with an Islamist activist who asked to remain anonymous due to his involvement in smuggling, Beirut, January 15, 2022.
50. Jana al-Dhaibi, "Akkar 'Khizan al-Jaysh' wa Muwazanat al-Hakuma: al-Mazid min al-Fuqr" [Akkar, 'the Army's Reservoir,' and the Government's Budget: More Poverty], *Al-Modon*, May 22, 2019, https://tinyurl.com/58yk52b4
51. Interview with Mustafa Alloush, Beirut, February 8, 2022.
52. Lebanese Forces Website, "Abnaa Trablos al-Ikhwan al-Hassan min al-Suwayd ila Souriya…wa Abou Muaaz Awal Intihari Lubnani Yufajir Nafsu ind Qalaat al-Husn" [The Sons of Tripoli, the Hassan Brothers, from Sweden to Syria, and Abu Muaz is the First Lebanese Suicide Bomber to Blow Himself Up at Qalaat al-Hosn], Lebanese Forces Website, August 3, 2013, https://tinyurl.com/4sxdarxe

4 NORTH PACIFIC: WHY LEBANON'S AKKAR REGION WEATHERED... 83

53. Cinderella Merhej, "Naam Daesh Qadima ila Loubnan" [Yes, the Islamic State is Coming to Lebanon], *El-Nashra*, March 29, 2017, https://tinyurl.com/yvuurr6m
54. Radwan Mortada, "Aayn Daesh ala Akkar" [The Islamic State's Eye Is on Akkar], *Al-Akhbar*, March 29, 2016, https://al-akhbar.com/Politics/6595
55. Ali Saad, "Arsal al-Loubnaniyya fi Qabdat al-Nusra wa Tanzim al-Dawla" [Lebanon's Arsal is in the Hands of the Islamic State and the Nusra Front], *Al-Jazeera*, August 3, 2014, https://tinyurl.com/yey5pct2
56. Halla Mohieddeen, "Syrian Refugees Entering Lebanon Face New Restrictions," France 24, January 5, 2015, https://www.france24.com/en/20150105-lebanon-syria-refugees-visa-restrictions
57. It was only toward the end of 2014 that the Lebanese government finally put together a refugee response that included the closure of official border crossings and publication of a Policy Paper on Syrian Refugee Displacement, the first document by the Lebanese government since the beginning of the crisis. The paper included new regulations that prevented Syrians from entering Lebanon and restrictions on residency and work permits for Syrians already in Lebanon. The aim was to reduce the number of Syrians in the country. See, General Directorate of General Security, Regulation of Entry and Residence of Syrians, General Directorate of General Security, https://www.general-security.gov.lb/ar/posts/33
58. Maha Yahya, Jean Kassir, and Khalil El-Hariri, *Unheard Voices, What Syrian Refugees Need to Return Home*, (Washington, D.C.: Carnegie Endowment for International Peace, 2018), https://carnegie-mec.org/2018/04/16/unheard-voices-what-syrian-refugees-need-to-return-home-pub-76050
59. Telephone interview with a representative of an international organization working in Lebanon who asked to remain anonymous, March 22, 2022.
60. Alice Fordham and Karen DeYoung, "Syrian Violence Spills into Lebanon and Turkey," *Washington Post*, April 9, 2012, https://www.washingtonpost.com/world/middle_east/syrian-violence-spills-into-lebanon-and-turkey/2012/04/09/gIQAxi5L6S_story.html
61. LBCI Lebanon News, "Aajel: Eshtibakat fi al-Baqi'ah bayna Mousallahin min al-Janib al-Loubnani wa al-Janib al-Souri" [Urgent: Clashes in Al-Baqi'ah in Akkar Between Gunmen From the Lebanese Side and From the Syrian Side], Facebook, July 3, 2012, https://tinyurl.com/5c9vhteb. See also, Moudir Tahrir Akhbar Akkar, "Katila wa Khamsat Jourha fi Qasf Souri ala Wadi Khaled Fajran" [Editor of Akkar News Facebook Page] One Dead and Five Wounded in Syrian Bombing of Wadi Khaled at Dawn], Facebook, July 7, 2012, https://tinyurl.com/389rabhp
62. Omar Habanjar, "Masader Tuwdah lil Anbaa Asbab Imtiaad Suleiman min al-Assad, wa Mikati Yuwajih Risalat Ihtijaj 'Ajila' li Souriya ala al-Khuruqaat

al-Amniyeh" [Sources Clarify for the Anbaa the Reasons Behind Suleiman's Anger With Assad, Mikati Sends an Urgent Message of Protest to Syria Because of the Security Breaches], *Al-Anbaa*, September 4, 2012, https://tinyurl.com/mss4465y

63. *Al-Jazeera*, "Awal Ihtijaj Loubnani ala Kharq Souriya lil Houdoud" [Lebanon's First Protest Against Syria's Breach of the Border], *Al-Jazeera*, July 23, 2012, https://tinyurl.com/2p85hm8v.

64. Interview with a former advisor to former prime minister Saad Hariri, who wished to remain anonymous, December 15, 2021.

65. El-Nashra, "Nouwab Akkar: Lil Israa bi Ikrar Majles Inmaa Akkar wa I'taa al-Mintaka Hissataha min Ta'in al-Fia al-Oula" [Akkar Parliamentarians: Expedite Approval of the Akkar Development Council and Give the Region its Share of Grade-One Civil Service Appointments], *El-Nashra*, September 20, 2019, https://tinyurl.com/2p965jad.

66. Given the potential for high income, a border position is desirable for officers, according to military and political sources. Interview with an advisor of Prime Minister Najib Mikati who asked to remain anonymous, Tripoli, January 20, 2022. Also, interview with a former Military Intelligence officer who asked to remain anonymous, Beirut, January 23, 2022.

67. National Democratic Institute, "Lebanon 2018 Parliamentary Elections," (Washington, D.C.: National Democratic Institute, 2018), 24, https://www.ndi.org/sites/default/files/Lebanon%202018%20Parliamentary%20Elections_Final%20Report%20%28v.3%29.pdf

68. Al-Alam News, "Aad la Yatrok Abwab Dimashq ... Andama Yatahaddath al-Hariri Aan Iadat 'Aamar' Souriya" [He Returned to Knock at the Doors of Damascus: When Hariri Talks About the "Reconstruction" of Syria], Al-Alam News, June 17, 2017, https://tinyurl.com/57994jah

69. Interview with Mustafa Alloush, Beirut, February 8, 2022.

CHAPTER 5

Transnationalization of a Borderland: Center, Periphery, and Identity in Western Iraq

Harith Hasan

INTRODUCTION

In 2003, when Saddam Hussein's Baath regime collapsed due to the US-led invasion of Iraq, Sherku Barakat was five years old.[1] He and his family were living in Sinjar, a large mountainous district located near Iraq's northwestern border with Syria and inhabited by the Yazidi minority, of which the Barakats were a part. Sherku grew up hearing about the agony of his family, which had been displaced from its village in Mount Sinjar and forcibly relocated to one of several collective townships built by the regime elsewhere in the district as part of its policy to Arabize and control the area.[2] The Yazidis are distinguished by their ancient religion, though they are generally regarded as ethnic Kurds. The regime's Arabization policies led Sherku's family to learn Arabic and begin to connect with Baghdad, where his elder brother wound up going for his university studies.

H. Hasan (✉)
Malcolm H. Kerr Carnegie Middle East Center, Beirut, Lebanon
e-mail: harith.hasan@carnegie-mec.org

© The Author(s), under exclusive license to Springer Nature Switzerland AG 2023
M. Yahya (ed.), *How Border Peripheries are Changing the Nature of Arab States*, https://doi.org/10.1007/978-3-031-09187-2_5

85

86   H. HASAN

After 2003, Sinjar became a disputed area. Though part of Nineveh Governorate, which is administered by the central government in Baghdad, Sinjar was claimed by the Kurdistan Regional Government (KRG), which governs Iraqi Kurdistan. This dispute sowed divisions within the Yazidi community, as some Yazidis saw themselves as Kurds and believed that Sinjar should be part of Iraqi Kurdistan, while others argued that Yazidis were a distinct community and must gain autonomy.[3] The question "Who are we?" began to occupy Sherku in 2014, when his town was attacked by the Islamic State. The attack had a horrific effect on the community. Islamic State fighters abducted Yazidi women and turned them into sex-slaves, forced large numbers of Yazidi men to convert to Islam, and killed those who refused.

Sherku and many members of his community managed to flee Sinjar. They were helped by the Kurdistan Workers' Party (PKK), a Kurdish rebel group that had fought the Turkish government for decades and, after it was driven out of Turkey, found shelter in northern Iraq. The PKK helped a large number of Yazidis escape Islamic State attacks by securing a corridor for them to cross the Iraqi border into northeastern Syria—where a PKK-backed group held sway—before they doubled back to Dohuk in Iraqi Kurdistan.[4] Many Yazidis were grateful for the PKK's help in saving them and also in fighting the Islamic State. Building on such goodwill, the PKK began to develop a military and administrative presence in Sinjar. This included forming a Yazidi militia called the Sinjar Resistance Units (YBS). The PKK's initiative exacerbated rifts within the Yazidi community and sharpened distinctions between Kurdishness, Iraqiness, and Yazidiness.

Sherku joined the Sinjar Resistance Units and became an adherent of the PKK's ideology. Initially a Marxist-influenced Kurdish nationalist group, the PKK embraced the idea of communalism and radical democracy following an intellectual shift on the part of its leader, Abdullah Öcalan. Communalism is based on democratic confederations between localities run by elected assemblies. Decisions are made at the local level, with no need for overarching state authority. In 2005, Öcalan had advocated the formation of municipal councils as a way of facilitating a democratic confederation of Kurdish and other communities across the state borders of Syria, Iran, Iraq, and Turkey.[5] He had also adopted anti-patriarchal feminist notions that influenced the ideology and composition of the PKK, a phenomenon that threatened the social stratification of the Yazidi community, which has for centuries remained highly hierarchical.[6]

The collapse of the Iraqi-Syrian border and the porousness of the Iraqi-Turkish border crystallized Sherku's identity.[7] He now viewed himself as part of an aterritorial Kurdish nation at odds not only with Turks, Arabs, and jihadis but also with the territorially bounded Kurdishness of the KRG and its leading proponent, the Kurdistan Democratic Party (KDP). In many ways, Sherku's personal story is emblematic of how the political center's diminishing influence in a borderland region and the consequent rise of non-state transborder actors reshape local identities. In Iraq, the solidification of subnational and transnational solidarities reflects the retreat of the capital Baghdad and deepening competition over defining collective identity in far-flung regions of the country. Peripheral groups seek to extend their influence to Baghdad, where most state resources of a rentier economy are located. At the same time, the weakness of the center emboldens the margins and enables them to constitute—or connect with—new centers.

Sinjar is a key example of this phenomenon, given that the district is situated near two types of borders—an international border between Iraq and Syria and an internal border between Baghdad and Erbil, the capital of Iraqi Kurdistan. In the words of an Iraqi politician with knowledge of Sinjar's situation, "It is hard to find three Yazidis who are in agreement about what is best for their community and where it should belong."[8] This confusion was generated in large part by the rise of new and competing forms of identity politics. The Yazidis, a besieged minority unsure of their relationship with Baghdad, Erbil, and Mosul, found themselves torn between ascendant Shi'i Islamism, insurgent Sunni jihadism, and irredentist Kurdish nationalism.

Other zones near the Iraqi-Syrian border (see Map 5.1), especially those—such as Al Qa'im and Baaj—home to a Sunni Arab majority, have witnessed similar dynamics. Indeed, Iraq's western borderland, with its roughly 800,000 inhabitants, represents a remarkable example of how a weakening of the center and a consequent fragmentation of state authority can lead to the rise of alternative solidarities revolving around alternative centers of gravity.[9] Thus, conflict and fluidity in this borderland are less a result of the artificiality of the border—as ideologies such as pan-Arabism, Islamism, and Kurdish nationalism would have it—than the outcome of a power vacuum that allowed for the emergence of non-state and even subaltern actors in the wake of the central government's receding authority.

In Al Qa'im and Baaj, Sunni jihadism exploited preexisting human trafficking networks and cultivated an increasing sense of alienation and

Map 5.1 General overview of the Iraqi-Syrian border

disempowerment among Sunnis to challenge the Shi'i-dominated government in Baghdad. Jihadi organizations found an opening through the civil war-induced collapse of order on the Syrian side of the border beginning in 2011. There followed the emergence of the Islamic State, which sought to implement a new "nation-building" project by making Sunni Islam, an identity shared by most of Iraq's western borderland inhabitants and most Syrians, the basis of its caliphate.

The Islamic State phenomenon has had a lasting impact on the center. Myriad subnational and transnational armed groups, such as the PKK and Iran-allied factions within the Popular Mobilization Forces (PMF), have sought to fill the vacuum left by the Islamic State's demise in much of the western borderland. These groups have mobilized societal support by propagating conceptions of ethnonational or religious identity that transcend borders and challenge geopolitical realities. Though operating largely out of a peripheral region, some such factions, especially the Iran-allied ones, have managed to infiltrate the state and entrench themselves in its ruling networks as well as its rent distribution machine, thereby strengthening their position in Baghdad and reconstructing the center from within.

To understand these developments, it is important to distinguish between the legal and the empirical reality of the border. Legally, the border remained unchanged following the Islamic State's demise. However, in practice, Baghdad and Damascus could no longer exert full control over the border area. Their authority was shared with, and even contested by, non-state and parastate actors. Indeed, the dynamics that shaped the emergence of the Islamic State, the PKK, and the Iran-backed factions of the PMF, all of which are transnational and thus transborder groups, remain at play in the Iraqi-Syrian border area. Among the local population, the retreat of the center has generated new allegiances, identity perspectives, and connections with alternative centers. Naturally, this has influenced the central government in Baghdad and its relationship with the periphery.

The Transformation of Center-Border Relations

The Iraqi-Syrian border has long been receptive to the appeal of transnational ideologies and transborder solidarities. The reasons for this include the history of cross-border sociocultural ties, the absence of natural barriers separating the two countries along much of the border, and the diffuseness of the ethnic and religious groups inhabiting the area. Prior to the creation of the two states following the end of the First World War in 1918, modern-day Iraq and Syria were part of the Ottoman Empire. During certain periods of Ottoman rule, there were extensive social and economic connections between western Iraq and eastern Syria.

As such, prior to the nineteenth century, Mosul was historically more connected to Aleppo than to Baghdad and Al Qa'im was more connected to Bukamal and Dayr Az Zawr than to Ramadi and Fallujah. The area known as the Jazeera cut across what would become the northern part of the Iraqi-Syrian border and was for centuries a distinct socioecological system despite periodic shifts in its center of gravity. Tribes such as the

Shammar migrated to this area, yet with the demarcation of the border between Iraq and Syria, they found themselves on either side of its northern stretch.

In the twentieth century, Arab nationalism emerged as a powerful ideology in these areas, reflecting, among other things, a sense of nostalgia for a time when the border did not exist. The irony is that the border between Iraq and Syria became inaccessible for lengthy periods during the rule of the two branches of the pan-Arab Baath party in Baghdad and Damascus. Between the late 1970s and late 1990s, the mutually hostile Baathist governments severed their diplomatic and commercial relations, increased securitization of the border, and viewed attempts at crossing the border with extreme suspicion.

However, political and ideological hostility does not explain it all. The transformations of the Iraqi-Syrian border have been largely shaped by the central Iraqi state's reach, or lack thereof. In general, nation-states project their power by subordinating geographical peripheries to the center. This process is best understood as a means by which the novel concept of nationhood is assiduously cultivated among these peripheries' inhabitants. When the central state controls and regulates the cross-border flow of people, goods, and even ideas, it injects into the borderland notions and establishes practices, through which the capital's sovereign authority turns into a reality. As the peripheral population learns to live by these norms, it internalizes the connection with the capital and behaves accordingly.

Thus it was in Iraq. Nation-building entailed the strengthening of domestic bonds between people within a national territory at the expense of cross-border ties. Notably, the increased weight that the central state began to acquire in the 1960s owed much to growing oil revenue, which allowed Baghdad to project its power more intensively in the border regions. This manifested itself primarily in two ways: social and ethnic reengineering, and economic integration. In Sinjar, the Arabization policies that were accelerated in the context of the confrontation between Baghdad and the Kurdish armed insurgency of the 1970s reflected the center's attempts to reshape the identity of the periphery. The authorities forced tens of thousands of Yazidis to leave their villages in Sinjar and live in collective townships with Arabic names.[10] And in Al Qa'im, Baghdad's integration of the district into a centralized economic system disrupted longstanding ties between the district and communities on the Syrian side of the border.

The Iraqi state's penetration of Al Qa'im district had begun in the 1940s, when the British-run Iraq Petroleum Company built an oil pumping station known as T-1 near the town of Al Qa'im. The pumping station served the Kirkuk-Haifa pipeline, which remained operational until the end of the 1940s.[11] In the mid-1970s, the Iraqi government established an industrial complex in Al Qa'im composed of a phosphate processing plant and a large cement plant, and expanded the railroad system connecting this zone to the capital so as to facilitate delivery of the two factories' products. About 4000 people from various governorates and ethnoreligious backgrounds worked in the complex, which accelerated the urbanization of this largely rural area and exposed its predominantly tribal Sunni Arab population to other communities.[12] Not only did western Iraq become more connected to Baghdad, but several influential military and security figures as well as many members of sensitive security organs such as the Republican Guards, the General Security Department, and the Iraqi Intelligence Service would originate from this area. Their involvement in politics and the military boosted Sunni Arab dominance and the impact of tribal culture and networks over the regime's internal structures.

STATE ATROPHY AND THE RISE OF TRANSNATIONAL JIHADISM

In Iraq, the weakness of the state's authority and its inability to shape border dynamics dates to the 1990s. With the Iraqi state reeling from the 1991 Gulf War and international sanctions that halted the exportation of oil, the country's main source of income, the regime's capacity to press ahead with its totalitarian policies of social engineering and the highly centralized management of the economic process was considerably diminished. This phenomenon created a power vacuum and a concomitant opportunity for the rise of countervailing forces with their own agendas. At the same time, the post-Cold War era, which was characterized by a worldwide decline of socialist political systems and centralized modes of governance, had an undeniable effect. Totalitarian projects such as those of the Baath came to be viewed by international organizations and the major world powers as incompatible with then-ascendant liberal values and the neoliberal model of governance.

Owing to its secular outlook, Baathism had attempted to submerge religious and sectarian differences within an ideology that fused Arab unity, socialism, and anti-imperialism. Yet Baathist rule was also characterized by exclusionary practices. Tribal, regional, and sect-based clientelism shaped access to power and resources, and ironically produced the conditions for the sociopolitical fragmentation that occurred when Baathism began to lose influence. Indeed, as soon as the central government was forced by the 1991 Gulf War's fallout to ease its grip on the western borderland, long-suppressed social and cultural ties, narratives, and memories resurfaced. Sunnism, Shiism, and Kurdish nationalism emerged as alternative political forms of identification, ultimately reconstructing sociopolitical boundaries along ethnosectarian lines.

Moreover, the state's retreat led to the activation of long-dormant smuggling and illicit trade networks. Internal Baath Party reports on the western borderland from the 1990s were rife with information on the smuggling of livestock, tobacco, and automobile spare parts across the border with Syria.[13] Those who engaged in such illicit activities were motivated by the plummeting value of the Iraqi dinar. In several instances, elements within the regime had a hand in the smuggling, especially when it came to oil, which allowed them and the higher-ups at whose behest they were acting to circumvent international sanctions.[14]

The US-led invasion in 2003 resulted in a much greater weakening of the state. The dismantling of the various security apparatuses of the Baath regime triggered a process of disaggregation of power and authority.[15] Inevitably, this undermined border control. It became easy for jihadis and foreign fighters to flow through the Iraqi-Syrian border between 2003 and 2008, feeding the Iraqi insurgency. The border quickly turned into a strategic asset that helped insurgents resist the US-sponsored state-rebuilding project and the Shi'i-dominated government to which it gave birth. The Iraqi branch of Al-Qaida, which at the time was led by a Jordanian national known by the *nom de guerre* of Abu Musaab al-Zarqawi, built new networks that operated across the border. The group also established an effective presence among the largely rural Sunni population of Al Qa'im and Baaj, which became strongholds for jihadi activities, providing logistical support and shelter for Sunni militants.[16]

The Islamic State phenomenon, which came to the fore in 2014, was driven by the Salafi-jihadi quest to resurrect the Islamic caliphate. Yet it was enabled by the rapidly shrinking role of the state on both sides of the border. In Iraq, the central government had lost control of the country's western regions to insurgents. Much the same had happened in eastern Syria following the militarization of an initially civilian uprising that erupted in 2011. The Islamic State sought to fashion a new territorial entity across the Iraqi-Syrian border. In the words of this new entity's self-styled caliph, Abu Bakr al-Baghdadi, "Syria is no longer for Syrians and Iraq is no longer for Iraqis."[17]

Thus, as the Islamic State transformed itself from a fringe group into a state, so too did another metamorphosis take place: a periphery became a center. In the border area, the Islamic State formed Wilayat al-Furat, which integrated the Iraqi town of Al Qa'im with the Syrian town of Bukamal. And to the north, it created Wilayat al-Jazeera, which separated Sinjar from Mosul and connected the former with districts such as Talafar and Baaj.[18] The Islamic State thus severed the connection between Iraq's western borderland and traditional administrative centers, whether governorates or Baghdad, and introduced the project of a multiethnic Sunni state in which a radical version of Sunni Islam became the main marker of collective identity. This state-building project included ethnoreligious cleansing, as with the Islamic State's attempt to eradicate the Yazidi community that inhabited the area between Mosul and the Syrian city of Ar Raqqah.

The PKK and the Transnationalization of Iraq's Northwestern Border

The Islamic State had celebrated the end of what it identified as the Sykes-Picot border, but the demise of the caliphate did not simply reestablish the border as a demarcation between two sovereign states.[19] A more complex configuration now materialized, one characterized by transactional alliances as well as mutating hostilities. At the time of this chapter's writing, Syrian government forces had very limited access to the Syrian side of the border. The Syrian Democratic Forces (SDF)—a coalition of Kurdish, Arab, and Syriac/Assyrian groups—blocked its access to the northeastern stretch and the Rabia-Yarubiyeh border-crossing, the only formally recognized entry and exit point along the northern section of the border. US troops restricted the access of Syrian government forces to the southern side near the Tanf border-crossing between Dayr Az Zawr and Anbar Governorates. In Iraq, the Iraqi Security Forces had no access to the area around Dohuk that lies between Mosul and the Turkish border, where the KDP was in control, and were obliged to coexist with the PKK-allied Sinjar Resistance Units in Sinjar and Iran-backed paramilitaries in Sinjar, Baaj, and Al Qa'im. Furthermore, the remaining cells of the Islamic State found the large and sparsely populated desert near the border ideal for regrouping with a view to resuming their activities.[20]

Defeating the Islamic State, a goal shared by the KDP, PMF, PKK, and the Iraqi Security Forces, was now replaced by competition over territorial control and access to the border. In 2017, the KRG unilaterally organized an independence referendum in Iraqi Kurdistan, triggering a political confrontation with Baghdad as well as border-area clashes between KDP forces and both the Iraqi Security Forces and the PMF.[21] Almost immediately, the Iraqi government sought to secure a corridor through Nineveh Governorate to the Iraqi-Turkish-Syrian border triangle and attempted to take over the Faysh Khabur border-crossing with Syria in order to control the flow of people and goods from Syria and even Turkey into Iraq.[22] This issue was linked to a longstanding dispute between Baghdad and the KRG regarding the management of border-crossings and the distribution of revenues. The Iraqi Security Forces and the PMF succeeded in seizing Faysh Khabur, only to again lose control of the crossing shortly thereafter to the KDP, which also operates the Ibrahim al-Khalil border-crossing with Turkey.[23]

Another attempt to refashion border dynamics occurred in 2020, when the Turkish army launched a campaign against PKK and PKK-affiliated fighters in northern Iraq and Syria. Ankara sought to open the road from Turkey to the Rabia-Yarubiyeh border-crossing between Iraq and Syria, which had been closed since the rise of the Islamic State in 2014. In this way, the Turks could clear the Iraqi-Syrian-Turkish border triangle of PKK fighters and expand their geopolitical influence.[24]

These tangles over borderland and border-crossings reflect a larger dispute between multiple local and transnational actors, as well as geopolitical powers, over territory and belonging. Sinjar is a microcosm of this dispute, with the KDP emphasizing its Kurdishness, the PKK linking the district to its transnational project, and both the Iraqi Security Forces and the PMF defending its connection with Baghdad even as they compete over shaping such a connection and defining its strategic objectives. The tug-of-war over Sinjar has had an adverse effect on Yazidi cohesion. This is especially apparent in the community's inability to agree on a political leadership. The traditional Yazidi authorities' power has been eroded by the rise of non-state actors and the appeal of conflicting ideologies.

In Sinjar, the anti-Islamic State efforts of the PKK and its allies, the Sinjar Resistance Units, resulted in temporary coordination with the PMF. In fact, hundreds of PKK-linked fighters were registered as PMF members. This phenomenon weakened the KDP, which had administered Sinjar District until 2014, and ultimately resulted in its ouster from the town, which then fell under a new de facto administration under the sway of the PMF and PKK.[25] The PKK's transnational vision and operational requirements in and around Sinjar clashed with the pragmatic approach of the KDP, which has strong political and economic relations with Ankara. The KDP continues to pressure the PKK to leave Sinjar and other areas so that it might forestall Turkish military attacks and reassert its authority over the Yazidis.[26] Yet the border zone near Sinjar has become one of the PKK's key lines for logistical support, smuggling, and the coordination of its activities in Iraq and Syria. With the central government both weak and disoriented due to Baghdad's constant tussles with Iran-allied paramilitaries, the PKK has emerged as a force capable of reengineering political and social life in this peripheral zone.

In October 2020, Baghdad and Erbil reached an agreement to normalize the situation in Sinjar and expel the PKK from the district, an agreement welcomed by Turkey. However, one problem in the implementation of this agreement was identifying fighters who were part of the PKK, given that the latter maintains that it has no military presence in Sinjar. For example, the Sinjar Resistance Units claim that while they are inspired by Abdullah Öcalan and his ideology, they have no organizational connection to the PKK. The confusion lies not just with the multiplicity of players and their disparate ideological claims but with the shifting and transactional nature of their alliances. At the time of this chapter's writing, several PKK-affiliated fighters had left the center of Sinjar but remained on its periphery. The Iraqi government sent two divisions of the federal police to secure the area, a move that may help it reassert its authority but runs the risk of leading to clashes with PKK-affiliated fighters.[27]

Iran-Backed Paramilitaries: The Periphery's Encroachment on the Center

Trying to embed themselves in the local environment and secure greater legitimacy in Iraq, the PKK and its local affiliates in Sinjar are said to have formed a political party that intends to run in future Iraqi elections. Moreover, there is already a sitting member of parliament who is reportedly connected to the PKK.[28] The attempt on the part of a peripheral group to gain a seat at the proverbial table in Baghdad is exemplified by the behavior of PMF factions. The PMF is, on the face of it, a formal security organ whose members receive Iraqi state salaries. Yet there is far more to the umbrella organization than its official status. In fact, the PMF is a unique phenomenon. On the one hand, it has mostly operated in coordination with the Iraqi government, whether during the fight against the Islamic State or during Baghdad's successful attempt—following the KRG referendum—to retake control of areas beyond Iraqi Kurdistan that Kurdish forces had previously seized. On the other hand, thanks to direct Iranian backing, the PMF has enjoyed a large degree of autonomy from the Iraqi government and the formal chain of command. Therefore, the PMF is a hybrid actor that operates as much within the Iraqi state as outside it.[29] Indeed, at one point, former prime minister Adil Abdul-Mahdi himself indicated that the PMF's main purpose was to protect the post-2003 Shi'i-centric order.[30] This makes the PMF a military-politico-ideological force whose aim is not merely to defend the Iraqi state but to shape it according to a pan-Shi'i vision of which the alliance with Iran's Islamic Revolutionary Guard Corps (IRGC) is a main pillar.

This alliance has manifested itself in the deployment of several PMF factions in Syria to fight alongside the Syrian regime against Sunni Islamist rebel groups. Since 2016, these PMF factions have been stationed on both sides of the Iraqi-Syrian border, especially in the Al Qa'im-Bukamal zone. Their deployment was planned and overseen by the IRGC, which maintains a behind-the-scenes presence in Iraq. Among the groups in question are Kata'ib Hezbollah, Kata'ib al-Imam Ali, Kata'ib al-Khorasani, Harakat al-Nujaba, and Liwa Fatimiyuun, which is composed largely of Shi'i Afghan fighters.[31] Though the Iraqi government claims to have no interest in intervening in the Syrian civil war or deploying forces in Syria, these groups frequently move across the border to do just that. In fact, some of their fighters in Syria are listed on the PMF's payroll.[32]

Despite official identification of the PMF as a state-affiliated body, the operations of PMF member groups such as Kata'ib Hezbollah and Harakat al-Nujaba are linked to Iran's regional ambitions. As such, the deployment of these factions near and across the border was not simply an extension of Baghdad's authority but an attempt by Tehran to secure a land corridor for the pan-Shi'i "resistance" axis it is building between Iraq, Syria, and Lebanon.[33] Iran's projection of its influence in this manner has had significant repercussions, with the Al Qa'im and Bukamal bases of PMF factions regularly targeted by US and Israeli airstrikes and drone attacks.

Essentially, the PMF succeeded in turning Iraq's western borderland, which had become the heart of the Islamic State's caliphate, back into an Iraqi periphery. Additionally, members of Kata'ib Hezbollah have managed to attain senior positions within the PMF and consequently provide political cover for their group's operations across the border.[34] And when Kata'ib Hezbollah's leader, Abu Mahdi al-Muhandis, was killed in the US drone strike that targeted the IRGC's Qassem Soleimani, his comrades replaced him with someone from within the group, Abdul-Aziz al-Muhammadawi, without consulting the prime minister, who is the Iraqi military's commander-in-chief. Moreover, according to Iraqi officials, Kata'ib Hezbollah continues to control a border post near Al Qa'im despite the fact that the government has reopened the official Al Qa'im-Bukamal border-crossing—and nobody is willing to challenge them.[35]

To counter what it considered Iranian influence on the Iraqi-Syrian border, the United States launched an airstrike on Kata'ib Hezbollah locations in Al Qa'im on December 29, 2019, killing about 25 of the group's members. Thousands of PMF members and sympathizers reacted by storming the US embassy in Baghdad. In retaliation, US President Donald Trump ordered the operation that resulted in the assassination of Soleimani, the head of the IRGC's Quds force, and Abu Mahdi al-Muhandis, who in addition to heading Kata'ib Hezbollah was PMF deputy leader and chief of staff. This incident escalated the tension between the United States and Iran, and deepened internal divisions in Iraq. As is clear, the center of power in Baghdad is still undergoing conflicts and rivalries that are strongly influenced by the geopolitical competition between the United States and Iran in a peripheral region along the Iraqi-Syrian border.[36]

Although Iran-allied paramilitaries are part of a transnational network of militias managed by the IRGC and often instrumentalized as a tool to project Iranian regional influence, they see themselves as part of the Iraqi state.[37] Some of these groups' political wings have become part of the Iraqi parliament and government. For example, the Fatah Alliance, which is made up largely of the political wings of PMF factions, was the second largest coalition in parliament and played a key role in forming both the government of Adil Abdul-Mahdi and that of Mustafa al-Kadhimi following the 2018 elections. Fatah's parliamentary members are known for defending the PMF and its existence as an autonomous security organ and even holding it aloft as the redeemer of Iraq, which otherwise would have been destroyed by the Islamic State. However, this narrative conceals the diversity and even disagreement within the PMF between Iran-allied factions and those of an Iraq-centric bent. Iran's allies control the key operational positions within the PMF.[38] They made common cause with other Iraqi state bodies in the fight against the Islamic State and have remained linked, albeit loosely, to the formal chain of command since the declaration of the PMF as a state institution under the supervision of the Iraqi prime minister.

The upshot of all this is that when the interests of Baghdad coincide with those of Tehran, as was the case during the war against the Islamic State, the PMF paramilitaries serve as an extension of the Iraqi government's authority. However, when the groups in question operate exclusively based on the IRGC's directives, as has been the case with their ongoing involvement in the Syrian conflict or their regular rocket attacks on US military and diplomatic facilities, they distinguish themselves from other Iraqi state organs and become akin to a parallel institution. Such hybridity reflects the ongoing processes of disarticulation and rearticulation within the center as well as between the center and geographical peripheries. In supporting the Iraqi state's efforts to recapture territory from the Islamic State, the PMF functioned as a centralizing force. Yet in resisting the same Iraqi state's attempts to impose more control over its structures and activities, the PMF acted as a centrifugal force. Indeed, under the leadership of Abu Mahdi al-Muhandis, the PMF underwent its own internal process of centralization that aimed to empower the IRGC-allied groups and weaken, subordinate, or even exclude those with different allegiances. This phenomenon echoes the struggle in Iraq between Tehran-centric Shiism and Iraqi nationalism, a struggle replete with competition over power, resources, and territorial control. The western borderland has emerged as an arena for Shi'i triumphalism, but has tangled the Iraqi state in strategies and alliances that embody the worldview of the IRGC-allied paramilitaries. In a sense, what is at play in the western borderland is an endeavor on the part of various and competing factions to reconfigure this periphery in a way that reshapes the identity of the center.

Conclusion: What Next?

In July 2020, Iraqi Prime Minister Kadhimi made a sudden and unusual visit to the Mandali border-crossing with Iran. While there, Kadhimi announced that he had ordered the security forces to take over all border-crossings and crack down on criminal groups that paid no heed to Iraq's borders.[39] This step came as part of a broader effort to restore the Iraqi government's authority throughout the length and breadth of the country. Given the multiplicity of actors deployed in the various border zones, their infiltration of state institutions, and the fragmentation and far-reaching corruption of security organs, Kadhimi's mission is a difficult one. However, it reflects a conviction that the center cannot be reempowered if the peripheries lie beyond its grasp. With Kadhimi's initiative in mind, we can envision two scenarios for Iraq's western borderland, which is the most unstable of the country's border regions. Should either come to pass, it will have implications for future configurations of power and local governance, as well as for the fate of borderland communities.

In the first scenario, Baghdad's efforts at centralization fail. As a result, the borderland remains subject to a hybrid and increasingly unstable regime of control and governance. The multiplicity of state, non-state, and parastate actors, with their ever-mutating relations and rivalries, continues to pull local communities such as the Yazidis and the Sunni Arabs in different directions. This tug-of-war deepens such communities' crisis over how to orient their identity, deprives their leadership of agency, and places hundreds of thousands of ordinary people at the mercy of militant groups with competing political visions. Baghdad's already faint influence further recedes even as the various antagonisms of the borderland's powerbrokers prevent the emergence of any sort of functional local governance. In parallel, ongoing economic deprivation weakens the rule of law, hastens the establishment of mutually hostile fiefdoms, and bolsters the illicit movement of both goods and militants across the border with Syria.

In the second scenario, the centralization drive succeeds. Motivated by the political imperative to monopolize power and the economic imperative to control cross-border trade, Baghdad asserts its authority over the western borderland. Yet such a project could have two very different outcomes. Should Baghdad achieve its objective independently of Iran-backed factions, it will *ipso facto* have severely curtailed such groups' power in the borderland, decoupled the anti-Islamic State mission from the US-Iranian rivalry, and taken a major step toward restoring Iraqi sovereignty.

However, should the Iraqi government prove unable to bring the borderland under its authority without the aid of IRGC-allied paramilitaries, a curious paradox will emerge, one of an Iraqi state that is at once more centralized and more beholden to Iran. In such a scenario, the PMF would solidify its presence in the borderland and serve the Iranian regime's ongoing assemblage of a Tehran-Baghdad-Damascus axis. This would further

100   H. HASAN

enable the Iran-backed umbrella organization to reengineer power structures within the center and could well strain Baghdad's already fraught relations with the United States and Iran's regional rivals.

NOTES

1. This is not his real name.
2. The main reason for this policy is that the mountain was a stronghold of the Kurdish rebels. For more details, see, Sangar Youssif Salih and Kayfi Maghdid Qadr, "How the Deprivation of Land Ownership Makes Minority Groups More Vulnerable: An Examination of the Case of Yazidis in Iraq," in *The Struggle for Socially Just Housing, Land and Property Rights in Syria, Iraq and Libya,* edited by Hannes Baumann, 103-120 (The Friedrich-Ebert-Stiftung's Regional Project, 2019). http://library.fes.de/pdf-files/bueros/tunesien/15664.pdf.
3. Author conversations with Yazidi activists and civil society leaders, Dohuk and Sinjar, November 26, 27, and 28, 2019.
4. Informal interviews with Yazidis in Dohuk who hail from Sinjar, November 26, 2019. Approximately 200,000 Yazidis continue to languish in such camps for the internally displaced.
5. Wez Enzinna, "A Dream of Secular Utopia in ISIS Backyard," *New York Times Magazine,* November 24, 2015, https://www.nytimes.com/2015/11/29/magazine/a-dream-of-utopia-in-hell.html. See also Abdullah Öcalan, *Democratic Confederalism* (London: Transmedia Publishing Ltd, 2011).
6. Radha D'Souza, "Preface," in Abdullah Öcalan, *Manifesto for a Democratic Civilization, Volume II: Capitalism, The Age of Unmasked Gods and Naked Kings* (Porsgrunn: New Compass Press, 2017), 11-24.
7. Some of the themes discussed in this chapter were also addressed by the author in this co-authored article: Harout Akdedian, Harith Hasan, "State Atrophy and the Reconfiguration of Borderlands in Syria and Iraq: Post-2011 Dynamics," *Political Geography* 80 (2020): https://doi.org/10.1016/j.polgeo.2020.102178.
8. Author interview with an Iraqi politician, Baghdad, April 30, 2020.
9. About 500,000 of the borderland inhabitants are Yazidis and Kurds, while 300,000 are Sunni Arabs. See Husham al-Hashimi, "ISIS on the Iraqi-Syrian Border: Thriving Smuggling Networks," *Center for Global Policy,* June 16, 2020, https://cgpolicy.org/articles/isis-on-the-iraqi-syrian-border-thriving-smuggling-networks/.
10. Author interview with Majid Shingali. Among these townships were Baath, Waleed, Ta'mim, Hiteen, Yarmuk, Qadissiyya, Uruba, and Andalus, For

5 TRANSNATIONALIZATION OF A BORDERLAND: CENTER, PERIPHERY... 101

more details, see UN Habitat, "Emerging Land Tenure Issues Among Displaced Yazidis from Sinjar, Iraq," November 2015, https://unhabitat. org/sites/default/files/documents/2019-04/emerging_land_tenure_ issues_among_displaced_yazidis_from_sinjar_iraq.pdf.

11. Author interview with Ayad Khalaf (via telephone), member of Al Qa'im local council, September 12, 2019. For more, see Jamed Bamberg, *The History of the British Oil Company: Volume 2 the Anglo-Iranian Years 1928-1954* (Cambridge: Cambridge University Press, 1994), 155-171.

12. Author interview with Ayad Khalaf.

13. Based on the author's research of the Baath Party archive at Hoover Institute-Stanford University, November 2017.

14. Phil Williams, "Criminals, Militias and Insurgents: Organized Crime in Iraq," *Strategic Studies Institute* 9, June 2009, https://www.globalsecurity.org/jhtml/jframe.html#https://www.globalsecurity.org/military/library/report/2009/ssi_williams.pdf|||Criminals,%20Militias,%20and%20Insurgents:%20Organized%20Crime%20in%20Iraq.

15. For more, see Peter Harling and Alex Simon, "Erosion and Resilience of the Iraqi-Syrian border," Robert Schuman Centre for Advanced Studies, 2015, https://cadmus.eui.eu/bitstream/handle/1814/37015/RSCAS_2015_61.pdf?sequence=1&isAllowed=y.

16. Harith Hasan and Kheder Khaddour, "The Transformation of the Iraqi-Syrian Border: From a National to a Regional Frontier," Carnegie Endowment for International Peace, March 31, 2020, https://carnegie-mec.org/2020/03/31/transformation-of-iraqi-syrian-border-from-national-to-regional-frontier-pub-81396.

17. BBC Arabic, "Al-Baghdadi: Souriya laysat li'l Souriyyeen wa'l Iraq laysa li'l Iraqiyyeen," [Al-Baghdadi: Syria is not for Syrians and Iraq not for Iraqis], July 1, 2014, https://www.bbc.com/arabic/middleeast/2014/07/140701_isis_leader_call.

18. Author interview with Husham al-Hashimi, expert on Islamist radical groups, Baghdad, September 29, 2019.

19. As demonstrated in several works of research, the border between Iraq and Syria is not identical to what was agreed upon in the Sykes-Picot agreement. Rather, it is the consequence of several events, conflicts, and negotiations that continued for decades after the agreement and altered to a large extent the original demarcation. See Sarah Pursley, "Lines Drawn on an Empty Map: Iraq's Borders and the Legend of the Artificial State," *Jadaliyya*, June 2, 2015, https://www.jadaliyya.com/Details/32140. Also David Siddhartha Patel, "Repartitioning the Sykes-Picot Middle East? Debunking Three Myths," Brandeis University Crown Center for Middle East Studies, Middle East Brief no. 103, November 2016, https://www.

102   H. HASAN

brandeis.edu/crown/publications/middle-east-briefs/pdfs/101-200/meb103.pdf.

20. Author interviews with members of Iraqi Border Guards and Iraqi National Intelligence, Baghdad, February 7 and 8, 2019.

21. Katie Klain and Lisel Hintz, "A Series of Miscalculations: The Kurdish Referendum and its Fallout," *Global Observatory*, December 19, 2017, https://theglobalobservatory.org/2017/12/series-miscalculations-kurdish-referendum-and-fallout/.

22. Muhammed Aziz Abdul Hasan, "Al-Ahamiyya al-Jiyustratijiyya li Maabar Fayshkhabur" [The Geostrategic Significance of the Fayshkhabur Border-Crossing], *Turk Press*, November 29, 2017, https://www.turkpress.co/node/42442.

23. Dailymotion, from *Al Mawsleya* via Storyful, "Iraqi Forces Advance Towards Kurdish-controlled Border Post of Faysh Khabur," https://www.dailymotion.com/video/x66hq2i.

24. Author interview with Hiwa Osman, Iraqi Kurdish journalist (via telephone), July 14, 2020.

25. Interviews by research assistant Jameel Barakat with Qassim Shashu, the head of a KDP-affiliated militia, Sinjar, December 7, 2019, and Zyad Haji, a Yazidi lawyer, Sinjar, July 28, 2019. Although the PKK-affiliated Sinjar Resistance Units are still part of the PMF, PKK militants clashed with the PMF in 2017 at a Sinjar checkpoint separating their strongholds, resulting in several casualties among PMF fighters.

26. Author interview with Talal Murad, a Yazidi activist and the head of the 24 media institute, November 21, 2019. Additionally, author interview with Dakhil Qassim Hasson, former mayor of Sinjar, November 23, 2019.

27. Samya Kullab, "In a Northern Town Brutalized by IS, Iraq Tests its Power," December 24, 2020, https://apnews.com/article/islamic-state-iraq-saddam-hussein-bf712bdec9b3328ccc3f99f1402f3607.

28. Off-the-record workshop on the Iraqi-Syrian border organized by the Carnegie Middle East Center and the Konrad-Adenauer-Stiftung, Beirut, June 11–12, 2019.

29. Renad Mansour, "The Popular Mobilization Forces and the Balancing of Formal and Informal Power," March 15, 2018, https://blogs.lse.ac.uk/mec/2018/03/15/the-popular-mobilisation-forces-and-the-balancing-of-formal-and-informal-power/. See also Fanar Haddad, "Iraq's Popular Mobilization Units," in *Hybrid Conflict, Hybrid Peace: How Militias and Paramilitary Groups Shape Post-Conflict Transitions*, edited by Adam Day, (New York: United Nations University, Center for Policy Research, 2020), 30-66, https://i.unu.edu/media/cpr.unu.edu/post/3895/HybridConflictFullReport.pdf.

30. Michael Knights, Hamid Malik, and Aymenn Jawad Al-Tamimi, "Honored, Not Contained: the Future of Iraq's Popular Mobilization Forces," *The Washington Institute for Near East Policy*, March 2020, 139, https://www.washingtoninstitute.org/uploads/Documents/pubs/PolicyFocus163-KnightsMalikTamimi-v3.pdf.
31. Harith Hasan and Kheder Khaddour, "The Transformation of the Iraqi-Syrian Border."
32. Author interview with security officials who preferred to remain anonymous, Baghdad, September 29, 2019.
33. Ibid.
34. Ibid.
35. Author interview with an official at Iraq customs service, Baghdad, May 14, 2020.
36. This is discussed in greater detail in Harith Hasan and Kheder Khaddour, "The Transformation of the Iraqi-Syrian Border."
37. Ibid.
38. Michael Knights, Hamid Malik, and Aymenn Jawad Al-Tamimi, "Honored, Not Contained: the Future of Iraq's Popular Mobilization Forces."
39. Qassim Abdul-Zahra and Samya Kullab, "Iraq's PM takes step in battle against border corruption," The Associated Press, July 11, 2020, https://apnews.com/c1ab4b9804aa14ada89050f3f3c9bcca.

CHAPTER 6

How Syria's War Extended Border Policies to Much of the Country

Kheder Khaddour and Kevin Mazur

INTRODUCTION

The conflict in Syria, which began as a popular uprising in 2011 and turned into an intrastate war, has reshaped how the regime, led by Bashar al-Assad, governs the country. Prior to 2011, the regime styled itself the custodian of a developmental state—taking upon itself the task of improving the nation's productive capacities and citizens' welfare—and ruled Syria through a mix of formal state institutions and direct security control.

Broadly speaking, two approaches were discernible. Communities on the country's borders, particularly in the sparsely populated northeast, were treated as potentially subversive and therefore policed with the cooperation of local notables. Communities in areas that were not

K. Khaddour (✉)
Malcolm H. Kerr Carnegie Middle East Center, Beirut, Lebanon
e-mail: kkhaddour@carnegie-mec.org

K. Mazur
Northwestern University, Evanston, IL, USA
e-mail: kevin.mazur@northwestern.edu

© The Author(s), under exclusive license to Springer Nature   105
Switzerland AG 2023
M. Yahya (ed.), *How Border Peripheries are Changing the Nature of Arab States*, https://doi.org/10.1007/978-3-031-09187-2_6

borderlands, but nonetheless peripheral in a societal or geographical sense, were generally considered less of a security risk and as such were somewhat more integrated into the bureaucracy of the state, with their inhabitants enjoying some access to state-provided goods. Governance of such communities could be described as hybrid—combining direct linkages to security forces with bureaucratic regulation and the provision of services.

Years of fighting have both exhausted the regime's resources and shattered any hope of a reconciliation with the large segments of the population that opposed it. In the borderlands, this has spurred Damascus to rely even more on traditionally powerful security agencies as a medium of governance. And in troublesome inland yet peripheral areas, the regime has ceased to use the old, hybrid form of governance in favor of a security-oriented approach resembling its method of managing the borderlands. In such inland areas, security networks now deal directly with populations under the regime's control, but provide virtually none of the services the regime offered (to varying degrees and often alongside significant coercion) before 2011.

Indeed, the change in governance is apparent across Syria's territory. In some instances it has proven slight and results less from a qualitative shift in administration than from Damascus simply dispensing with its long-standing rhetoric of cooperation between state and citizenry, thereby laying bare its security-focused priorities. The regime's approach to the northeastern border area of Hasakah, for instance, reflects such a turn. Hasakah is home to an Arab population largely organized along tribal lines as well as a significant concentration of the country's Kurdish minority, which the regime, with its Arab nationalist orientation, has long viewed with suspicion. Historically, the regime's approach to governing the region consisted in relying on informal linkages to traditional local leaders and maximizing its control of territory, all in the service of pacifying the local population rather than attending to people's needs and providing them with services. This has not substantially changed as a result of the conflict; it is simply more blatant.

In inland areas and towns that fall within regime-controlled territory, the war has also led to more direct involvement of state security agencies. Here, however, the phenomenon manifests itself in two distinct ways. When dealing with areas that are loyal to the regime or at least ambivalent toward the opposition, Damascus has allowed its security services, which emerged from the war with enhanced powers, to assume a more hands-on role in administration and the provision—or at least facilitation—of basic services. This is very much the case in Jaramana and Tal, where the regime has empowered the security services to deal with local leaders. As for the security forces themselves, the new development has proven lucrative, in that it enables them to extract rents from locals by providing basic services or merely granting them permission to obtain such amenities from external actors.

The role of the security forces is even more pronounced in the regime's treatment of former bastions of rebel activity, particularly urban quarters densely populated by Sunni Arabs. In such areas, the new, direct security relationship has taken an extreme form that reproduces and even surpasses Damascus' method of administering its northeastern and eastern borderlands. Razing an entire district of a town or city, expelling its inhabitants, reconstructing it exclusively in accordance with perceived security imperatives, and resettling a regime-aligned community there is now the order of the day. Arguably the most salient example of such wholesale reengineering, whether in terms of demographics or urban layout, is the Baba Amr district of Homs.

The forms of governance adopted in postwar Syria do not constitute a clean break with the country's pre-2011 governance; rather, they are the accentuation of one aspect of rule at the expense of another. Since Hafez al-Assad, father of Syria's current president, seized power in a 1970 coup, Syria has been dominated by the military and various security services, but one with all the trappings of a modern—if undemocratic—state. During the uprising, regime loyalists often sought to undercut the opposition's criticism of the regime by extolling the latter's achievements in securing the safety and wellbeing of Syrians. They described such achievements as the fruits of "Assad's Syria" (*Suriya al-Asad*). The recent war destroyed the formal administrative hierarchies of the state that provided such benefits, but kept the core relations underlying it largely intact. As such, the most significant development in the governance of Syria since the war began is that the dominant role of the security services is no longer partly concealed, that such security services have extended their reach to the most mundane of matters, and that they operate with greater intensity. Seen from this angle, the contemporary Syrian state—shorn of any administrative trappings or developmental promises and ruled directly by the regime's violent apparatuses—has become Assad's Syria in a far more literal sense. Governance is no longer substantially differentiated in style from one area to another; the difference is the degree of involvement by the security

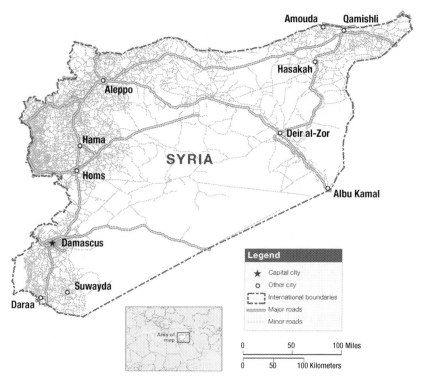

Map 6.1 General map of Syria

services. Today, administrative divisions exist only on paper, while the reality almost everywhere on the ground is direct control by the center (Map 6.1).

Center-Periphery Relations Before 2011

Prior to 2011, the regime's approach to managing territories along its northeastern and eastern borders consisted primarily in utilizing direct relationships between senior security officials and local notables. Whereas state employment and development projects played an important role in the implicit social contract extended to local populations in other peripheral areas of the country, border areas received far fewer of these services, and their residents were often prohibited from selling or developing land near the border.[1] In this respect, the regime's method evinced a degree of continuity with earlier forms of governance by other actors. Just as the French Mandate and independent but pre-Baath Syrian governments often sought to empower local tribal authorities to maintain the state's influence along the border, the Baath vested in borderland tribes far greater authority than it did in their counterparts in other regions of the country.[2] Demography played an important role in maintaining links between the center in Damascus and peripheral regions, in that the regime was able to foster relations with Arab tribes in ethnically mixed areas. But the most important element of these links was that they were maintained directly, without state institutions as intermediaries.

The ways in which the regime dealt with the Tayy tribe in the northeastern governorate of Hasakah exemplify this type of approach. Leading members of the tribe have long wielded significant influence in an area known as the Syrian Jazira, which historically stretched from Nusaybin in modern Turkey to Sinjar in modern Iraq, with modern-day Syria's Hasakah Governorate at its center. In the twilight years of the Ottoman Empire, local Arab tribes had their own administrative district in the area. Thus, when international boundaries were drawn in a series of treaties and deals in the 1920s, it seemed as though Tayy leaders would be shorn of much of their power.[3] Yet the tribe managed to adapt to the new situation by making itself useful to Syria's rulers. For instance, under Hafez al-Assad, many members joined the Baath Party—as did members of other tribes in the border regions—and participated in party-sponsored activities, thereby providing the regime with a local support base.

One example of the direct links between Damascus and this region came after Muhammad al-Faris, a Tayy sheikh, ran for parliamentary elections in 1998 but lost.[4] After his loss, Ali al-Hassan, a commander in the Republican Guard, called Faris to reassure him that the regime was still on his side and that he would ultimately succeed in his ambitions. In other words, even if regime support was not always immediately forthcoming, direct communication and links between the center and peripheries remained uninterrupted.[5]

Later, in 2004, tensions flared in Hasakah's most populous city, Qamishli, during a football match between the local club, composed mostly of Kurdish and Syriac/Assyrian players, and the Deir al-Zor club, which was mostly Arab. The game took place in the context of the US invasion of Iraq, which had resulted in increased autonomy for Iraqi Kurds. The tensions around the game were fueled by events across the border, with local Arabs displaying support for former Iraqi president Saddam Hussein and Kurds showing support for the Iraqi Kurdish leader Massoud Barzani, and eventually led to Arab-Kurdish clashes. Although the regime called in the Republican Guard to separate the mutually hostile groups, members of the Tayy tribe—who were allowed to bear arms and were far more familiar with the area's social landscape than outsiders—played an instrumental role in restoring order.[6]

Matters were different in areas that were nowhere near the border but nonetheless peripheral in terms of their social composition as well as their location on the outskirts of inland cities. Here, the Syrian regime did not deal with inhabitants exclusively through its security organs. Consequently, in such non-borderland peripheral areas, Syrians could access government services through a mix of formal procedures and informal networks, most of which did not have to go through security channels. Many services and resources provided by the state were obtained through codified bureaucratic procedures. This included subsidized bread and fuel, inclusion in civil registries, and employment benefits accorded civil servants and professional union members, who together constituted over one-third of the workforce. Other state-controlled resources—including many of the most valuable—were accessed through personal networks with state officials. For example, although formal procedures were in place for requesting state employment and permission to open a business or travel abroad, pursuing such projects was generally considered fruitless unless one had the backing of employees within a ministry who could see to it that the request was granted.[7]

This distinction between formal and informal access was not hard and fast. Personal ties might enable one to jump the queue for a widely but slowly delivered service, and a ministry whose leaders diverted enormous amounts of resources to personal use might adhere to formal rules in some areas of its operation. For example, a manager at a state construction company might allow vast amounts of material to be stolen by politicians to construct villas, but also carry out the company's main public works projects successfully.[8] This suggests a spectrum of governance in pre-2011 Syria, with some institutions tending toward adherence to formal rules and bureaucratic procedure, others run almost exclusively according to personal ties and the whims of individual leaders, and hybrids in between these extremes.

The city of Jaramana exemplifies the hybrid form of governance. Jaramana lies just a few kilometers from Damascus, the country's capital

6 HOW SYRIA'S WAR EXTENDED BORDER POLICIES TO MUCH... 111

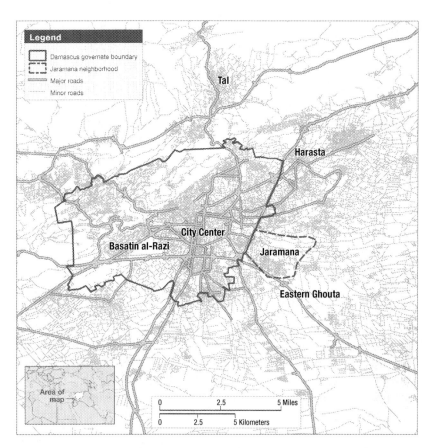

Map 6.2   Damascus and its environs

and the regime's nerve center (Map 6.2). Yet it is socially peripheral to the capital; the networks of most of its residents are based in Jaramana or localities from which they have collectively moved to Jaramana, and they are generally less affluent and connected to powerful political actors than residents of central Damascus.[9] In Ottoman times, Jaramana was a small village inhabited by members of the Druze community. Chain migration to Jaramana from heavily Druze Suwayda, located in the southeastern part of Syria, began in the 1960s. Damascene Christians who were priced out of their historical neighborhoods began migrating to Jaramana in the 1990s.[10] The 2003 US invasion of Iraq and subsequent insurgency and violent conflict led to an influx of Iraqis, who rented homes and opened shops, further developing commerce and also adding a new layer to the town's social makeup.[11]

These newcomers of the 1990s and 2000s drove a major expansion of the city's footprint, settling in what local residents refer to as "agricultural" (*zira'i*) neighborhoods, which contrasted with "official" (*nizami*) neighborhoods situated along the city's central squares and main street. Agricultural neighborhoods, so named because they were built on lands recently used for agriculture, expanded in violation of formal planning regulations, on the initiative of local residents rather than by design of the state. This pattern of settlement also gave rise to spatial and social distinctions between the original residents of Jaramana and the newcomers. Crucially, these distinctions did not map neatly onto religious difference—while all generational Jaramana residents are Druze, recent migrants from Suwayda of Druze background were no more considered Jaramanis than Christians from Damascus.[12]

Though the population diversified considerably in the 2000s, large-scale commercial activity and political connections remained primarily in the hands of generational residents. Relations with regime agents, and thus the political center, flowed through established businessmen and the heads of prominent extended families. These figures typically owned large tracts of land and enjoyed local influence and prestige, making them attractive clients for the regime. These businessmen and heads of prominent extended families retained power by cultivating informal relations with security officials, but also by dominating the city council, which was invested with considerable influence.[13]

Though they lacked the high-level connections to regime figures enjoyed by the town's elite, many migrants to Jaramana used their informal relations with the state to carve out a niche for themselves. The strategies of one municipal employee, a street cleaner who migrated from Suwayda in the late 1970s, exemplify such an approach. Owning no land in Jaramana and lacking any prospect of buying any, this man built a home on land in an officially restricted area surrounded by high-tension electrical power lines. He also used his ties to individuals within the municipal government to foil other city employees' attempts to demolish the building due to the danger it presented to his family and the electrical grid. Though the building had a small footprint, he eventually built four stories so that his extended family could all live there, with the top floor coming within meters of the power line.[14]

Ruling through local notables, as practiced in the country's northeast, looked quite different from the combination of governance techniques employed in Jaramana. Yet the strategies of rule employed by the Syrian regime over its various territories before 2011 constituted an effective patchwork, honed over decades, for maintaining political stability. Fast-moving changes set in motion by the 2011 uprising compelled the regime to alter this mix in all areas under its authority. Increasingly, direct security control of the sort that characterized border regions emerged as the regime's new approach to governance.

THE BORDERLANDS POST-CONFLICT: ACCENTUATING THE SECURITY-BASED APPROACH TO GOVERNANCE

The Syrian conflict laid bare the relationship between the political center in Damascus and the country's borderlands, exposing the regime's overriding interest in retaining control of territory rather than establishing a functioning bureaucracy or catering to inhabitants' needs. This priority was present before the 2011 uprising, but the regime was able to partially obscure this fact through high-minded language about the rights of all Syrians and the duty of both state and citizens to defend the nation's borders. Its behavior during the war, however, revealed that its focus was always on maintaining control of territory. The war also strengthened the direct linkages between regime security figures and certain local elites, at times turning the borderlands, even those that are sparsely populated, into a resource through which Damascus could gain financial or other compensation from foreign actors in return for allowing them to spread their influence there.

The regime still has a direct relationship with far-flung eastern and northeastern parts of the country—Albu Kamal on the border with Iraq and Qamishli on the border with Turkey. In Albu Kamal, historically populated by Arab tribes straddling the border with Iraq, the regime has essentially granted Iran-backed Iraqi militias free rein to operate in the area and thereby secure it. This accentuates a practice already common in the region before 2011, whereby the regime dealt with the people more as security risks to be managed than as citizens with rights and obligations to the state. The regime has traditionally been wary of Albu Kamal, in large part because the town is home to Arab tribes active on both sides of the border with Iraq, one of Syria's regional rivals until the US-led invasion in 2003 toppled Saddam Hussein's regime. Alongside its security presence, the regime cultivated ties to loyalist tribal leaders in order to keep a close watch on matters. As in much of the rest of the country, nepotism and clientelism constituted an essential basis for all forms of employment, with the leaders and notables of the region as the main service providers.[15]

Before the war, Albu Kamal was largely self-sufficient, with its residents engaging in agriculture and raising livestock.[16] The commercial market for their agricultural products was restricted to the Syrian interior—mainly Aleppo and Hama—as border crossings with Iraq were not fully operational due to fraught Syrian-Iraqi relations. As the 2011 uprising transformed into a civil war, conditions changed, especially once the Islamic State occupied the area and effectively erased the border between Syria and Iraq. Many residents left their homes and migrated to rural areas or to neighboring governorates, including Hasakah and Rural Aleppo Governorate, to escape the Islamic State's harsh rule and airstrikes targeting its domain. Some families were displaced to camps in Iraq or went to live with relatives there. On a social level, the erasure of the border enabled certain families to reunite after long periods and also led to a rise in Syrian-Iraqi marriages. As for the economic situation, it changed drastically.[17] Trade with Iraq expanded to involve cigarettes, weaponry, food, and other products. The manufacture of military fatigues for Islamic State fighters also became widespread. And a new industry focused on refining crude oil and extracting fuel quickly emerged.[18] This process was a major source of livelihood for people in a region generally characterized by harsh and unstable economic conditions.

In 2016, Syrian government forces and Iran-backed militias expelled Islamic State fighters and regained control over Albu Kamal. Today, the border city is nearly empty of local residents. Instead, it is brimming with Iran-backed Iraqi militias that have established bases in and around Albu Kamal.[19] Despite adverse economic conditions, investment is on the rise. Investors are communicating with absentee citizens who are unable to return or are wanted by the police in order to buy their lands and properties.[20] As many people have refused to sell their assets to foreigners, Iranian businessmen are coordinating with locals in order to stealthily acquire land by convincing property owners to sell their land to a local who will in return give it to an Iranian entrepreneur and receive a commission. This has enabled Iranian nationals to systematically purchase abandoned lands and houses in line with a strategy to build a social base loyal to Iran in a

6 HOW SYRIA'S WAR EXTENDED BORDER POLICIES TO MUCH... 115

strategic area straddling the Syrian-Iraqi border, one with no preexisting such base.[21]

The situation in Albu Kamal shows how war has enhanced the security-based form of control the regime exerts over borderlands. Following its founding at the end of the nineteenth century, Albu Kamal was administratively and economically tied to the city of Deir al-Zor. The center-periphery relationship was between Deir al-Zor-based security officials on the one hand and local notables and tribal leaders on the other. But today the strongest and most apparent relationship is with Damascus. Elite forces from Damascus are stationed in and around Albu Kamal, tying the city directly to the capital. The presence and power of these forces means that the regime no longer sees a need to use Deir al-Zor intermediaries to mask its security-based approach to governance in Albu Kamal.

In Hasakah, Damascus no longer retains its previously firm grip on local affairs. An entity called the Self-Administration, which is affiliated with the Syrian Democratic Forces (SDF), a Kurdish-dominated military formation, is the main power broker. As a result, the regime cannot rely exclusively on its security organs to exert control. Hasakah thus constitutes an exception—albeit a partial one born of circumstances beyond the regime's control—to the ongoing trend in which Damascus channels its relationship with a borderland through its security services. The regime is one of several political actors in the area, and its ability to exert control over the governorate is hampered by a limited military capacity and a shrunken geographical presence. Indeed, Qamishli is governed by the Self-Administration. Yet despite having lost power and territory to the SDF and other groups, the regime continues to wield influence in parts of Hasakah, including a section of Qamishli itself, both directly and indirectly. In Qamishli specifically, the regime maintains its presence through security agencies and various state institutions, an airport that connects the area to the rest of Syria and the outside world, and tribal links.

The regime's security branches are located in a part of the city known colloquially as the "security square" (*al-murabbaa al-amni*). These security forces control institutions such as the city's hospital, civil registry, the migration and passports agency, and educational facilities.[22] Additionally, two Syrian army units are stationed in Hasakah Governorate, the first near Qamishli and the second near Hasakah city, and regime forces also control the Qamishli airport, which connects the area to Damascus and Beirut. And then there is the loyalist Tayy tribe, which is considered something of a Trojan Horse for Damascus in the heart of the SDF's canton. The leader of the Tayy tribe in Qamishli, Sheikh Mohammed al-Faris, has a close relationship with the security branches there and in Hasakah. Faris saw to it that the tribe and its subsidiaries cooperated with the National Defense Forces (NDF), a militia established by the regime, during the height of the conflict. Notably, however, the regime's relationship with the Tayy tribe extends well beyond the Assaf clan, from which its top sheikhs have historically been drawn, and includes other clans or subtribes.[23] For instance, the regime maintains close ties to Hamid al-Asaad, from the Bani Sabaa subtribe, in addition to leaders such as Mohammed Abdelrazzaq from the Assaf clan. In this way, Damascus prevents the Assaf leadership of the tribe from growing too powerful. Indeed, in 2020, the regime-backed Asaad prevailed in parliamentary elections against Faris.[24]

In Qamishli and Hasakah city, the regime and the Self-Administration vie for influence, but are also socioeconomically entangled. For example, in Qamishli, the regime's security services put up pictures of Assad, while in the areas of the city controlled by the Self-Administration, the latter puts up images of SDF fighters killed in battles against the Islamic State group. There is a tacit agreement between the two sides to facilitate transit on all the main routes—there are, for the most part, no checkpoints inside the city, which leads to swifter transport of goods and movement of residents. In Hasakah city, the Assad regime maintains a security presence. The city is historically home to Arabs, Kurds, and Syriacs/Assyrians and currently also houses a large number of displaced people. This composition has led to an expansion of the Self-Administration at the regime's expense. For example, the central market no longer constitutes the heart of the city, as three other markets have sprung up in quarters under the Self-Administration—Salahiyyah, Mufti, and Tal Hajjar.[25] Even in the central market, traders have since 2014 paid taxes to the Self-Administration in exchange for security and services.

In April 2021, the SDF clashed with NDF members of the Tayy tribe in a district of Qamishli. Russian military police, which at the request of the regime maintain a presence in Qamishli Airport and in nearby Amouda, intervened to stop the fighting and brokered a ceasefire.[26] This incident demonstrates that despite the rise of the SDF, the Tayy tribe effectively remains allied to the regime. From the perspective of Damascus, this is immensely beneficial, as it means that the regime's presence is not limited to its security apparatus—as manifested in the "security square" of Qamishli—and remaining state institutions but includes a distinctly societal element, namely, many members of a large and influential tribe.

Through direct and time-tested links to the Tayy tribe, the regime ensures that it maintains some sway at the northeastern reaches of Syria.

EMPLOYING BORDERLAND TACTICS IN NON-BORDERLAND PERIPHERIES

While eight years of war have accentuated preexisting relations and forms of governance in Syria's borderlands, they have fundamentally reshaped the regime's method of governing non-borderland peripheral areas. The old relationship between the regime and peripheral populations, which saw the state provide services and security in exchange for Syrians' obedience, has partially collapsed. War has destroyed the state's ability to fund many of its institutions and the development projects with which it previously cultivated ties with peripheral communities. This has placed an enormous strain on the housing stock and public services of cities. Adding to the burden, the cities that escaped widespread destruction have seen their population swell with Syrians displaced from other areas of the country.[27] With its coffers depleted, the regime has proven unable to ensure that public spending and services have kept up with these developments and has had to devise new strategies for managing inland peripheral populations.

The most significant change lies in the state's inability to provide social services and its consequent decision to permit local communities to fill gaps created by its absence, with the proviso that such efforts go through security officials. Indeed, what relationship remains between state and citizenry depends less on institutions and municipal authorities than direct, informal ties between citizens and security agents. To implement the service-based projects that formerly fell within the purview of the municipal authorities—including repair of roads, water delivery, and waste management—local actors are obliged to navigate a host of challenges. They must secure their own funding and then obtain permission from central authorities in the form of the governorate-level Political and Security Committee. Even more importantly, they must ensure that local security actors do not block their project, often by paying them significant sums of money. This is because even when the committee grants its approval, high-ranking local security officials can intervene and veto a project.[28]

In areas whose inhabitants have openly resisted the regime, the latter has adopted a nakedly security-oriented approach reminiscent of its

118   K. KHADDOUR AND K. MAZUR

method of governing borderlands. The objective is to ensure that the area in question remains firmly under the control of the state, with little regard for the inhabitants or the urban layout. In Kurdish towns on the northeastern border with Turkey, for example, security services traditionally intervened extensively in the lives of local residents and generally provided lower-quality public services.[29] This is now the norm in areas, including urban districts, that were until recently strongholds of rebel forces. Before 2011, these areas' residents were ruled by the same hybrid model of governance—bureaucracy and security oversight—as other districts in Syria's interior and enjoyed similar levels of public services. Today, however, they are subjected to the sort of stringent security measures and constraints previously restricted to northeastern and eastern border regions.

How the Regime Manages Loyal and Ambivalent Peripheral Areas

The town of Tal, in Damascus' northern hinterland, exemplifies the new relationship binding non-borderland peripheral areas to the central authority. Tal, a community with dense local networks and established intermediary relations with the center, fell out of regime control during the uprising. Crucially, however, several of its most influential inhabitants retained ties to the regime.[30] As such, when the town was retaken in 2016, it was not subjected to the full-scale displacement seen in other formerly rebellious suburbs of Damascus, such as Harasta.[31] Yet this did not mean that much-needed services were forthcoming. The town's water supply required major repairs, but state authorities were unable or unwilling to make those repairs. Instead, a council of local notables gathered funds from the town's diaspora in the Gulf and obtained permission from the relevant government ministries to carry out the project. The project faced delays from local security officials, but ultimately was able to proceed after local notables lobbied these security officers and paid them considerable bribes.[32] Such private provision of essential services in a peripheral area like Tal would have been rare and superfluous before 2011, with over 96 percent of people living in towns with a population larger than 10,000 having had home access to the public water supply.[33]

The roundabout means by which services are now obtained in Tal and the necessity of bribing security officials to receive the all-important permission to proceed exemplify the major changes in relations between the center of power and peripheral communities across postwar Syria. These relations increasingly bypass state institutions and municipal government. Less is exchanged between center and periphery, but the exchange is negotiated far more directly than before the uprising. Moreover, the exchange tends to take place between the periphery's notables and one or another security arm of the state.

A similar phenomenon is apparent in Jaramana. Changes in the patterns of governance there demonstrate the ways in which both established local notables and new actors have come to play an important role, performing functions formerly within the remit of the administrative state—but almost always with the permission of the security services, with which they have forged direct links. As violence engulfed the Eastern Ghouta region surrounding Jaramana in 2012, elite regime forces, including Air Force and Military Intelligence and the Republican Guard, set up checkpoints to control the flow of people and goods in and out of the city. Such measures served their stated purpose of preventing attacks on nearby Jaramana, but also opened up new profit-making opportunities for these security and military personnel, who benefitted from issuing construction permits and skimming off building materials and consumer goods. Getting goods into tightly controlled Jaramana and, especially, the besieged towns of Ghouta required the permission of security authorities, secured through informal ties and substantial bribes. Businessmen allied with proregime militias controlling the city's main entry points monopolized the sale of staple goods such as bread, splitting the profits with the militias.[34] The siege of neighboring towns in Eastern Ghouta further promoted the emergence of traders benefitting from the smuggling economy.[35]

Jaramana became a haven for displaced Syrians as its preconflict population of 185,446 swelled to an estimated 621,000 in 2019. This led to a massive vertical and horizontal expansion of the city, as well as major changes in land use. Floors were added to many buildings in "agricultural" neighborhoods, and new buildings were constructed from scratch, often in a matter of weeks, in order to be rented to new arrivals. The footprint of the city expanded by 16 percent between 2011 and 2019. The ground floors of many existing buildings were also turned into workshops, commercial facilities, and sites for street vendors. All of these changes occurred with little state support and in violation of formal planning rules.[36] Permission was sought from high-ranking officials in the security services whose power had eclipsed that of the state bureaucracy. In this respect, Jaramana has come to partially resemble the borderlands prior to

2011, where the security services were, for all intents and purposes, the state.

Parallel to the unregulated expansion of the city's footprint, residents of Jaramana took to securing for themselves what were previously provided as public services. Electricity is frequently delivered from the central grid on a scheme of several hours on, several hours off, and many street lights are not functioning.[37] This has given rise to a "generator economy," compelling residents to purchase both the machines and fuel on the black market. State provision of subsidized cooking and heating fuel has similarly become infrequent, forcing residents to endure long waits or pay several times the official, subsidized price on the black market.[38]

This new norm has deprived the traditional Jaramana business classes of the ability to engage in many kinds of commerce and has outlived the dismantling of the security infrastructure associated with the siege of Eastern Ghouta. In March 2019, following the Syrian military's defeat of rebels in the surrounding area, regime checkpoints were removed from Jaramana. Yet many of the partnerships between businessmen and heads of proregime militias and security officials remain in place, particularly when it comes to the trade in construction materials. In addition, while the proregime militias from outside Jaramana that participated in the siege of Eastern Ghouta have largely withdrawn, Hezbollah and a number of local militias based in Jaramana and in Druze communities beyond have retained an informal presence in the city.[39] Today, the old networks of Jaramana natives continue to exercise some economic power and political influence, but a wider and more diffuse range of new regime clients and security officials have come to exert significant influence and extract considerable rents from the city's residents. Both old and new influential local actors have been drawn into a relationship with security forces that is more direct than the one that existed prior to 2011.

How the Regime Treats Rebellious Peripheral Areas

In many areas that engaged in open rebellion, the regime's distrust of residents is so great that it will not entertain the notion of reverting to the pre-uprising mode of governance. In such areas, the regime is now asserting its authority in the manner it has traditionally done along its borders—focusing on preventing territory from being used to challenge its authority rather than attempting to integrate the local community into its institutions and networks. The regime's plans for reconstructing such urban neighborhoods make this strategy plain: Damascus has promulgated laws giving it broad authority to seize property and has announced plans to redevelop these areas in ways that would radically reshape their social fabric. This represents a drastic change. Whereas the regime tightly controlled construction in border areas prior to 2011, it maintained a lenient approach in inland areas. For example, it allowed rural families that had migrated to Homs to build homes on the city's outskirts—in considerable density and in violation of formal planning regulations.[40]

To see how the regime has altered its method of operation, one need look no further than Homs itself. In the Homs district of Baba Amr, the regime's historical approach to the borderlands—focusing on the control and retention of territory, with little regard for integrating the often suspect local inhabitants into the bureaucracy of the state—is being replicated. Baba Amr was a locus of opposition to the regime and was heavily damaged during fighting. The dense local networks of extended family solidarity found in Baba Amr were critical to its residents' ability to sustain their fight against the regime. These networks are intimately connected to the patterns of building and settlement. Indeed, extended families built informally in the same area, allowing them to keep these networks and control the space.[41]

Such resistance will no longer be possible. Large areas of Baba Amr that were heavily damaged in fighting have been expropriated under Law No. 10 of 2018, ostensibly for purposes of reconstruction. This law gives the state the right to expropriate any property in certain zones, demolish all structures located there, and compensate owners with shares in a joint-stock company owning the new property.[42] It is reminiscent of a pre-uprising law, Decree 49 of 2008, that froze all property transactions in proximity to the border, thereby allowing security forces to directly control the economic affairs of local residents in Qamishli, but also in Daraa near Syria's southwestern border with Jordan.[43] In the place of winding, informally developed streets and buildings that housed large extended family networks and ended up facilitating resistance, the regime aims to construct high-rise luxury towers for wealthy nuclear families—dwellings that would make the kind of social relations and resistance that emerged from Baba Amr in 2011 impossible.[44] The luxury tower projects are unlikely to ever be completed, but the demolition that is nominally a precursor to their construction serves to keep these strategic territories—on the periphery of the country's largest cities—free of the communities and social networks that challenged the regime.

Such demolition is contentious because many of the owners of property in the informally constructed areas subject to these laws lack formal property deeds and others actively opposed the regime and have been displaced by war.[45] They fear returning to claim what is theirs, yet the state has passed laws depriving them of their property if they do not return and claim their properties in person. Syrians outside the country or those considered associated—even indirectly—with the opposition are unlikely to do so, for fear of subjecting themselves to imprisonment at the hands of the regime. As such, they are unlikely to ever recover possession of their properties.[46]

The Baba Amr plan bears striking similarity to a plan for a similarly rebellious area of Damascus, Basatin al-Razi, which was razed under Law No. 10 in order to construct a development called Marota City. It also recalls the "Homs Dream," a plan formulated in 2007 to demolish large areas of the city and reconstruct them in the image of Dubai.[47] Promotion of redevelopment on this scale signals a hardening of the regime's attitude toward spontaneous, informal settlement. The logic of the Homs Dream, which was shelved but recently revived, has become central to how the regime seeks to govern areas like Baba Amr after years of war. It seeks to uproot segments of the local society that it cannot control through its informal methods of governance, namely, those densely linked Sunni Arab communities that rose against it in 2011.[48]

Whether the regime will be able to complete construction of the Marota City or Homs Dream projects, much less populate them with white-collar, individuated nuclear families, remains to be seen.[49] Yet in merely breaking ground on the projects, the regime has completed the work of uprooting their residents. Baba Amr was largely destroyed by fighting and regime bombardment, and few of its residents have returned. Demolition would make their return impossible. Between 2015 and 2017, all residents of areas within the planned Marota City were displaced, with around 6700 properties demolished. In many cases, workers were accompanied by security agents to prevent residents from halting demolition.[50]

The urban development plans for Baba Amr and Basatin al-Razi, formulated under Law No. 10, differ radically from those in other areas of the country. For example, demolition of egregiously unsafe buildings and shakedowns by individual civil servants and military officers notwithstanding, spontaneous building is still largely tolerated in Jaramana. The master plan for Jaramana, formally announced in October 2019, integrates and formalizes all areas of "collective violation" except those deemed dangerous and provides some support through the local engineers' syndicate and municipal government to correct building code violations.[51] The difference between the two approaches to urban planning underscores the full informalization of governance. Where the regime can control populations through informal networks, it is content to mold formal structures around those arrangements. However, among populations in which it lacks such ties, the regime is using planning to reshape communities or, indeed, create them anew.

CONCLUSION

The hybrid prewar structures of governance in Syria's inland peripheral areas—which combined the arbitrary violence of security forces with clientelistic personal relations and the formal administrative hierarchies of state institutions—are no longer in force. Whereas prewar inland Syria was ruled through a patchwork of formal and informal arrangements filtered to a certain extent through state institutions, today a far less differentiated manner of rule is in effect. Essentially, the regime, which no longer attempts to obscure its security-driven rule of the borderlands, has to varying degrees replicated this method of governance elsewhere. Damascus now rules much of the country through its security organs.

Far from abating as the conflict recedes in intensity, this new trend seems set to accelerate and to spread throughout Syria. From the perspective of Damascus, it is precisely and perhaps *only* by governing in such a manner that the regime will sustain itself. Chastened by an uprising that took it by surprise, drew in foreign state and nonstate actors, and lasted for nearly a decade, Bashar al-Assad and his regime have concluded that the most effective way of guarding against another such scenario is by taking the security approach to its logical extreme. For all intents and purposes, the security services in Syria have become the state. And given that the state was always authoritarian, these security services now intrude into myriad aspects of citizens' lives.

War has divided Syria into four zones controlled by four distinct actors: the Syrian regime; the SDF; Turkey and its Syrian militia proxies; and Syrian and foreign Islamists, who run Idlib Governorate. To outside observers as well as many ordinary Syrians themselves, it is the zone under the regime's control that constitutes the heart of Syria. This is the area over which discussions of the country's political future occur in international forums and to which most Syrians abroad yearn to return. It is the

124 K. KHADDOUR AND K. MAZUR

part of Syria that is home to the country's historic cities, major population centers, and chief economic engines. The regime trades on its continued control of these territories to bolster its self-projected image as the ruler of the core of Syria, but it has little to offer international players in return for their recognition of its legitimacy and offers virtually nothing to Syrians under its authority. Indeed, the regime has reduced much of this portion of Syria—by far the largest—to *Suriya al-Asad*. It is land possessed by the Assad regime, without any semblance of a compact between state and citizenry.

Notes

1. Sam Dagher, *Assad or We Burn the Country: How One Family's Lust for Power Destroyed Syria* (New York: Little, Brown and Company, 2019), 164.
2. Dawn Chatty, "The Bedouin in Contemporary Syria: The Persistence of Tribal Authority and Control," *The Middle East Journal* 64, no. 1 (2010): 29–49.
3. Mohammed Jamal Barout, *Al-Takawwun al-Tarikhi al-Hadith li'l-Jazira al-Suriyya: As'ilah wa Ishkaliyyat al-Tahawwul min al-Badwana ila al-Umran al-Hadari* [The Contemporary Historical Formation of the Syrian Jazira: Questions and Issues Concerning the Transformation from Nomadism to Sedentary Urbanization] (Beirut: Arab Center for Research and Policy Studies, 2013), 133.
4. Authors' interview with a member of the Tayy tribe (via WhatsApp), Urfa, September 3, 2020.
5. These links have remained intact down to the present. Faris made numerous public appearances in support of the regime throughout the uprising and civil war. In April 2021, he went on state television to call on all members of the Tayy tribe to leave the Kurdish-dominated Syrian Democratic Forces (SDF) and announced the formation of a popular resistance to American occupation. See "Al-Shaykh Muhammad al-Faris, Shaykh Qabilat al-Tayy, Phone Communication [Shaykh Muhammad al-Faris, Shaykh of Tayy Tribe, Phone Communication], YouTube video, 10:19, posted by *syria alikhbaria*, April 23, 2021, https://www.youtube.com/watch?v=ArfbD7_ZL7g.
6. Authors' interview with a member of the Tayy tribe (via Skype), Erbil, June 29, 2020. Muhammad Mansoura, head of Military Security (one of the regime's four overlapping security branches) for Hasakah Governorate from 1980 to 2002, exemplifies these security relationships. Mansoura knew the leaders of the region's tribes and local families intimately and was a master at manipulating them and setting them against one another.

Commonly called the "absolute ruler" of the Jazira, Mansoura developed a reputation for deescalating conflicts through cooptation, earning himself the appellation "Key to the Solution." See Al-Majlis al-Watani li'l-Haqiqa wa'l-Adalah wa'l-Musalaha—Profile Siyasi-Amni li'l-Liwa' Muhammad Mansoura (Taqrir Khas bi-Munasabat Taayinihi Ra'isan li-Shu'bat al-Amn al-Siyasi fi Suriyya" [National Council for Truth, Justice, and Reconciliation in Syria—Politico-Security Profile of Major General Muhammad Mansoura (Special Report on the Occasion of His Appointment as Head of the Political Security Branch in Syria], *Al-Hiwar Al-Mutamaddin*, January 19, 2005, http://www.ahewar.org/debat/show.art.asp?aid=30163.

7. Kevin Mazur, "Networks, Informal Governance, and Ethnic Violence in a Syrian City," *World Politics* 72, no. 3 (July 2020): 501.

8. Muhammad Nur al-Din, "Al-Mujtama' wa'l-Siyasa wa'l-Thaqafa Qabl Aam 2011," [Society and Politics and Culture Before the Year 2011], *Siar Suriyya* (blog), Sharq.org, Tarikhi, July 4, 2017, https://tarikhi.org/inte rview/%d9%85%d8%ad%d9%85%d8%af-%d9%86%d9%88%d8%b1-%d8%a7 %d9%84%d8%af%d9%8a%d9%86/?lang=ar.

9. Peripheries in Syria, as we understand them in this chapter, are less a spatial concept—though they are often located far away from Damascus—than a social structure and a pattern of relating to outside powers, including state authorities and regime figures. Specifically, the social structure of peripheral communities is based largely on extended families; there are typically dense personal linkages among members, and collective memories play a central role in promoting group solidarity. Influential local community members typically play an intermediary role linking these communities to outside powers. In the center, by contrast, relationships are often between individuals of widely different backgrounds without such shared formative context—and many of the residents of central areas of Damascus are themselves in positions of economic and political power. These actors depend, in turn, on linkages to the periphery to govern, extract resources, and market their goods. Whereas peripheral actors largely remain within their locality, the center is the site linking peripheries. To return to the example at hand, Jaramana is only a few kilometers from the city center, but stands outside of it socially. It is connected to the center through networks of powerful individuals rooted in the local community, exemplifying how the center and periphery are related to and depend upon one another in contemporary Syria.

10. Cyril Roussel, "Jeramana (Syrie)," *Confluences Méditerranée* no. 85 (July 3, 2013): 117–18.

11. UrbAN-S, "Jaramana City Profile," Urban Analysis Network for Syria, December 2019, https://urban-syria.org/#city-profiles, 14.

12. Authors' interview with a Jaramana resident, Beirut, April 2020.

126 K. KHADDOUR AND K. MAZUR

13. UrbAN-S, "Jaramana City Profile."
14. Authors' interview with Jaramana architect, Beirut, April 2020.
15. Harith Hasan and Kheder Khaddour, "The Transformation of the Iraqi-Syrian Border: From a National to a Regional Frontier," Malcolm H. Kerr Carnegie Middle East Center, March 31, 2020, https://carnegie-mec.org/2020/03/31/transformation-of-iraqi-syrian-border-from-national-to-regional-frontier-pub-81396.
16. Ibid.
17. Firas al-Umri, "Taghayyur Nauʻi Yalhaq bi Aswaq Dayr al-Zur...Tawaqquf Tasdir al-Naft ila al-Shamal, wa Infitah ala Aswaq al-Iraq" [A Qualitative Change to the Markets of Deir al-Zor...A Halt to Oil Exports to the North, and an Opening onto the Markets of Iraq], *Ain al-Madina*, September 1, 2014.
18. Harith Hasan and Kheder Khaddour, "The Transformation of the Iraqi-Syrian Border: From a National to a Regional Frontier."
19. Ziad Awad, "Iran fi Deir al-Zor: Al-Istratijiyya wa'l-Tamaddud wa Furas al-Taghalghul [Iran in Deir al-Zor: Strategy, Expansion, and Opportunities for Infiltration], *Middle East Directions*, October 7, 2019, https://medirections.com/index.php/2019-05-07-15-50-27/%20wartime/2019-10-07-07-56-40.
20. Ibid.
21. This practice is also widespread in Aleppo. Hani Abdallah, "Al-Aqarat fi Halab Tantaqil min Ashabiha li-Qabdat Iran wa'l-Asad" [Properties in Aleppo Go from their Owners to the Clutches of Iran and Assad], *Focus Halab*, January 25, 2021, https://focusaleppo.com/2021/01/25/ العقارات-في-حلب-تنتقل-من-أصحابها-القبضة/.
22. Ibid.
23. Turki Ali Al-Rabiʻu, "Nahwa Taʾsis Inasa li-Dirasat al-Mujtamaʻ al-Badawi: Qabilat Tayy Namudhajan" [Toward the Creation of an Anthropology that Studies Bedouin Society: The Tayy Tribe as an Example], *Al-Ijtihad* 4, no. 17 (Autumn 1992), https://search.mandumah.com/Record/506056.
24. Authors' interview with a member of the Tayy tribe (via WhatsApp), Qamishli, June 18, 2020.
25. Ibid.
26. Authors' interview with a resident of Qamishli (via phone), October 2020.
27. The population of coastal Latakia, for example, roughly doubled from its pre-war level, reaching 859,340. See UrbAN-S, "Latakia City Factsheet," 2019, https://api.urban-syria.org/uploads/a33d7407797a48ffb5e1158d9ab323a8.pdf.
28. The legislative apparatus for municipal governance reflects these on-the-ground realities. The regime undertook a major decentralization initiative in 2011, at the beginning of the uprising; it issued Decree 107, giving local

6 HOW SYRIA'S WAR EXTENDED BORDER POLICIES TO MUCH... 127

administrators more control over planning, funding, and monitoring development projects—on paper. In practice, the regime did little to decentralize governance. This stasis was formalized by Baath Party Decree 108 in 2018, requiring that almost all candidates for municipal councils come from a "National Unity List," which reasserted the power of the Party. See COAR (Center for Operational Analysis and Research), "Arrested Development: Rethinking Local Development in Syria," March 31, 2020, https://coar-global.org/2020/03/31/arrested-development-rethinking-local-development-in-syria/.

29. Authors' interview with journalist from Kobane based in Sulaimani, April 27, 2014; see also Harriet Allsopp, *The Kurds of Syria: Political Parties and Identity in the Middle East* (London: I.B. Tauris, 2014), chapter 1.

30. Kheder Khaddour, "Localism, War, and the Fragmentation of Sunni Islam in Syria," Malcolm H. Kerr Carnegie Middle East Center, March 28, 2019, https://carnegie-mec.org/2019/03/28/localism-war-and-fragmentation-of-sunni-islam-in-syria-pub-78714.

31. COAR, "Political Demographics: The Markings of the Government of Syria Reconciliation Measures in Eastern Ghouta," 2018, https://coar-global.org/2018/12/30/2018dec13-political-demographics-the-markings-of-the-government-of-syria-reconciliation-measures-in-eastern-ghouta-coar/.

32. COAR, "Arrested Development."

33. Central Bureau of Statistics of Syria, "2004 National Census," 2004, http://www.cbssyr.org/indicator/hp-f.htm. By contrast, residents of the northeastern border areas often drilled their own wells to access water for drinking and irrigation—a common complaint among Kurdish residents of the region was that Damascus ignored their pleas for the state to provide these services. Authors' interview with journalist from Kobane based in Sulaimani, April 27, 2014.

34. UrbAN-S, "Jaramana City Profile," 42–43.

35. Ayman al-Dessouky, "What We Can Learn from the Rise of Local Traders in Syria," in *Local Intermediaries in Post-2011 Syria: Transformation and Continuity*, edited by Kheder Khaddour and Kevin Mazur (Beirut: Friedrich-Ebert-Stiftung, 2019), 43–66.

36. UrbAN-S, "Jaramana City Profile," 15, 32, and 34; authors' interview with architect from Jaramana "agricultural" neighborhood, Beirut, April 2020.

37. Abdullah al-Bashir, "Tauzi' ghayr Adil li'l-Kahruba' fi Madinat Homs Wast Suriyya" [Unjust Distribution of Electricity in the City of Homs, Central Syria], *Al-Araby Al-Jadeed*, May 13, 2021, https://www.alaraby.co.uk/society/توزيع-غير-عادل-للكهرباء-في-مدينة-حمص-وسط-سورية.

38. UrbAN-S, "Jaramana City Profile," 79.

128   K. KHADDOUR AND K. MAZUR

39. "Dimashq.. Jaramana Nadhifa min Hawajiz al-Asad wa Istimrar al-Sariqat wa'l-Tashbih" [Damascus... Jaramana is Cleansed of Assad's Checkpoints and Fears of the Continuance of Theft and Thuggery], *Zaman al-Wasl*, March 4, 2019, https://www.zamanalwsl.net/news/article/102354/; UrbAN-S, "Jaramana City Profile," 28.

40. Kevin Mazur, "Networks, Informal Governance, and Ethnic Violence in a Syrian City," 495.

41. Marwa al-Sabouni, *The Battle for Home: Memoir of a Syrian Architect* (London: Thames & Hudson, 2016).

42. The process builds upon the model employed in central Beirut to create the Solidere development, suggesting important points of comparison with this controversial project as well as the Lebanese experience of reconstruction, generally. See Noor Hamadeh and Krystel Bassil, "Demolishing Human Rights in the Name of Reconstruction: Lessons Learned From Beirut's Solidere for Syria," Tahrir Institute for Middle East Policy, September 16, 2020, https://timep.org/commentary/analysis/demolishing-human-rights-in-the-name-of-reconstruction-lessons-learned-from-beiruts-solidere-for-syria/.

43. This made the sale of property in Kurdish border areas of the northeast effectively impossible and also enmeshed locals in the southern border area of Daraa in relations of complicity with security officers. See Myriam Ababsa, "The End of a World: Drought and Agrarian Transformation in Northeast Syria (2007–2010)," in *Syria from Reform to Revolt*, edited by Raymond A. Hinnebusch and Tina Zintl (Syracuse, N.Y: Syracuse University Press, 2015), 217; also Dagher, *Assad or We Burn the Country*.

44. "Tandhim Thalathat Ahya' fi Homs bi Mujab al-Qanun Raqm 10" [Organization of Three Districts in Homs in Accordance with Law No. 10], *Enab Baladi*, December 12, 2019, https://www.enabbaladi.net/archives/348583.

45. Omar Abdelaziz Hallaj, "Urban Housing and the Question of Property Rights in Syria," in *State of Syrian Cities 2016–2017* (European Union Working Paper, 2017), https://syrianechoes.com/2017/12/21/urban-housing-and-the-question-of-property-rights-in-syria/; Etienne Léna, "Mukhalafat in Damascus: The Form of an Informal Settlement," in *Popular Housing and Urban Land Tenure in the Middle East*, edited by Myriam Ababsa, Baudouin Dupret, and Eric Dennis (Cairo: American University in Cairo Press, 2012), 13–46.

46. Sawsan Abou Zainedin and Hani Fakhani, "Syria's Reconstruction Between Discriminatory Implementation and Circumscribed Resistance," in *Contentious Politics in the Syrian Conflict: Opposition, Representation, and Resistance*, edited by Maha Yahya (Beirut: Carnegie Middle East Center, 2020), https://carnegie-mec.org/2020/05/15/syria-s-reconstruction-

6 HOW SYRIA'S WAR EXTENDED BORDER POLICIES TO MUCH... 129

between-discriminatory-implementation-and-circumscribed-resistance-pub-81803.
47. Homs Governor Ayad Ghazal made this comparison explicit in an interview given to a Kuwaiti newspaper. See "Ghazal: Hilm Homs Mashru' li-Tatwir al-Madina wa-Tahqiq Hajat Abna'iha wa-Tumuhatihim" [Ghazal: The Homs Dream is a Project to Develop the City and Meet the Needs and Ambitions of Its Sons], December 22, 2007, *Alanbaa*, https://www.alanba.com.kw/ar/arabic-international-news/20811/22-12-2007-. At the time, the project was primarily the initiative of Ghazal and received little support from senior regime figures—virtually no work was done to implement it prior to the onset of the uprising, and Ghazal was fired, and the project formally canceled in April 2011, within weeks of the first major demonstrations in the country. See "I'lan Wafat Hilm Homs Rasmiyyan" [Official Announcement of the Death of the Homs Dream], *Zaman al-Wasl*, July 24, 2011, https://www.zamanalwsl.net/news/20564.html.
48. "Al-Nidham Yaqul Innahu Lam Yulghi 'Hilm Homs' .. Wa Satwat al-Qanun Raqm 10 Tasil ila al-Madina" [The Regime Says It Has Not Canceled the 'Homs Dream' ... And the Influence of Law No. 10 Reaches the City], *Eqtisad*, July 22, 2019, //www.eqtsad.net/news/article/26080/.
49. The most advanced of these projects, Marota City, remains at the stage of basic infrastructure construction and lacks sufficient investment. Omar Abdulaziz Hallaj, "Formality, Informality, and the Resilience of the Syrian Political Economy," Geneva Centre for Security Policy, Syria Transition Challenges Project, Research Project Report 8, June 2021, 33, endnote 76, https://dam.gcsp.ch/files/doc/syrian-political-economy.
50. Sawsan Abou Zainedin and Hani Fakhani, "Syria's Reconstruction," 26; Moutasem Jamal, "Urban Planning Project Obfuscates Demographic Shift Unfolding in Southwest Damascus, Says LCC Member," *Syria Direct*, January 21, 2016, https://syriadirect.org/news/urban-planning-project-obfuscates-demographic-shift-unfolding-in-southwest-damascus-says-lcc-member/.
51. Ghaliya Sharaf, "Baladiyyat Jaramana: Sanuwassi' al-Mukhattat al-Tandhimi li-Yashmul Kamil al-Madina" [Jaramana Municipality: We Will Broaden the Organizational Plan So that It Encompasses the Entire City], *Al-Iqtisadi* (Majra), May 31, 2019, https://manhom.com/1424631-دراسة-تنظيم-جرمانا/; Muhammad Manar Hamiju, "Wazir al-Iskan: Mukhattat Tandhimi Jadid li Madinat Jaramana fi Rif Dimashq" [Minister of Housing: A New Organizational Plan for Jaramana on the Outskirts of Damascus], *Al Watan Online*, October 16, 2019, https://www.alwatanonline.com/وزير-الإسكان-مخطط-تنظيمي-جديد-لمدينة-ج/.

CHAPTER 7

Hadramawt's Emergence as a Center: A Confluence of Yemeni Circumstances and Hadrami Resourcefulness

Ahmed Nagi

INTRODUCTION

The conflict in Yemen—which began in 2014, drew in regional countries in 2015, and shows no sign of abating—has reinforced a desire for self-rule in several disaffected parts of the country. One such region is Hadramawt, a governorate occupying around 38 percent of Yemen's total area.[1] Hadramawt's tendency toward autonomy derives from its history. Having enjoyed semi-independence for centuries prior to the creation of South Yemen (into which it was subsumed) in 1967, Hadramawt has a legacy of serving as a center for surrounding areas. And crucially, its people, the Hadramis, have a distinct sociopolitical identity.[2] Hadramawt's neglect at the hands of the Aden-based government of South Yemen, and, following the unification of North and South Yemen in 1990, the Sanaa-based government, has not substantially changed Hadramis'

A. Nagi (✉)
Malcolm H. Kerr Carnegie Middle East Center, Beirut, Lebanon
e-mail: ahmed.abdullah@carnegie-mec.org

© The Author(s), under exclusive license to Springer Nature Switzerland AG 2023
M. Yahya (ed.), *How Border Peripheries are Changing the Nature of Arab States*, https://doi.org/10.1007/978-3-031-09187-2_7

131

132   A. NAGI

self-perception. Moreover, Hadrami sociopolitical movements of both Yemen and the diaspora have long used their people's particularity as a launching pad for an aspirational political program centered on autonomy.

Indeed, the Hadramis were angling for greater autonomy even before the outbreak of the current conflict. The National Dialogue Conference (NDC) in Sanaa, held from March 2013 until January 2014, is a case in point. The NDC's purpose was to bring all Yemen's political groups together to discuss the future of Yemen following the civil uprising of 2011 and to agree on the form of governance that Yemen should adopt. The NDC's "Outcomes Document,"[3] which included recommendations for reforms such as the adoption of a federal system, with Hadramawt as a center for the eastern governorates (Hadramawt itself, Shabwa, and Mahra), were received with much enthusiasm among Hadramis and other aggrieved peoples of Yemen's peripheries. Although the NDC's recommendations were never implemented, the Hadrami community came to consider them a point of departure for future negotiations.

Perhaps ironically, Yemen's descent into war in 2014 brought autonomy-seeking Hadramis closer to realizing much of their vision and initiated the governorate's transformation from a periphery into a center. To begin with, Hadramawt has emerged as an island of relative stability in war-torn Yemen. Indeed, the governorate has witnessed only battles between Al-Qaeda in the Arabian Peninsula (AQAP) and Yemeni government forces supported by a Saudi-led Arab military coalition—and that was in 2015 and 2016. (Only Mahra, which is Yemen's easternmost governorate, has seen less fighting.) Hadramis themselves have shown a marked unwillingness to participate in the country's main conflict, which pits the Saudi-led coalition against Ansar Allah, better known as the Houthis, a Zaydi Shiite Islamist political movement and militia backed by Iran. Furthermore, the establishment of two local paramilitary groups, the Hadrami Elite Forces by the United Arab Emirates (UAE) and the Hadrami Security Battalions by Saudi Arabia, has empowered Hadramis to manage security issues in their region, meaning that it is unlikely Hadramawt will ever turn into a battleground between the Houthis and Yemeni government forces. Economic developments have, if anything, proven even more significant. The blockade imposed by the Saudi-led coalition on those of the country's ports controlled by the Houthis has led Hadramawt's ports to assume a much more important role in commercial traffic. Finally, the relative stability of Hadramawt has drawn in internally displaced Yemenis as well as those obliged to leave Saudi Arabia due to its "Saudization" policy. Those with means have established businesses, enhanced the governorate's economy, and furthered its growth into a center.

It is important to note that, unlike Yemen's southern separatist movement, the Hadramis are not out to recreate a southern Yemeni state. Despite differences between various Hadrami political groups, most of them agree on the point that Hadramawt should remain a part of Yemen, provided it enjoys autonomy. As such, Hadrami groups' political agitation is focused on enlarging the margin of maneuverability they have when it comes to governing themselves, particularly with a view to Yemen's future as a decentralized state.[4] And given that Hadramawt is responsible for about half of Yemen's total oil production and is home to fisheries and other economic assets, the governorate's steady accrual of autonomy and steady growth as a center cannot but have major consequences for the country as a whole (Map 7.1).

A HISTORICAL TENDENCY TOWARD AUTONOMY

For centuries, Hadramawt served as a center of power and commerce in the Arabian Peninsula. Its strategic location, overlooking the Arabian Sea and extending deep into the desert area of the Empty Quarter (Al-Ruba' al-Khali), enabled it to hold sway over surrounding areas. Hadramawt lay along the incense trade route, by which incense, spices, and other goods made their way from the Indian Subcontinent to the Arabian Peninsula.[5] The long coastline of Hadramawt contributed to strengthening its role on this route through a multiplicity of seaports which facilitated trade with South and East Asia in one direction and the Horn of Africa in the other. This remained the case until 1967, when South Yemen was established.

Hadramawt's cultural stature was no less important than its economic position. Home to ancient Sufi schools, Hadramawt served as an important religious and cultural center for scholars and researchers from many regions of Yemen and beyond. The historic city of Tarim, which lies in the middle of the Hadramawt Valley, remains one of the most famous Sufi centers in the Islamic world. And it still has many religious education centers and historical and cultural libraries.[6] The migration of Hadramis to the Horn of Africa and even farther afield to East and South Asia had an impact among the communities in whose midst they settled, contributing greatly to the promotion of Hadrami schools and religious traditions in their new places of residence and strengthening Hadramawt's trade links to countries near and far.

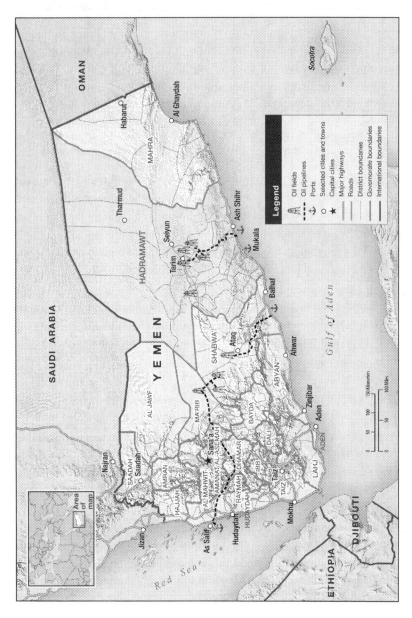

Map 7.1 NDC map of a proposed federal Yemen

The most important factor reinforcing Hadrami identity, maintaining the political unity of the Hadrami people and endowing them with a narrative, was a ruling system long prevalent in Hadramawt. The valley of Hadramawt was home to several inter-related kingdoms and sultanates, the two most famous of which were the Kathiri Sultanate, founded in 1379, and the Quaiti Sultanate, established in 1820. Their historical legacy remains strong. Although Britain controlled much of southern Yemen from 1839 until 1967, the region's sultans and sheikhs were granted a kind of autonomy after entering into protection agreements with the British, as the latter had no desire for direct domination or the removal of local rulers.[7] Despite the tribal style of governance that prevailed during the period of the rule of the Hadrami sultanates, it contributed to keeping Hadramawt as a territory distinct from its neighbor and a correspondingly distinctive population.

This history is embedded in the collective memory of the governorate's inhabitants. Along with that memory is a feeling of resentment owing to the perceived peripheralization of Hadramawt in modern Yemeni history. Most Hadramis consider the situation in which they have found themselves since 1967 to have diminished their homeland's historically consequential role. Until then, Hadramawt had not been a satellite of another center; on the contrary, it was a center in its own right.[8] There was little to no indication that this would change when the British left southern Yemen in November 1967 and a new state was born. Yet the People's Democratic Republic of Yemen (PDRY), commonly known as South Yemen, immediately abolished all the sultanates and sheikhdoms that were associated with the British, including the Quaiti and Kathiri sultanates. This alienated Hadramis of traditional bent. At the same time, Hadramis of a "revolutionary" orientation, many of whom had fought in the ranks of the National Liberation Front (NLF), a Marxist guerrilla group that sought freedom from the British, were not satisfied either. They had expected whatever entity the NLF established to give their region its perceived due.

Instead, the form of governance pursued by the regime in the capital, Aden, diminished Hadramawt's standing. Hadramawt became simply one of several governorates in the new republic. Moreover, the regime adopted a socialist system that called for the strict centralization of administration in all its forms. This turned all governorates into satellites of Aden Governorate. The policy of nationalizing individual property, a measure taken in line with the regime's Marxist orientation, added to Hadramis' woes and contributed greatly to the emigration of merchants who feared

136 A. NAGI

losing their wealth. Despite the appointment of individual Hadramis to the upper echelons of the state hierarchy in a bid to demonstrate inclusiveness, the regime's ideological rigidity when it came to socialist governance and centralized administration made it impossible for notions of decentralization and autonomy to gain traction.

On a regional level, South Yemen found itself isolated from its neighbors. The Gulf countries were often at loggerheads with Aden, especially over the latter's adoption of a revolutionary political line in opposition to their monarchical and feudal system of governance.[9] In fact, the government of South Yemen became a major supporter of an insurgent group—the Popular Front for the Liberation of the Arabian Gulf, or PFLOAG in its most well-known iteration—that was particularly active in Oman's Dhofar region from 1965 until 1975 and whose supply lines ran through Hadramawt's most important city, Mukala.[10] And in 1969, Hadramawt's Wadiah region became the scene of border skirmishes between South Yemen and Saudi Arabia.[11] These skirmishes alarmed many Hadramis, who feared for those of their kin who lived and worked in more prosperous Saudi Arabia and sent remittances home. The sons of the Hadrami sultans, who were hosted by Saudi Arabia after their removal at the hands of the NLF, contributed to stirring regional discontent with South Yemen and encouraging domestic dissent among their many supporters in the homeland.[12]

The Hadramis were not the only South Yemenis dissatisfied with the state of affairs in their country. The regime was aware of the legacy of regional identities that outlasted the rule of the British and wished to subsume them into a single South Yemeni identity. To that end, Aden decided in 1967 to issue a decree replacing the names of the country's governorates with serial numbers. (Hadramawt's number was five.) Yet far from dissolving regional identities and merging distinct societies into one, the move backfired. Along with other South Yemenis, Hadramis demonstrated regularly against the renaming of their homeland. The decree was rescinded in 1979.[13]

In 1990, a watershed moment took place in modern Yemeni history. That year, the People's Democratic Republic of Yemen in the south and the Yemen Arab Republic in the north declared the unity of the two countries. Accordingly, the name of the unified state became the Republic of Yemen, and Sanaa was declared the capital. In the first years of unity, Hadramawt's economic importance increased. Oil was discovered in the governorate in 1991. Production and export began two years later, even as further discoveries of oil were made.[14] Many Hadramis saw this development as heralding Hadramawt's return to prominence, this time as an economic resource for a new state. But the state did not allow Hadramawt to benefit much from the wealth it came to generate. Under the regime of then-president Ali Abdullah Saleh, little investment was made in Hadramawt, despite the regime's stated interest in launching development projects in all governorates. Hadramawt continued to be a periphery to the new center, which was now Sanaa instead of Aden.

Amid simmering resentment among Hadramis, the government in Sanaa made a decision that inflamed tensions. The large geographical area of Hadramawt and its people's distinct identity created an incentive for the political authorities to divide it. In 1997, a proposal to divide Hadramawt into two parts was put forward by the ministry of local administration, which was reorganizing the division of governorates and districts following a civil war between the state and southern secessionists in 1994. In response to the proposal, a delegation of nearly 200 people, including parliamentarians, tribal leaders, officials, and party leaders from various Hadramawt districts, led by parliamentarian Faisal bin Shamlan, headed to Sanaa and succeeded in aborting the move after meeting Saleh, who was inclined to accept the division proposal.[15] Even under an autocratic president, the Hadrami community was able to establish a red line, as it had done when it rejected a similar plan that had been considered by South Yemen.[16]

Turning Hadramawt from a Periphery into a Center

Hadramawt's metamorphosis from a periphery into a center is essentially an account of the Hadrami quest to achieve the related yet far less ambitious objective of autonomy. Indeed, a years-long and increasingly organized push for autonomy by a significant number of Hadramis left them poised to take advantage of war-related circumstances that facilitated their governorate's transformation into a center. Ultimately, the increased importance Hadramawt enjoys today is due to the weakness of the Yemeni government, and specifically the war-induced disintegration of state institutions since 2014, combined with the initiative of Hadramis themselves.

The Hadrami drive toward autonomy predates the events of 2014–2015, when the Houthis overran Sanaa, a Saudi-led Arab military force intervened, and Yemen descended into all-out conflict. It began shortly after the protests that erupted against Saleh in 2011, when Yemen was swept up in the Arab Spring. In several governorates, including Hadramawt, the protests remained peaceful. Yet in Sanaa, where such protests posed a direct threat to Saleh's hold on power, the president instructed the security services to forcibly disperse them. Given that a large portion of Yemen's male citizenry is armed, the move provoked a violent response. Ultimately, the 2011 uprising did not achieve its goal of changing the political regime, especially after Sanaa witnessed conflict between government forces and tribes that supported the uprising.[17]

The clashes and ensuing chaos prompted Hadrami political and tribal leaders to organize a conference dedicated to discussing their governorate's future in light of the country's deteriorating situation. The Hadramawt Vision and Path Conference took place in Mukala in June 2011 and received extensive media coverage. Hadrami groups with a secessionist agenda refused to participate because the question of Hadramawt becoming an independent state was not on the table, but they were in the minority. Indeed, the gathering was widely attended by autonomy-minded Hadramis and brought together political parties, tribal elders, religious figures, women, and youth groups from across the governorate.[18]

The conference's main outcome was nine essential points that attendees pledged to disseminate in a bid to rally support among Hadramis as well as non-Hadrami political actors. All points followed from the first and most important one, which stipulated that Hadramawt was to be an autonomous region within the framework of a federal Yemen. It would enjoy representation at the highest levels of government—in accordance with its area, wealth, coastal length, historical position, and contribution to the federal budget—but would have the right to pass its own laws. The broad form of autonomy envisaged by the document further allowed the governorate to manage its own revenue—it demanded that 75 percent of the wealth generated by Hadramawt should revert to the governorate, instead of the 20 to 25 percent that had been decided by the government—and even permitted it to maintain its own security forces. Despite the fact that there was no way to enforce these resolutions, the conference was a milestone that brought the main demands of autonomy-seeking Hadramis to the fore and unified their vision. For the next several years, Hadrami autonomy movements relied on the conference's outcomes as a reference point for their activism.[19]

The idea of an autonomous Hadramawt received a further boost two years later, as part of a conference on governance that took place at the national level. In line with a Gulf Cooperation Council power-sharing initiative and the mediation of the United Nations,[20] the Comprehensive National Dialogue Conference (NDC) was held in Sanaa between March 2013 and January 2014 and brought together 565 participants from different political and geographical backgrounds. For marginalized political and social groups, the NDC was a good opportunity to air grievances and present alternative visions of how their regions should be governed. No delegation was devoted exclusively to pressing the issue of Hadramawt's autonomy, as there was no Hadrami bloc. Nevertheless, individual Hadramis attended as members of delegations from several political parties—including the General People's Congress, Islah, and the South Yemen Movement—that endorsed some form of devolution of power from the center to the peripheries.[21]

Some Hadramis were concerned that the NDC would not go far enough. In July 2013, while the conference was still underway, a group of prominent tribal leaders representing most of Hadramawt's tribes formed an alliance called the Hadramawt Tribes Alliance (HTA). Headed by Sheikh Saad Bin Habrish, the HTA was intended in part to pressure Hadramis involved in the NDC to adopt a firm position on Hadramawt's autonomy and touted itself as the protector of Hadramis' rights.[22] Six months after the HTA's founding, Habrish was killed by Yemeni soldiers at a checkpoint in unclear circumstances in Hadramawt's Seiyun.[23] His death enraged Hadramis, particularly the tribes, and led to a popular uprising, *Al-habbah al-shaabiyyah*, centering on the demand that the government hand over his killers. In order to maintain the momentum of their movement, the Hadrami tribes chose Habrish's son, Amer, to succeed him and lead the HTA. The Yemeni government tried to contain the tribes' anger, but the HTA refused all mediation initiatives so long as the government refused to hand over the people accused of killing Habrish.[24] The government's refusal stirred resentment across Hadramawt, including among non-tribal Hadramis, and enhanced demands for autonomy. Following the dispute, HTA activities—including public gatherings, rallies, and even armed protests—increased in several districts of governorate. The government managed to defuse tensions by using tribal mediation to give the Hadrami tribes financial compensation and other peace offerings (vehicles and rifles).[25]

The major outcome of the NDC was wide agreement that moving from a centralized to a decentralized form of rule would resolve the phenomenon of marginalization that many communities and regions of Yemen had experienced. According to the NDC's resolutions, Yemen should become a federal state containing six regions—two in the south and four in the north. Hadramawt and the eastern governorates of Mahra, the Socotra Archipelago, and Shabwa were to constitute a single region called "Hadramawt."[26] This name was changed to the "Eastern Region" following objections raised by social and political entities in Mahra and Socotra (Map 7.2).

Not all Yemenis supported federalism, specifically of the kind endorsed by the NDC. The main objection was that, because the NDC's proposal envisioned natural resource federalism, it was promoting an arrangement that would lead to economic inequality between the country's regions. For example, whereas Hadramawt is rich in oil and gas fields, a region such as Azal—which the NDC's outcome document envisioned as comprising Saadah, Hajjah, Amran, Dhamar, and Sanaa—would suffer for its lack of natural resources. This realization prompted some parties, most prominent among them the Houthis, to reject the proposal of a federal state.[27] The Houthis, who had already engaged in several rounds of conflict with the central government, translated their rejection of the NDC and its outcomes into an all-out assault on Sanaa in September 2014.

The major Hadrami political organizations condemned the Houthis' attack on the capital and announced their support for President Abed Rabbo Mansour Hadi, who had replaced Saleh following an election in February 2012 in which he emerged as a consensus president backed by the Gulf Cooperation Council.[28] Yet these same Hadrami groups continued to press their demands. Moreover, in December 2014, the second anniversary of Habrish's death, the HTA upped the ante. In a bid to demonstrate that it was capable of seizing Hadramawt's vital facilities, the HTA took over Ash Shihr seaport, deployed armed men in Mukala and other cities in the governorate, and even fought with Yemeni military forces.[29] This put pressure on the government, which was already contending with the Houthis' takeover of Sanaa, to make concessions. Hadi granted Hadramis affiliated with the HTA positions in his government, including in the all-important ministry of petroleum, of which they would now have partial oversight.[30] This enhanced the HTA's reputation as a defender of Hadrami rights and the standard-bearer of Hadramawt on the national level.

The fall of Sanaa to the Houthis in September 2014, and subsequent events culminating in Hadi fleeing the city in February 2015, brought Hadramis face-to-face with a major and quite possibly long-term political

7 HADRAMAWT'S EMERGENCE AS A CENTER: A CONFLUENCE OF YEMENI... 141

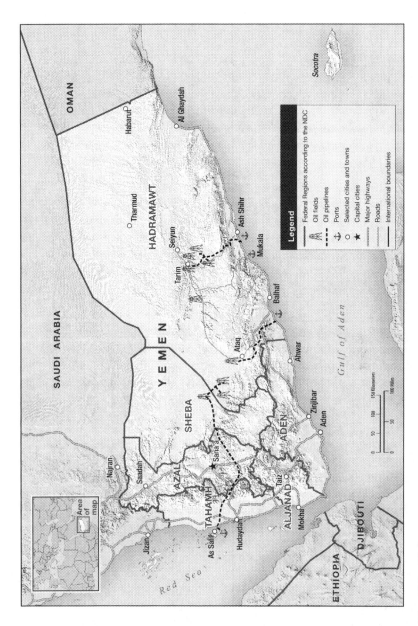

Map 7.2 Hadramawt governorate map

142 A. NAGI

disruption. The NDC resolutions were a dead letter, and a force implacably hostile to the idea of federalism had seized control of the nation's capital. The government, from which the Hadramis had managed to extract concessions, and which might have eventually proven amenable to an autonomous Hadramawt, had been dislodged. As such, the center no longer governed the peripheries, Hadramawt included. Moreover, it remained to be seen whether the Houthis, who now controlled the center, would eventually prove able to restore its reach. Increasingly, it appeared as though de facto autonomy had fallen into the Hadramis' lap.

In March 2015, shortly after the Houthis' capture of Sanaa, an additional development further scrambled Yemen's political map. A Saudi-led Arab military coalition intervened in the country in order to reverse, or at least halt, the Houthi advance, and also to prevent the possible collapse of Hadi's government, which had reassembled in Aden. Battles pitting the Saudi-led coalition and Yemeni government forces against the Houthis erupted throughout large areas of Yemen, but did not spread to Hadramawt. Nevertheless, it was at this critical moment that AQAP sought to benefit from a situation in which the center exercised little control over Hadramawt.[31] In April 2015, AQAP advanced on Mukala from surrounding mountainous areas and seized the city. The group was careful to justify its move as both defensive and protective in nature. Indeed, the stated objective of AQAP was to shield Mukala from potential Houthi advances in Hadramawt.[32]

This did not sit well with most Hadramis, who were aware that, whatever the Houthis' ultimate intentions, they were in no position to seize Mukala, much less all of Hadramawt.[33] Yet there was not much they could do to counter AQAP. Several elements of the army and state security agencies that had previously maintained a presence in Hadramawt had either melted away or redeployed elsewhere after receiving orders to confront the Houthis. Those that had remained were not equal in size or strength to the AQAP and were located in areas outside its control, meaning that defeating the group would entail devising a strategy to retake and hold territory. This left only the possibility of homegrown resistance. Yet urban areas, including Mukala, were ill-suited for mounting any such resistance, as the more powerful and organized Hadrami tribes had little to no presence there.[34]

In a bid to increase its power by coopting ideological kin among Hadramawt's various religious entities and personalities and also to temper criticism emanating from disaffected Hadramis, AQAP tasked a faction of local Salafi clerics, the Majlis Ahl al-Sunnah Wa'l Jamaa, with forming a council that would manage the daily administration of areas under AQAP's control.[35] In May 2015, having established the loyalty of the Majlis, AQAP handed it control of Mukala, including the city's seaports, airport, and other vital facilities. AQAP retained control of all-important security matters. This gesture toward community-based governance went some way toward containing resentment, at least for a while, as Hadramis had long sought a decentralization of power. The move also enabled the group, which already included Hadramis in its ranks, to recruit more of them.

Nevertheless, most Hadramis opposed AQAP, whose militant version of Islam differed from, and vilified, the Sufism popular among locals. As a result, resistance was not long in coming. Crucially, there was foreign backing for such a development. The Hadrami resistance movement was supported by members of the Saudi-led coalition. While the Saudis themselves created and equipped the Hadramawt Brigades in Seiyun and Hadramawt Valley, the UAE did the same with the Hadrami Elite Forces (HEF), which operated in and around Mukala and took the lead in fighting AQAP.[36] In April 2016, the HEF succeeded in ousting AQAP from Mukala.[37]

This was a milestone in Hadramawt's quest for autonomy. A homegrown force had driven out an occupying one. Moreover, this homegrown force was supported by a regional power, the UAE, that for its own reasons had begun to warm to the idea of an autonomous Hadramawt. The HEF began to deploy beyond Mukala and throughout the governorate's coastal districts, conducting mopping-up operations but also permanently taking charge of security. Recognition from what remained of the center was not long in coming. In 2017, a much-weakened Hadi, at once eager to appear as still in control and wary of alienating Hadramis, appointed HEF commander Faraj Salimeen al-Bahsani to the position of governor of Hadramawt.[38]

In 2017, a year after the HEF had expelled AQAP from Mukala and cemented its control over much of the governorate, a group of Hadrami public figures—including tribal leaders, political personalities, and academics—organized another conference in order to bring the issue of Hadramawt's autonomy to the fore of Yemeni public discussions. The Hadramawt Inclusive Conference took place in Mukala in April 2017, following six months of preparation.[39] In terms of attendance, it was even larger than its 2011 predecessor, with some 3000 attendees of political or social note, including many from the diaspora, which led the event's organizing committee to call it "the first of its kind since the 1960s."[40] The conference reiterated the nine points of the 2011 Vision and Path Conference, but added more to them in the form of a document listing a total of 40 agreed-upon points, most of which were concerned with the issue of ensuring and expanding Hadramawt's autonomy. This outcomes document also specified the governorate's relationship with the country's future federal government and called for the Hadramis' representation to reach 40 percent in all higher-level state positions, in accordance with Hadramawt's area and its contribution to the national budget. Noticeably, in an apparent effort to secure complete freedom for Hadramis should their relations with such a government sour, the outcomes document, which referred to Hadramawt as an autonomous region within a federal state, stipulated that the Hadrami people's right to self-determination included that of secession.[41]

For many Hadramis, the Inclusive Conference became a benchmark for any public discussion of their governorate. In the latest round of negotiations between the Yemeni government and the Southern Transitional Council in Riyadh, the Saudi sponsors of the talks pointedly invited a Hadrami negotiating team—comprising HTA members and a delegation from the Inclusive Conference—to the table.[42] In the Yemeni unity government that emerged from these talks in December 2020, the Inclusive Conference/HTA was granted a cabinet post. Although having one minister out of 24 was not in and of itself a major achievement, it signified the arrival of the Hadrami movement on the national stage.[43]

It is no coincidence that all these developments solidifying mechanisms of self-rule in Hadramawt and formalizing their acceptance by the nominal center took place as Hadramawt was emerging as an actual center. Examples of this transformation abound. The Houthis' capture of Sanaa in September 2014 and the precarious position of Aden, which turned into a battlefield on more than one occasion, created a need for a larger role for Hadramawt's Seiyun Airport, whose administrators proved able to accommodate increased air traffic. At various times, the airport overtook those of Sanaa and Aden in importance, what with all the flights diverted to it.[44] Similarly, as the only border crossing with Saudi Arabia that the Saudi authorities have allowed to remain open, Hadramawt's Wadiah crossing has since 2015 had to contend with a surge in the two-way flow of goods and travelers, a challenge its Hadrami personnel have successfully met. Annual revenue generated from the Wadiah crossing rose from 6.5

Yemeni billion rials in 2014 to over 29 billion rials in 2016.[45] As for Mukala, it began to receive commercial ships that used to dock at the country's main seaports in Aden and elsewhere. Despite the modest infrastructure of the Mukala seaport, freight traffic witnessed a significant spike.[46]

All these developments contributed to a modest economic boom in Hadramawt, as did an influx of people of means. Some of these were middle-class Yemenis displaced from other regions who chose to move to Hadramawt because it was relatively safe and stable. Others were Yemeni returnees from Saudi Arabia. In 2017, when Saudi Arabia launched a Saudization drive across several economic sectors, tens of thousands of Yemeni expatriates, many of whom were businesspeople and entrepreneurs, left the kingdom for their native country.[47] Yet they did not all go back to their home governorates. Rather, Hadramawt was the most popular destination. From India to the Horn of Africa, Hadrami migrants and their descendants have long been renowned as successful traders and businessmen, and now many of them, along with other Yemenis who wished to recreate in Yemen what they had built for themselves in Saudi Arabia, streamed into Hadramawt, particularly Mukala and Seiyun, with funds in hand and projects in mind.[48]

In yet another indication of Hadramawt's emergence as an alternative center, it has turned into the preferred location for meetings between members of the very entity—the Yemeni government—embodying the country's nominal center. Although the government relocated to Aden shortly after Sanaa fell to the Houthis in September 2014, most of its members left Yemen altogether in March 2015, when the Houthis launched an assault on Aden itself. Since then, the government has operated largely out of Saudi Arabia, where Hadi is based, and Egypt. With the deterioration of the security situation in Aden and the Houthi advance on Ma'rib and Shabwa, Hadramawt has also increasingly become the place of residence for non- and anti-Houthi Yemeni political figures who have chosen to remain inside the country.[49]

Perhaps the most important convergence of Hadramawt's growing autonomy and its growing role as a politicoeconomic center in Yemen has occurred in the oil sector. As with civil service jobs of various kinds across Hadramawt, employment in the governorate's oil and natural gas sector has gradually become the almost exclusive preserve of Hadramis. Except for those positions that require certain technical skills and knowledge that Hadrami employees do not (yet) possess, Yemenis from other regions are no longer hired to work in this sector.[50] This trend is of potentially great consequence for the future, given Hadramawt's outsized role in oil production, which is a major source of revenue for Yemen. The governorate produces around 100,000 barrels of a crude oil a day, which constitutes half the country's overall production.[51]

An eye-opening indication of what Hadramis might do should they feel slighted by the government of a postwar reconstituted Yemen was provided by a statement issued by Hadramawt Governor Bahsani in September 2018, following a dispute over payments. When Yemen exports oil products, the companies buying them pay the Yemeni government, which then transfers a certain allotment of the sum to the governorates from which the products were extracted. However, the government often delays such transfers, resulting in the governorates finding themselves unable to pay their staff. In Hadramawt, which had witnessed repeated protests regarding this issue, locals began to exert pressure on the governor to provide the government with an ultimatum. Eventually, he obliged, declaring, "If the economic situation in Hadramawt continues without the internationally recognized government adopting urgent solutions to lift the people's suffering, the local authority will be forced to halt the export of oil from Hadramawt."[52]

On the face of it, this was an extraordinary threat for a supposedly peripheral governor to direct at his country's central government—whose head, Abed Rabbo Mansour Hadi, had appointed him to his position a year earlier. But it was of a piece with a major transformation of center-periphery relations that had occurred in Yemen. The traditional sources of central authority, who had been pushed out of Sanaa and then Aden, no longer existed. Meanwhile, Hadramawt, long a periphery, had managed not only to gain autonomy but to position itself as a center-in-the-making.

Hadramawt at the Mercy of Saudi-Emirati Rivalry

Hadramawt's journey to becoming a center and enjoying de facto autonomy has included obstacles and detours, and will continue to do so. The most significant challenges have to do with security and political rivalry. When it comes to security, the threats to Hadramawt's status come from the Houthis and AQAP. The Houthis have not given up on their goal of taking over Yemen in its entirety, in which case they would almost certainly abolish Hadramawt's prerogatives.[53] The Houthis were not engaged in any kind of offensive on Hadramawt at the time of writing. Yet they were continuing their efforts, through one battle after another, to gain control of the governorates of Ma'rib and Shabwa, both of which border Hadramawt. Seizing either or both of these governorates would solidify the Houthis' hold on Yemen—Ma'rib, for example, has significant oil and natural gas deposits—as well as stand them in good stead to launch an assault on Hadramawt.

The other security concern, AQAP, may constitute a threat from within Hadramawt itself. Although AQAP was expelled from Mukala in April 2016, questions remain as to where the group disappeared. Many observers in Hadramawt and outside believe that AQAP is still around; it just moved from the cities to the mountainous areas in Hadramawt or the neighboring governorates.[54] If this is in fact the case, it would place Hadramawt at continued risk of attack. In the past four years, the governorate has witnessed several bombings and assassinations that many people believe were orchestrated by AQAP.[55] The deployment of the HEF and the Hadramawt Brigades militates against any large-scale maneuvers by AQAP, such as a 2015-style assault on Mukala, yet foiling future bombings and assassinations requires a detailed and long-term security plan.

For all the risks posed by the Houthis from one end and AQAP from the other, the fact that neither party exerts direct influence in Hadramawt means that the governorate has more pressing concerns, particularly when it comes to protecting its hard-won autonomy and continuing to develop its status as a center. Chief among these concerns is the regional rivalry between Saudi Arabia and the UAE. Almost as soon as the Saudi-led military coalition, of which the UAE is a member, entered Yemen, the Saudi-Emirati rivalry manifested itself throughout the country and became especially apparent in Hadramawt. For Saudi Arabia, it was important to wield influence in Hadramawt, given its location along the Saudi border and its important position on Yemen's economic and geopolitical map. As for the UAE, its interest lay mainly in the coastal regions and their seaports, which have taken on increased significance for major shipping routes. Today, Hadramawt is effectively divided into two spheres of influence: Mukala and the coast, where the UAE holds sway, and Hadramawt Valley, including Seiyun, where Saudi Arabia is the main power broker.

By defeating AQAP, the HEF did not simply demonstrate its usefulness to its Emirati backers but gained a good deal of prestige among locals. In the minds of many Hadramis, the HEF recalls the historical army of Hadramawt, the Hadrami Badia Army, which was formed by the British in 1939, when they were in control of the southern Arabian Peninsula and granted the Hadramis much leeway in running their own affairs. Moreover, the HEF controls Mukala. As Hadramawt's capital, Mukala is the most important and populous city. The seaports on Yemen's southern coast, including that of Mukala itself, have emerged as the country's busiest and most dependable during the conflict. The UAE's interest in the coastal part of Hadramawt derives from the Emiratis' economic imperative to secure shipping routes in the region and place themselves in a position to intervene when maritime trade is threatened. To this end, the UAE also maintains an active presence in the Horn of Africa.

In Hadramawt Valley, the Saudis exercise influence through the Hadi-led Yemeni government, which remains in nominal control of the region and maintains a security presence there in the form of the Hadramawt Brigades, which are in reality beholden to their Saudi backers.[56] The Saudis also fund Salafi schools, which regard Saudi Arabia as the religious center of the Islamic world and interpret Islam in line with the teachings of the country's official religious establishment.[57] From a religious perspective (irrespective of their political orientation), Salafis tend to vilify Sufism, which is the most popular strain of Islam in Hadramawt, especially in coastal cities and their environs. Most of Hadramawt's oil deposits are located in the valley, as is Seiyun, the governorate's second-most populous city and the only one with a commercial airport. For Saudi Arabia, the importance of Hadramawt Valley is rooted in its location as a borderland with the Saudi governorate of Najran. Historically, Riyadh has maintained a good relationship with the Hadrami tribes in the valley as part of its border security strategy. During the conflict, the Saudis expanded their influence and did not allow any other regional actor to establish a foothold in the area.[58]

The Saudi-Emirati rivalry is playing out on a historical social and geographical fault line between the valley and the coast, which means that Hadramis have their own political and tribal reasons for aligning themselves with either party in order to settle generally petty domestic scores.[59] In and of themselves, differences between Hadramis need not thwart the governorate's quest for official recognition of its autonomy or hinder its growing role as a center, and there is little indication that Hadramis on either side of the coast-valley equation wish to institutionalize this division. Moreover, the division itself is not hard and fast; for example, many members of the HEF are drawn from the tribes of the valley.[60] Nevertheless, in taking place on a social and geographic fault line, the Saudi-Emirati rivalry may well deepen differences that already exist—to the ultimate detriment of Hadramawt's unity. And if Hadramawt cannot remain effectively united, its autonomy as well as its ability to function as a center will suffer. As such, the question is not only whether the Saudis and Emiratis will arrive at a *modus vivendi* but whether, in the event of their continued rivalry, Hadramis will allow their affiliation with Saudi Arabia or the UAE to trump Hadramawt's interests.

In addition to the Saudi-Emirati rivalry, Hadramis have to contend with an aspect of the UAE's Yemen policy that may have serious implications for Hadramawt. The Emiratis back the Southern Transitional Council (STC), which is the main organization within the South Yemen Movement. Thanks to Emirati support for the STC, southerners have an opportunity to work toward secession from a Yemen that, since its unification in 1990, has marginalized them. The fact that the STC and other groups within the South Yemen Movement wish to reestablish an independent state that includes Hadramawt within its borders has impelled Hadramis to set themselves apart from southerners. Considering that many Hadramis view the South Yemen era as the beginning of their own marginalization, there is little affinity on their part for a planned resurrection of that political entity, even if chances are slim that it will revert to its earlier Marxist incarnation.[61] Indeed, Hadrami political movements are noticeably less inclined than their counterparts in other former South Yemen governorates, such as Aden and Al-Dhale, to support the secession of the south, particularly when Hadramawt is included in the secessionists' designs. In some ways, the dynamic here recalls the developments of the early 1960s, when Britain established the Federation of South Arabia and the sultanates of Hadramawt refused to join this entity. Together with other eastern sultanates, they formed the Protectorate of South Arabia, a separate federation also overseen by the British.[62]

The key components of the South Yemen Movement, including the STC, are aware of Hadrami sensitivities and have tried to allay them. For instance, to reassure Hadramis that in an independent South Yemen Hadramawt would enjoy significant latitude when it comes to managing its own affairs, the STC consistently states that it envisions a decentralized form of governance.[63] Yet this has failed to win over most Hadramis, who realize that Hadramawt would have even more clout as an autonomous center of a united Yemen. Tensions over the issue exist within Hadramawt itself, where locals have not supported secession in large numbers.[64] In 2017, the STC attempted to convince the HTA, which was growing in power and influence, to join the ranks of the South Yemen Movement, but the HTA declined.[65] Ultimately, the STC and other groups devoted to the south's secession believe that without Hadramawt, their projected state would not achieve economic viability. What remains unclear is how the UAE, which withdrew most of its military forces from Yemen in 2019 but retains much sway in the country, will adjudicate the dispute between these groups on the one hand and the majority of Hadramis on the other and whether Hadramawt will have to make concessions to a future southern entity or state.

CONCLUSION

Given that Yemen is embroiled in a conflict that has led to the emergence of self-contained and often warring fiefdoms throughout the country, the question of this or that periphery redefining its relationship with the center is moot. Cantonization has effectively done away with the official center, Sanaa, and further diminished the modest stature of the country's second center, Aden. Nonetheless, Hadramawt is in the midst of a far-reaching transformation of direct relevance to future center-periphery dynamics in Yemen. Here, a former periphery has not simply ceased to be such owing to circumstances but has gone so far as to position itself to become a center, perhaps even *the* center, of postwar Yemen. The most salient indication of this is the Hadramis' methodical and largely successful campaign to take control of their region's oil and natural gas industry, which constitutes one of the pillars of Yemen's economy.

On April 7, 2022, President Hadi announced that he was stepping aside in favor of a newly formed Presidential Leadership Council (PLC), a Saudi- and Emirati-backed governing body comprising eight members drawn from powerful political factions in those regions of Yemen not under the Houthis' control. Hadramawt's representative on the council is none other than Bahsani, who is close to both the Saudis and the Emiratis. With the PLC assuming its intended governing role, Saudi Arabia and the UAE hope to reduce the intensity of their conflict with the Houthis, something that has emerged as a priority for both countries following the group's repeated drone and missile attacks on Saudi and Emirati soil. The PLC may eventually expand to include members of the Houthis themselves, but the continued representation of Hadramawt and its role as a key entity in any future political agreements or compromises are virtually assured. And for Hadramis to accept any agreements or compromises regarding the future of Yemen, decentralizing the country, which would mean greater latitude for Hadramawt and other peripheral governorates, is imperative.

This does not mean that challenges do not remain. In angling for a more influential position within Yemen, Hadramawt must navigate the regional competition between Saudi Arabia and the United Arab Emirates, which remains strong despite the two countries' cooperation over the PLC. There also hovers the threat posed by AQAP, which may have regrouped in the governorate's mountainous areas, the complicating factor of internal divisions among Hadrami movements themselves, and the Houthis' designs on nearby Ma'rib and Shabwa. But more than anything else, Hadramawt's *de jure* attainment of autonomy hinges on whether the Hadramis retain control of their region's oil and natural gas industry should Yemen reconstitute itself as a functioning unitary state. If they succeed in retaining such control, this would allow for a situation in which, theoretically at least, a formerly peripheral governorate emerges as more powerful than Sanaa and Aden Governorates, the two poles of modern Yemen, and possibly even reclaims its historical status as a politicoeconomic center in the Arabian Peninsula.

NOTES

1. National Information Center (Yemen), "Nubdha Ta'rifiyya 'an Muhafadhat Hadramawt" [Profile of Hadramawt Governorate], https://yemen-nic. info/gover/hathramoot/brife/.
2. Saleh Ba Surra, *Tarikh Hadramawt al-Hadith wa'l Mu'asir* [The Modern History of Hadramawt] (Aden: Aden University Printing and Publishing House, 2001), 83-115.
3. Office of the Special Envoy of the Secretary-General for Yemen (OSESGY), "National Dialogue Conference," https://osesgy.unmissions.org/national-dialogue-conference.
4. Author interview with Hadrami journalist Waleed al-Tamimi (via telephone), July 23, 2020.
5. Gamal Shnitr, "Yemeni Frankincense: Historical Mark on the Road of Frankincense," *Independent Arabia*, October 8, 2021, https://www.independentarabia.com/node/266241/%D8%AA%D8%AD%D9%82%D9%8A%D9%82%D8%A7%D8%AA-%D9%88%D9%85%D8%B7%D9%88%D9%84%D8%A7%D8%AA/%D8%A7%D9%84%D8%A8%D8%AE%D9%88%D8%B1-%D8%A7%D9%84%D9%8A%D9%85%D9%86%D9%8A-%D8%B9%D9%84%D8%A7%D9%85%D8%A9-%D8%AA%D8%A7%D8%B1%D9%8A%D8%AE%D9%8A%D8%A9-%D8%B9%D9%84%D9%89-

152 A. NAGI

%D8%B7%D8%B1%D9%8A%D9%82-%D8%A7%D9%84%D9%84%D8%A8
%D8%A7%D9%86.

6. Author observation during a field visit to Tarim, May 2019.
7. R. N. Mehra, "The Emergence of the Aden Protectorate—Some Views Examined," Proceedings of the Indian History Congress 38 (1977): 631–37, http://www.jstor.org/stable/44139125.
8. Almasdar Online, "Ra'is al-'Usba al-Hadramiyya Abdullah Bahaj: Hawiyyat Hadramawt Mukhtalifa Kull al-Ikhtilaf 'an al-Hawiyya al-Janubiyya wa'l Yamaniyya" [Head of the Hadrami League Abdullah Bahaj: Hadramawt's Identity Differs Completely from Southern and Yemeni Identity], March 14, 2013, https://almasdaronline.com/articles/97877.
9. Bruce Riedel, "Saudi Arabia and the Civil War within Yemen's Civil War," Brookings, August 15, 2019, https://www.brookings.edu/blog/order-from-chaos/2019/08/15/saudi-arabia-and-the-civil-war-within-yemens-civil-war/.
10. Geraint Hughes, "A Proxy War in Arabia: The Dhofar Insurgency and Cross-Border Raids into South Yemen," Middle East Journal 69, no. 1 (2015): 91–104, http://www.jstor.org/stable/43698211.
11. Herbert K. Tillema, International Armed Conflict Since 1945: A Bibliographic Handbook of Wars and Military Interventions (New York: Avalon Publishing, 1991), 135.
12. Mutahar Al-Sofari, "Janoub wa Sharq al-Yaman .. Jughrafiya Tatanaza'uha Qiwa Iqlimiyya" [South and East Yemen: A Geography Fought Over by Regional Powers], Strategic Fiker Center for Studies, February 4, 2020, https://fikercenter.com/2020/02/04/%D8%AC%D9%86%D9%80%D9%88%D8%A8-%D9%88%D8%B4%D9%80%D9%80%D8%B1%D9%82-%D8%A7%D9%84%D9%8A%D9%85%D9%86-%D8%AC%D8%BA%D8%B1%D8%A7%D9%81%D9%8A%D8%A7-%D8%AA%D8%AA%D9%86%D8%A7%D8%B2%D8%B9%D9%87%D8%A7-%D8%A7/.
13. Ibid.
14. Republic of Yemen, Ministry of Oil and Minerals, "Productive Sectors," https://mom-ye.com/site-en/%d8%a7%d9%84%d9%82%d8%b7%d8%a7%d8%b9%d8%a7%d8%aa-%d8%a7%d9%84%d8%a5%d9%86%d8%aa%d8%a7%d8%ac%d9%8a%d8%a9/.
15. Almashhad Alyemeni, "Taqsim Hadramawt ila Muhafadhatain Ya'oud ila al-Wajiha min Jadid" [Dividing Hadramawt into Two Governorates Returns to the Fore Once Again], November 24, 2019, https://www.almashhad-alyemeni.com/150520.
16. Ibid.
17. Peter Finn, "Elite Yemeni Families at Center of Clashes," Washington Post, June 2, 2011, https://www.washingtonpost.com/world/middle-east/

elite-yemeni-families-at-center-of-clashes/2011/06/02/AGKi1ZHH_ story.html.

18. Nabeel Bin Iyfan, "Al-I'lan bi'l Mukalla 'an Muswaddat Mashrou' Wathiqat (Hadramawt al-Ru'ya wa'l Masar" [Announcement in Mukala of Draft Document "Hadramawt Vision and Path"] *Aden Alghad*, June 13, 2011, https://adengad.net/posts/2366.

19. Ibid.

20. UN Peacemaker Platform, "Agreement on the Implementation Mechanism for the Transition Process in Yemen in Accordance with the Initiative of the Gulf Cooperation Council (GCC)," December 5, 2011, https://peacemaker.un.org/sites/peacemaker.un.org/files/YE_111205_ Agreement%20on%20the%20implementation%20mechanism%20for%20 the%20transition.pdf.

21. The Office of the Special Envoy of the Secretary-General for Yemen (OSESGY), "National Dialogue Conference," https://osesgy.unmissions. org/national-dialogue-conference.

22. Al-Tagheer, "Qira'a fi Masirat Hilf Hadramawt '22' " [Reading the Trajectory of the Hadhramaut Tribes Alliance '2'], June 2014, https:// www.al-tagheer.com/art27054.html.

23. Al-Mashhad Alyemeni, "Man Huwa Bin Habrish al-Ladhi Habbat Hadramawt wa Daqqat Tuboul al-Harb ba'd Maqtalih??" [Who Is Bin Hibrish, Following Whose Killing Hadramawt Rose Up and Beat the Drums of War??], December 19, 2013, https://www.almashhad-alyemeni. com/7598.

24. *Aden Alghad*, "Tasrih Rasmi min Ri'asat Hilf Qaba'il Hadramawt" [Official Statement from the Leadership of the Hadramawt Tribes Alliance], December 17, 2013, https://adengad.net/post/amp/82519.

25. Almasdar Online, "Ittifaq 'ala Tahkim Qaba'il Hadramawt fi Maqtal ((Bin Habrish)) wa'l Daman: Milyar wa 202 Bunduqiyya wa 20 Sayyara" [Arbitration Agreement with the Tribes of Hadramawt in the Killing of Bin Habrish, and the Guarantee: One Billion and 202 Rifles and 20 Vehicles], March 5, 2014, https://almasdaronline.com/article/55344

26. National Dialogue Conference, Outcomes Document, https://www.peaceagreements.org/viewmasterdocument/1400.

27. Euronews, "Al-Houthiyyoun wa'l Janoubiyyoun Yarfudoun Taqsim al-Aqalim al-Sitta fi'l Yaman" [The Houthis and the Southerners Reject the Division of the Six Regions in Yemen], February 11, 2014, https://arabic. euronews.com/2014/02/11/yemen-the-new-governments-plan-to-form-the-new-federation.

28. *Yemen Press*, "Iqlima Hadramawt wa'l Janad Yu'linan al-Harb 'ala al-Houthiyeen (Nass al-Bayan)" [Hadramout and Al-Janad Regions

154   A. NAGI

Announce War Against the Houthis, (Text of Statement)], November 10, 2014, https://yemen-press.net/news37841.html.

29. Fares al-Jalal, "Al-Yaman: Tumuhat Tawasuiyya li-Hilf Qabail Hadramawt Yemen" [Expansionist Ambitions of the Hadramawt Tribes Alliance], *Al-Araby Al-Jadeed*, December 24, 2014, https://www.alaraby.co.uk/%D8%A7%D9%84%D9%8A%D9%85%D9%86-%D8%B7%D9%85%D9%88%D8%AD%D8%A7%D8%AA-%D8%AA%D9%88%D8%B3%D9%91%D8%B9%D9%8A%D8%A9-%D9%84%D8%AD%D9%84%D9%81-%D9%82%D8%A8%D8%A7%D8%A6%D9%84-%D8%AD%D8%B6%D8%B1%D9%85%D9%88%D8%AA.

30. Ibid.

31. Baraa Shiban, "Hadhramout from Federalism to Civil War: Demands and Realities," LSE's Middle East Centre Blog," March 29, 2017, https://blogs.lse.ac.uk/mec/2017/06/26/hadhramout-from-federalism-to-civil-war-demands-and-realities/.

32. "Kharitat Qiwa Hadramawt al-Yamaniyya" [The Map of Yemen's Hadramawt Forces], *Al-Araby Al-Jadeed*, July 4, 2015, https://www.alaraby.co.uk/%D8%AE%D8%A7%D8%B1%D8%B7%D8%A9-%D9%82%D9%88%D9%89-%D8%AD%D8%B6%D8%B1%D9%85%D9%88%D8%AA-%D8%A7%D9%84%D9%8A%D9%85%D9%86%D9%8A%D8%A9.

33. Aref Bamoumin,"Hadramawt Tatahassan Didd al-Madd al-Houthi" [Hadramawt Fortifies Itself Against Houthi Expansion], *Al-Araby Al-Jadeed*, July 4, 2015, https://www.alaraby.co.uk/%D8%AD%D8%B6%D8%B1%D9%85%D9%88%D8%AA-%D8%AA%D8%AA%D8%AD%D8%B5%D9%91%D9%86-%D8%B6%D8%AF%D9%91-%D8%A7%D9%84%D9%85%D8%AF%D9%91-%D8%A7%D9%84%D8%AD%D9%88%D8%AB%D9%8A.

34. Radhi Sabeeh, "Hadramawt Tataqasamuha al-Qa'ida, al-Qabail, wa'l Quwat al-'Askariyya" [Hadramawt is Shared by al-Qaida, the Tribes, and the Military Forces], Aljazeera.net, November 23, 2015, https://www.aljazeera.net/news/reportsandinterviews/2015/11/24/%D8%AD%D8%B6%D8%B1%D9%85%D9%88%D8%AA-%D8%AA%D8%AA%D9%82%D8%A7%D8%B3%D9%85%D9%87%D8%A7-%D8%A7%D9%84%D9%82%D8%A7%D8%B9%D8%AF%D8%A9-%D9%88%D8%A7%D9%84%D9%82%D8%A8%D8%A7%D8%A6%D9%84.

35. Radhi Sabeeh, "Hal Tansahib al-Qa'ida min Mukalla al-Yamaniyya?" [Will al-Qaida Withdraw from Yemen's Mukala?], Aljazeera.net, August 25, 2015, https://www.aljazeera.net/news/reportsandinterviews/2015/8/26/%D9%87%D9%84-%D8%AA%D9%86%D8%B3%D8%AD%D8%A8-%D8%A7%D9%84%D9%82%D8%A7%D8%B9%D8%AF%D8%A9-

7 HADRAMAWT'S EMERGENCE AS A CENTER: A CONFLUENCE OF YEMENI... 155

%D9%85%D9%86-%D8%A7%D9%84%D9%85%D9%83%D9%84%D8%A7-%D8%A7%D9%84%D9%8A%D9%85%D9%86%D9%8A%D8%A9.

36. Officially, these units are the First Military Zone forces of the Yemeni government. See National Information Center (Yemen), "Qarar Ra'is al-Jumhouriyya bi Taqsim Masrah al-'Amaliyyat al-'Askariyya li'l Jumhouriyya al-Yamaniyya wa Tasmiyat al-Manatiq al-'Askariyya wa Ta'yin Qiyadatiha" [The President's Decision to Divide the Republic of Yemen's Theater of Military Operations and the Naming of the Military Zones and their Leaders], https://yemen-nic.info/NIC/detail.php?ID=37801.

37. Saeed Al-Batati, Kareem Fahim and Eric Schmitt, "Yemeni Troops, Backed by United Arab Emirates, Take City From Al Qaeda," *New York Times*, April 24, 2016, https://www.nytimes.com/2016/04/25/world/middleeast/yemeni-troops-backed-by-united-arab-emirates-take-city-from-al-qaeda.html.

38. Shabakat Sawt Al-Huriyya (Yemen), "Al-Bahsani Yu'addi al-Yamin al-Dusturiyya bi Munasabat Ta'yinihi Muhafudhan li Haramawt" [Al-Bahsani Takes the Constitutional Oath on the Occasion of his Appointment As Governor of Hadhramaut], April 2016, https://www.freedom-ye.com/new/60286.

39. Adam Baron and Monder Basalma, "The Case of Hadhramaut: Can Local Efforts Transcend Wartime Divides in Yemen?" The Century Foundation, April 20, 2021, https://tcf.org/content/report/case-hadhramaut-can-local-efforts-transcend-wartime-divides-yemen/.

40. Almasdar Online, "Mu'tamar Hadramawt al-Jami' Yan'aqid al-Yawm wa Tawaqqu'at bi I'lan Ru'yah li 'Mustaqbal Hadramawt' " [Hadhramawt Inclusive Conference is Held Today Amid Expectations of Announcement of a Vision for the 'Future of Hadramawt'], April 22, 2017, https://almasdaronline.com/article/90597.

41. Nashwan News, "Nass Qararat Wathiqat Mu'tamar Hadramawt al-Jami': Iqlim Mustaqill la Janoub wa la Shamal" [The Text of the Decisions of the Hadhramawt Inclusive Conference Document: An Independent Region, Neither South Nor North], April 22, 2017, https://nashwannews.com/75380/%D9%86%D8%B5-%D9%82%D8%B1%D8%A7%D8%B1%D8%A7%D8%AA-%D9%88%D8%AB%D9%8A%D9%82%D8%A9-%D9%85%D8%A4%D8%AA%D9%85%D8%B1-%D8%AD%D8%B6%D8%B1%D9%85%D9%88%D8%AA-%D8%A7%D9%84%D8%AC%D8%A7%D9%85%D8%B9-%D8%A5%D9%82.

42. Yemen News Portal, "Al-Sa'udiyya Tushrik Hadramawt Tarafan Thalithan fi Mufawadat al-Riyadh" [Saudi Arabia Involves Hadramawt As a Third Party in the Riyadh Negotiations], July 15, 2020, https://yemnews.net/index.php/news/2020-07-15-13-34-30.

156   A. NAGI

43. Ibrahim Jalal, "The Riyadh Agreement: Yemen's New Cabinet and What Remains to Be Done," Middle East Institute, February 1, 2021, https://www.mei.edu/publications/riyadh-agreement-yemens-new-cabinet-and-what-remains-be-done.
44. Abdulmajeed Bakhurisah, "Limadha Yufaddiloun al-Kathiroun al-Safar Abrah.. Kayf An'ash 'Matar Say'oun' al-Haraka al-Tijariyya wa'l Siyahiyya fi'l Madina!" [Why Many Prefer to Use it for Travel...How Seiyun Airport Revived Commercial and Tourist Traffic in the City!], TaizonLine, May 24, 2019, https://taizonline.com/news19014.html.
45. Ahmed Nagi, "Manfadh al-Wadi'ah al-Hudoudi la Yurahhib Bikum" [Wadiah Border Crossing Does Not Welcome You], Malcolm H. Kerr Carnegie Middle East Center, April 23, 2021, https://carnegie-mec.org/diwan/84389.
46. Saeed Al Batati, "A Year After Liberation, Business Up at Mukalla Seaport," *Gulf News*, June 30, 2017, https://gulfnews.com/world/gulf/yemen/a-year-after-liberation-business-up-at-mukalla-seaport-1.2051154.
47. Sumaiya Ahmed, "Hadramout Maladh al-'A'idin min al-Ightirab" [Hadramawt, a Refuge for Returnees from Abroad], Khuyut, August 1, 2021, https://www.khuyut.com/blog/yemeni-labor-ksa.
48. Mohammed Rajeh, "Awda Qasriyya li Alaf min al-Yamaniyyin min al-Sa'udiyya: Tahawiy al-Tahwilat" [Forced Return of Thousands of Yemenis from Saudi Arabia: The Collapse of Remittances], *Al-Araby Al-Jadeed*, August 19, 2021, https://www.alaraby.co.uk/economy/%D8%B9%D9%88%D8%AF%D8%A9-%D9%82%D8%B3%D8%B1%D9%8A%D8%A9-%D9%84%D8%A2%D9%84%D8%A7%D9%81-%D8%A7%D9%84%D9%8A%D9%85%D9%86%D9%8A%D9%8A%D9%86-%D9%85%D9%86-%D8%A7%D9%84%D8%B3%D8%B9%D9%88%D8%AF%D9%8A%D8%A9-%D8%AA%D9%87%D8%A7%D9%88%D9%8A-%D8%A7%D9%84%D8%AA%D8%AD%D9%88%D9%8A%D9%84%D8%A7%D8%AA.
49. Saba News Agency, "Ra'is al-Wuzara Yasil al-Mukalla fi Ziyara Tafaqudiyya li Muhafadhat Hadramawt wa Tadshin Adad min al-Mashari' " [The Prime Minister Arrives in Mukala for a Visit of Inspection and the Inauguration of Several Projects], April 24, 2018, http://sabanew.net/story/ar/32220.
50. Additionally, many non-Hadramis have asked their employers to transfer them to other governorates owing to a feeling on their part that they are no longer welcome in Hadramawt. See "Milaf Nufty Hadrami Muhimm (Al-Halaqa al-Thaniya) Ahaqiyyat Tawdhif Abna' Hadramawt fi'l Sharikat al-Nuftiyya" [An Important Hadrami File (The Second Episode): The Sonds of Hadramawt's Right to Be Hired by the Oil Companies], *Al-Jarida Post*, October 15, 2020, https://www.aljaridapost.com/site/2020/10/1 5/%D9%85%D9%84%D9%81-%D9%86%D9%81%D8%B7%D9%8A-%D8%AD%D8%B6%D8%B1%D9%85%D9%8A-

7 HADRAMAWT'S EMERGENCE AS A CENTER: A CONFLUENCE OF YEMENI... 157

%D9%85%D9%87%D9%85-%D8%A7%D9%84%D8%AD%D9%84%D9%8
2%D8%A9-%D8%A7%D9%84%D8%AB%D8%A7%D9%86%D9%8A%
D8%A9-%D8%A3%D8%AD%D9%82%D9%8A/

51. Reuters, "Yemeni Provincial Official Threatens to Halt Oil Shipments from Southern Hadramout Region," September 6, 2018, https://www. reuters.com/article/us-yemen-security-oil-idUSKCN1LM2C0.
52. Ibid.
53. Debriefer, "Jama'at al-Houthi: Jahizoun li Iqtiham Ma'rib wa'l Andhar Tattajih Sawb Hadramawt wa'l Mahra" [The Houthi Group: We Are Ready to Storm Ma'rib, All Eyes on Hadramawt and al-Mahra], September 25, 2021, https://debriefer.net/news-27103.html.
54. Giorgio Cafiero, "Al-Qaeda in Yemen Three Years after Mukalla's 'Liberation,' " *Inside Arabia*, April 22, 2019, https://insidearabia.com/ al-qaeda-yemen-three-years-mukallas-liberation/.
55. Abu Bakr al-Yamani, "Hadhramaut Valley Forces Recruit Locals to Fight al-Qaeda," Al-Mashareq, August 23, 2017, https://almashareq.com/en_ GB/articles/cnmi_am/features/2017/08/23/feature-02.
56. Ahmed Al-Shalafi, "Al-Sa'udiyya wa Istratijiyyat al-Tawasu' al-'Askari 'ala al-Ard fi'l Yaman [Saudi Arabia and the Strategy of Military Expansion in Yemen], Aljazeera.net," August 16, 2020, https://www.aljazeera.net/ blogs/2020/8/16/%D8%A7%D9%84%D8%B3%D8%B9%D9%88%D8%A F%D9%8A%D8%A9-%D9%88%D8%A7%D8%B3%D8%AA%D8%B1%D8% A7%D8%AA%D9%8A%D8%AC%D9%8A%D8%A9-%D8%A7%D9%84%D8 %AA%D9%88%D8%B3%D8%B9-%D8%A7%D9%84%D8%B9%D8%B3%D9 %83%D8%B1%D9%8A.
57. Adam Yehia, "Al-Salafiyya.. Adat Tahaluf "al-Riyadh wa Abu Dhabi" li Tatwi' al-Yaman" [Salafism: The Tool of the "Riyadh and Abu Dhabi" Alliance to Subdue Yemen], *Alestiklal*, March 17, 2019, https://www. alestiklal.net/ar/view/441/dep-news-1552674710.
58. Wael Magdi, "Ba'd Mubaya'at al-Qaba'il.. Hal Tandamm Hadramawt li'l Sa'udiyya?" [Following the Tribes' Pledge of Loyalty, Will Hadramawt Join Saudi Arabia?], Masr Alarabia, September 2, 2015, https://masralar-abia.net/%D8%A7%D9%84%D8%B9%D8%B1%D8%A8-%D9%88%D8%A 7%D9%84%D8%B9%D8%A7%D9%84%D9%85/716845-%D8%A8%D8%B9%D8%AF-%D9%85%D8%A8%D8%A7%D9%8A%D8%B9 %D8%A9-%D8%A7%D9%84%D9%82%D8%A8%D8%A7%D8%A 6%D9%84-%D9%87%D9%84-%D8%AA%D9%86%D8%B6%D9%85-%D8%AD%D8%B6%D8%B1%D9%85%D9%88%D8%AA-%D9%84%D9%84 %D8%B3%D8%B9%D9%88%D8%AF%D9%8A%D8%A9%D8%9F.
59. Adam Baron and Monder Basalma, "The Case of Hadhramaut: Can Local Efforts Transcend Wartime Divides in Yemen?" The Century Foundation,

158   A. NAGI

April 21, 2021, https://tcf.org/content/report/case-hadhramaut-can-local-efforts-transcend-wartime-divides-yemen/?session=1.

60. Ali Ahmad al-Ghurabi, "Man Assas al-Nukhba al-Hadramiyya??" [Who Established the Hadrami Elite?], Tarebh Today, April 8, 2021, https://www.tarebhtoday.com/2021/04/blog-post_961.html.

61. Author field interviews with locals from various areas of Hadramawt, including Seiyun, Mukala, Wadi Dawaan, Shibam, and Qeten between April 25 and May 5, 2019.

62. Jacob Abadi, "Britain's Abandonment of South Arabia—A Reassessment," *Journal of Third World Studies* 12, no. 1 (1995): 152–80, http://www.jstor.org/stable/45197412.

63. The Vision of the Southern Transitional Council (STC), https://stc-eu.org/en/unsere-vision/.

64. Helen Lackner and Raiman Al-Hamdani, "War and Pieces: Political Divides in Southern Yemen," European Council on Foreign Relations, January 22, 2020, https://ecfr.eu/publication/war_and_pieces_political_divides_in_southern_yemen/.

65. Mareb Press, "Al-Majlis al-Intiqali al-Janoubi Aqaba Wujoudiyya fi Hadramawt" [The Southern Transitional Council is an Existential Obstacle in Hadramawt], May 17, 2017, https://marebpress.org/amp-news.php?sid=128233.

CHAPTER 8

The Center Gives: Southern Syria and the Rise of New Peripheral Powerbrokers

Armenak Tokmajyan

INTRODUCTION

The conflict in Syria has fundamentally transformed relations between the center and the country's peripheral southern border region of Daraa Governorate. Almost ten years of war have weakened Damascus' control over Daraa and given rise to new peripheral powerbrokers independent from the Syrian government and antagonistic toward the restoration of its full authority in the south.

The war has also transformed the periphery's political geography. The southern border has become a zone of regional contention, where the interests of foreign actors are converging and conflicting. This has imposed a new framework for center-periphery relations in which the return of the state's full sovereignty and the fate of peripheral powerbrokers are now strongly tied to regional factors.

Before the uprising in 2011, the state had penetrated Syria's peripheries in an unprecedented manner. Under the late president Hafez al-Assad

---

A. Tokmajyan (✉)
Malcolm H. Kerr Carnegie Middle East Center, Beirut, Lebanon
e-mail: armenak.tokmajyan@carnegie-mec.org

© The Author(s), under exclusive license to Springer Nature   159
Switzerland AG 2023
M. Yahya (ed.), *How Border Peripheries are Changing the Nature of Arab States*, https://doi.org/10.1007/978-3-031-09187-2_8

(1970–2000), there was a high degree of centralization, as well as a massive expansion of formal institutions and services throughout the country, including its distant peripheries. All of this enabled greater state domination over society.[1] The infiltration of many state institutions by the security services after the Muslim Brotherhood initiated a campaign of violence against the regime beginning in the late 1970s reinforced this trend.[2] Assad's ability to exercise sovereign power over Syrian territory as no previous Syrian leader had done helped to transform the country into a leading regional actor, after it had been a playing field for regional and global rivalries during the 1940s, 1950s, and early 1960s.[3]

In the shadow of the state, influential community-rooted personalities continued to enjoy a degree of informal authority over their families, towns, and larger social networks. This was especially true in the rural peripheries of the country. Among them were the notables in Daraa, who were often relatively older men of means. They tended to hail from large extended families or clans from the region, were engaged in public and communal affairs, and enjoyed influence in their locality and sometimes even beyond. Despite the presence of formal institutions in Daraa, the Syrian state maintained a complex network of unofficial relationships with these notables and could utilize their local authority to curb any challenges to the state from within their communities.

The importance of these informal networks was very clear at the onset of the Syrian uprising. In March 2011, when protests broke out in Daraa against the regime of President Bashar al-Assad, government officials contacted notables and asked them to help contain the situation. Despite repeated efforts by the central authorities and these local figures to do so, deliberate state violence and the rebellion of local youths against the notables' authority undermined these actions. The conflict that followed fragmented the political center, marginalized the notables as intermediaries, ended the old mechanism of state domination over the periphery, and enabled the rise of new local powerbrokers.

The Syrian conflict created similar dynamics in other rebel-held areas. However, there many of the local strongmen who had become prominent during the fighting were crushed between 2016 and 2018, when government forces and their allies, especially Russia, recaptured rebel-held enclaves. The Syrian government's retaking of territory concluded in summer 2018 with the campaign in Daraa and Quneitra Governorates, where developments were different than elsewhere in Syria. In Daraa particularly some of the new local powerbrokers are still present today and are constantly renegotiating their relationship with the center.

The distinctive nature of the regime's return to the south, manifested most clearly in Daraa, was largely a result of its geography. Daraa is located in a sensitive border region near the Israeli-occupied Golan Heights and Jordan. This proximity forced the government to adopt a different strategy of return during its military campaign, one that excluded the participation of Iranian and pro-Iranian forces. Russia, which pushed for this approach, understood that had Iranian forces and their allies entered recaptured border areas, it could have provoked a violent reaction from Israel, Jordan, and perhaps even the United States, hindering the return of the Syrian military. Consequently, the Russians encouraged a process that emphasized dialogue, soft power, and compromise, unlike in other regions.[4] By avoiding major battles, they managed to exclude Iranian participation in the military campaign. However, this led to a situation in which the government's control on the ground was weakened, preserving a role for some of the powerbrokers who had gained stature during the conflict. The status quo has thus far been maintained thanks to Russia's commitment to keeping things as they are.

It is in this internationalized context that the Syrian government's quest for greater control over the periphery is taking place. It is part of a wider effort to reverse the erosion of its authority nationally—both with respect to local leaders and foreign actors, whether allies or foes—and is tied to its projection of power at the center and what this entails. The Syrian government's failure to fully control Syria's geographical border areas effectively casts doubt on the credibility of the state as a sovereign entity. Such an impression has been harmful to a Syrian leadership that has struggled to affirm that its military victories against the rebels in recent years represented a return to the situation existing prior to 2011.

LOCAL INTERMEDIARIES AS INSTRUMENTS OF STATE DOMINATION BEFORE 2011

Daraa Governorate's hitherto marginalized rural population welcomed the arrival of the Baath in the 1960s and the reforms that followed. The inhabitants filled official positions within state institutions locally and outside the governorate.[5] Embracing the new political system, however, did not mean an end to informal authority. In fact, informal networks played

162   A. TOKMAJYAN

a crucial role in center-periphery relations, and a mutually beneficial relationship existed between the central authorities and local intermediaries who agreed to advance the state's policies. The state granted these figures a degree of local authority and access to privileges while using them to contain challenges to its domination.[6] This took place in the context of an unequal relationship between the state and communities on the peripheries and where the state would resort to violence in instances where it failed to restore its authority through its informal networks.

A large familial dispute in early 1996 in the city of Inkhil, in northern Deraa Governorate, illustrates how informal networks of relations could be used by the authorities to end a situation that could have destabilized the order imposed by the state.

A personal fight escalated into a large-scale confrontation involving two extended families, in which three people were killed and ten injured. Policemen were deployed to calm the two sides, and in a bizarre albeit common step, they moved into the houses of the conflicting families to prevent a further escalation while eating and drinking at their expense until the conflict was resolved. The authorities arrested 200 people, including women. Some of those involved fled Syria until an informal reconciliation took place, formalized by the state.

An eyewitness and a close associate of one of the notables who mediated a solution recalled what happened:

> The chief of police in Daraa called my father and said, 'We tried but failed to resolve the dispute. You [as a respected notable] are accepted among the people. Come and try to resolve it.' We went to Inkhil, formed a reconciliation committee that included members from each family, but failed to find a resolution. My father told the police chief: 'No one wants to reconcile. A few ignorant people are spoiling the process and I don't have the necessary authority to force a solution.' The chief replied: 'Consider that you have all the authority. The state wants this problem resolved, quickly.' My father gave the chief the names of ten prominent members from both families and said, 'Take them and put them in prison.' The police chief imprisoned [those on the list] and told them, 'You will not leave until there is a solution.' After a few hours in jail, they agreed to resume the reconciliation process, which led to a resolution.[7]

The way the state reacted revealed much about how it cooperated with local notables. While the conflict resolution methods were primarily informal, there was something methodical in what took place. The interaction between the police chief and the local notable indicated that relations had existed before the dispute. In fact, informal appeals for local assistance would sometimes come from more senior officials in Damascus, such as ministers.[8] The opposite, too, could be true, when notables used their network to reach out to the central authorities to raise certain demands.[9] In addition, the measures that the police and the notable adopted indicated that both had previous experience in dealing with such cases.

There were many factors that motivated the two to cooperate in facilitating social peace. The police chief had to show his superiors that he was in control of the situation.[10] The notable, in turn, wanted to underline that he could make things happen locally, thereby meriting his political role as mediator between state and society.[11] There was also the question of social duty and prestige. To the notables, intervention to resolve conflicts is almost an obligation for an honorable man.[12] Moreover, several Qur'anic verses encourage reconciliation.[13] In practical terms, the notable contacted by the authorities sought to preserve his access to the centers of power, which empowered him within his extended family, clan, community, and locality. Such access also served to spare his community from state violence and provided him with a valuable alternative channel to state authorities—sometimes even to the president himself—as a way of bypassing official institutions when required.

The resolution in Inkhil also showed a desire to circumvent official institutions because the outcome was seen as being more organic, therefore more sustainable. By adopting a traditional form of reconciliation rather than resorting to the Syrian legal system, both the authorities and local powerbrokers had parallel interests. The state knew that going to the courts would have burdened the judiciary and taken up valuable time, while any judgment would have failed to prevent future revenge killings. For the notables too a reconciliation was preferable, because of their role in such a process. As one police officer from Daraa later put it, "Reconciliation is the master of all rulings."[14]

What made cooperation possible between the central authorities and peripheral notables, however, was not the state's employment of violence but the implied threat that it might do so. Placing policemen in the private homes of individuals engaged in the Inkhil dispute while women and children were there was, and is, a sensitive issue in a conservative rural and tribal setting. The aim was to create a greater impetus for the sides to reconcile.[15] One Daraa notable explained the logic behind such a move. The personnel, according to him, might "remain [in the homes] for a month or two. When they see a lamb they slaughter it, causing deliberate inconvenience to push the sides to reconcile."[16]

The arrest of the family elders followed a similar rationale. In a formal judicial process, an arrest could lead to an official investigation, a complex court case that could involve paying bribes, and possibly a long jail term. In an informal setting, however, this was not necessarily true. Arrests are merely demonstrations of force by the authorities to pressure rival families into accepting a resolution. Once a reconciliation takes place, the state can reduce the sentence.

For the state to threaten violence rather than have recourse to it was the cog that kept informal conflict resolution mechanisms alive. The incident in Daraa in March 2011 that provoked the first spark of the Syrian uprising showed the price that was paid when abandoning this logic. At the time, Atef Najib, the chief of the Political Intelligence Directorate in Daraa, ordered the arrest and torture of children who had written anti-regime slogans on walls, and he humiliated the Daraa notables who visited him to secure their release.[17] By opting for violence, Najib undermined the informal balance that had been in place between the state, local notables, and their communities. This led to Syria's first major protest on March 18 in Daraa city, causing the earliest victims of the uprising.[18]

A few days after the children's arrest in Daraa, another event in Sanamayn, a town in northern Daraa Governorate, underscored how the regime had shifted toward engaging in deliberate violence. After Friday prayers protestors headed toward the local police station shouting anti-government and sectarian slogans. Then someone from the security forces, who was known for being ruthless, began firing his automatic weapon at the protestors.[19] This transgression of the implicit red lines on the use of violence soon became the norm, undermining the informal mechanisms that had been in place previously to neutralize conflict.

Soon after the first protests in Daraa city, senior government officials contacted local notables asking them to control the situation. Many of them were the same longtime intermediaries who had facilitated the state's actions in their localities. A close relative of one very prominent notable claimed that the man had received a call from a senior Baath official who told him, "There are protests in Daraa. Go and try to resolve the problem. You are mandated by the president."[20] Such efforts by the central authorities were common. For months, the state activated individuals and delegations from Daraa.[21] However, their efforts largely failed to yield results, and when they did the impact was short-lived. As a consequence the state used more violence, and in time, pushing the protestors to resort to violence themselves.

Another example from Inkhil, this time in May 2011, shows how the dynamics at the local level began to change as the uprising escalated. There, protestors opposed to the state disregarded the authority of the old powerbrokers. This meant that even when these powerbrokers had an opportunity to prevent the spread of violence, the instruments which they had used, namely, higher levels of state violence, were no longer effective. The son of one of these notables, who was a witness to what happened, recalled how the situation unfolded in Inkhil.

> A representative from the [local] Political Intelligence branch came to my father [a prominent figure in the town]. They knew each other. He told him, 'You know what would happen if the army stormed the town. We need twelve wanted people. They shall come to the branch accompanied by local notables, undergo a security clearance, and leave.' My father agreed, and invited the youths to our home. [My father and the intelligence officer] told them that if the regime entered the town, it would do so with tanks and that they [the youths] had nothing with which to defend themselves. They refused. The regime stormed the town with tanks and arrested 300 instead of the twelve.[22]

Once conflict resolution mechanisms based on a threat of violence and informal intermediaries did not yield meaningful results, the process that could have neutralized tensions at the local level in 2011 collapsed. What ensued was a much bloodier conflict. In the case of Daraa, as in many other places in Syria, this marked a turning point in relations between the Syrian state and society.

How the Syrian Conflict Transformed Center-Periphery Relations

The spiral of violence after March 2011 triggered large-scale protests around Syria and soon transformed the situation into a civil war that drew in regional and international actors. The once powerful central state gradually lost territorial control over most of Daraa. Instead, it sought to maintain its presence in administratively important, mainly urban, defensible areas. The military-security apparatus took on an even greater role in handling relations with society. In opposition-held territory a new generation of powerbrokers emerged that was very different than the traditional notables. Most were young and not necessarily from a privileged social background. They tended to be rebel combatants who had emerged independently from the central government and were hostile to its authority. Significantly, many enjoyed transnational links to regional and international actors who supported the anti-Assad war effort in the south.

The war did not merely transform the key actors constituting Syria's central authorities and the peripheral leadership, it also transformed the political geography of the periphery itself. In that way it altered the context in which the center and periphery had interacted. Syria's south in general was transformed from a border area within a sovereign state into a regional frontier. The area's closeness to Israel and Jordan, these two countries' concerns about the deployment of Iranian forces and their allies near to territories they controlled, and Russian involvement effectively turned local dynamics into regional ones.

The Rise of New Peripheral Powerbrokers in Daraa

At the beginning of 2013, almost two years after the start of the Syrian conflict, rebels in Daraa Governorate changed their tactics from hit-and-run attacks against government forces to gaining and holding territory.[23] At around that time, countries opposed to the Assad regime established a joint operations room in Jordan, which they called the Military Operations Center (MOC). It served as an umbrella to coordinate support for the southern rebels, with the United States and Jordan being the most influential members.[24] The MOC's military and financial backing brought foreign support for rebel groups to a whole new level.

By mid-2015, the Syrian government had lost control of its border with Jordan. Its presence was reduced to a strip of land along the M5 highway that connected Damascus with Daraa city and divided the governorate into eastern and western halves. Daraa city, the governorate's capital, was itself divided into two, with government-controlled Daraa al-Mahatta in the north and rebel-controlled Daraa al-Balad in the south.[25] These boundaries remained more or less constant until the military campaign of 2018, when government forces returned to the south.

With the withdrawal of the state in 2011 and foreign-supported armed organizations dominating the south, center-periphery relations were completely transformed. As one notable from Nawa put it, "After the armed factions took over the area, the role of the notables ended completely.

With the influx of huge foreign funds, no one listened to us ... none [of the notables] had influence over anyone."[26] This ended the notables' political role as intermediaries with the state. Although some notables supported the rebellion behind the scenes, or enjoyed respect within their clan, locality, or communities in exile, they played a marginal political role in leading the revolt and in the subsequent armed conflict.

The influence of youths in the uprising came early on as most of the new powerbrokers were young men. A protestor, who was in his twenties and lived in southwest Daraa, explained that in his clan "those who took the lead were not the [clan] sheikhs. It was the young [who included] university students, teachers, and officers."[27] This pattern continued throughout the conflict, though the civilian dimension of the social movement became weaker as the violence grew. Military men became the decision-makers on the ground. Before the return of government forces in 2018, the average age of a cross-section of 18 personalities who had become prominent during the conflict in Daraa Governorate was around 42 years, with two-thirds of them being armed rebels [1, see Table 8.1].

These new powerbrokers did not necessarily hail from the large clans in their area or from prominent families in their clan. Nor did they have a long record of social, communal, or political engagement. For this younger generation the sources of legitimacy had less to do with tribal background and social status and more with having been at the forefront of protests and, later on, the military conflict. Legitimacy was also based on their ability to survive, attract foreign support, and impose themselves as new leaders—a process that often involved fighting other rebel factions or competitors, aside from government forces.[28]

Another crucial difference is that new powerbrokers rose not because they had been empowered by the central authorities, as the old notables had been, but because they were opposed to them. Though not tied to the center in Damascus, the new powerbrokers were also not independent. Their status was determined by the transnational links they had forged. Transnationalism was not entirely new. Strong connections had long extended to communities across the border with Jordan as well as to diaspora communities in the Gulf countries. However, the war introduced a whole new level of ties between the emerging local powerbrokers and outside countries opposed to the Assad regime. The move from a war funded through locally generated resources and diaspora support to one in which combatants received financial, military, and political support

168 A. TOKMAJYAN

Table 8.1 Characteristics of the new powerbrokers in Daraa

THE MOST INFLUENTIAL NEW POWERBROKERS

	Ahmad al-Audeh أحمد العودة	Adham al-Krad أدهم الكراد	Bashar al-Zubi بشار الزعبي	Mohammed Murshid al-Baradan محمد مرشد البردان	Abu Munzir al-Duhni أبو منذر الدهني
Approximate Age in 2011	30	37	40	24	45
Civilian or Military	Military	Military	Military	Military	Military
Occupation Before 2011	English Language Teacher	Engineer in the UAE	Owner of Travel Company	Farmer	Colonel in the Syrian Army
Education	MA, English Literature	BS, Mechanical Engineering	School Degree (baccalaureate)	9th grade	
Social Background Small/big family or clan	Small al-Hamdi clan	Influential al-Krad clan	Al-Zubi clan (one of the biggest in the Governorate)	Al-Baradan (biggest in Tafas)	Small clan
Home Locality	Busra al-Sham	Daraa city (Daraa al-Balad)	Taybeh	Tafas	Daraa city (Daraa al-Balad)
Notable in a Family/ Clan/Locality	Not a notable	Not a notable	Not a notable	Not a notable	Yes, thanks to his military rank
Other Relevant Information	Many of his relatives migrated to the UAE for work	Worked in the UAE	In the Syria-Gulf land transport business	Had some indirect links to Syrian Muslim Brotherhood movement.	
Organizational Background During Rebellion	Founder and leader, Forces of Sunni Youth, which dominated eastern Daraa	Founder and leader of Engineering and Rockets Battalion that produced rockets locally	Founder of the Yarmouk Army, which became biggest coalition of forces in the south	Founder and leader of Mutaz Billah Army, the strongest in south-west Daraa Governorate	Founder and leader of 18 March Brigade, most influential in Daraa al-Balad
Transnational Ties Before 2018	• Diaspora networks in the Gulf • Military Operation Centre (MOC) • United Arab Emirates	• Diaspora networks in the Gulf • Military Operation Centre (MOC) • (Most likely) United Arab Emirates	• Diaspora networks in the Gulf • Military Operation Centre (MOC) • Several Gulf countries • Syrian Muslim Brotherhood	• Military Operation Centre (MOC) • Syrian Muslim Brotherhood	• Military Operation Centre (MOC)
Relations With Russia After 2018	Very strong (patronage)	Working relations through Daraa Central Committee (tasked to re-negotiate the Russia and the regime)	He left Daraa in 2018	• Incorporation attempt by Russia • Working relations through Daraa Central Committee	Good working relations in Daraa al-Balad
Incorporation By the Regime	Head, Russian-backed 8th Brig. 5th Corps. Nominally part of the Syrian Army		He left Daraa in 2018		
Assassination Attempts	No	Yes, assassinated in October 2020. Regime is the main suspect	He left Daraa in 2018	Several attempts, ISIS was suspected for the latest attempt (June 2020)	No

LESS INFLUENTIAL POWERBROKERS (CIVILIANS)

	Adnan al-Masalmeh عدنان المسالمة	Sheikh Faysal Abazed الشيخ فيصل أبازيد	Sheikh Ahmad Bqayrat الشيخ أحمد بقيرات	Ala' al-Zoani علاء الزوياني	Yaarub Abu Sefan يعرب أبو سعيفان	Mahmoud al-Ibrahim (Mahmoud al-Bannat) محمود الابراهيم
Approximate Age in 2011	50	50	45	26	45	45
Civilian or Military	Civilian	Civilian	Civilian	Civilian	Civilian	Civilian
Occupation Before 2011	Lawyer	Mosque imam, Daraa al-Balad	Mosque imam, Tal Shihab	Mosque imam, Yadouda	Member of Daraa Governorate Council	High School Principal in Mzerib
Education	Law	Sharia	Sharia	Sharia	BS, Agricultural Engineering	Sharia
Social Background Small/big family or clan	Influential al-Masalmeh clan	Influential Abazed clan	His locality's biggest clan			
Home Locality	Daraa city (Daraa al-Balad)	Daraa city (Daraa al-Balad)	Tal Shihab	al-Yadouda	Al-Shajara	Mzerib
Notable in a Family/ Clan/Locality	Notable in his clan	Notable in his clan	Notable in his clan	Notable in the clan due to his position	Notable in his Yarmouk Basin region	Notable in the locality given his position as a school principle
Other Relevant Information						
Organizational Background During Rebellion	Daraa Provincial Council (part of opposition's Turkey-based interim government)	Daraa Provincial Council Member of other civilian organizations	Judge, (opposition) Hawran Courthouse	Judge, (opposition) Hawran Courthouse	Daraa Provincial Council	Judge, (opposition) Hawran Courthouse
Transnational Ties Before 2018	• No strong transnational relations	• No strong transnational relations • How about Muslim Brotherhood?	• No strong transnational relations • How about Muslim Brotherhood?	• No strong transnational relations • How about Muslim Brotherhood?	• No strong transnational relations	• No strong transnational relations • How about Muslim Brotherhood?
Relations With Russia After 2018	Working relations through Daraa Central Committee	Working relations through Daraa Central Committee	Working relations through Daraa Central Committee	Working relations through Daraa Central Committee	Working relations through Daraa Central Committee	Working relations through Daraa Central Committee
Incorporation By the Regime						
Assassination Attempts	No	No	No	Yes. Assassinated in February 2019. Pro-Iranian forces were suspected	No. Died in March 2020 due to health problems	Several attempts

(continued)

Table 8.1 (continued)

	LESS INFLUENTIAL POWERBROKERS (MILITARY)						
	Mustafa al-Masalmeh (Al-Kasem) مصطفى المسالمة (الكسم)	Walid al-Zahra وليد الزهرة	Abu Bakr al-Hassan أبو بكر الحسن	Abdul Hakim al-Id عبد الحكيم العيد	Othman Mohammed Smer جدي	Imad Abu Zureiq عماد أبو زريق	Fadi al-Asimi فادي العاسمي
Approximate Age in 2011	18	29	27	26	41	28	35
Civilian or Military	Military	Military	Military	Military	Military	Military	Military
Occupation Before 2011	Conscript in the Syrian Army		Recent graduate	Captain in the Syrian Army	Farmer	School Teacher, Physical Education	Mosque khatib, Dael
Education			MA, Administration		Sharia (did not finish)	Physical Education	Sharia
Social Background Small/big family or clan	Influential al-Masalmeh clan		small educated family	second biggest clan in his hometown	From a big clan in his locality	Fifth biggest clan	
Home Locality	Daraa city (Daraa al-Balad)	Sanamayn	Jasem	Inkhil	Inkhil	Nassib	Dael
Notable in a Family/Clan/Locality	Not a notable		Not a notable	Not a notable	Not a notable	Not a notable	Notable in his clan, thanks to his religious position
Other Relevant Information							
Organizational Background During Rebellion	Head of a small faction that joined several coalitions	Head of a small faction in Sanamayn	The speaker of the Army of the Revolution, armed alliance	Head of Islam's Lions Brigade, strong armed group in northern Daraa and Quneitra until 2015	From the leadership of Mujahidin Hawran Brigades, strong armed group in northern Daraa and Quneitra until 2015	Second tire commander in the Yarmouk Army	Second tire commander in the Army of the Revolution, an armed alliance
Transnational Ties Before 2011	• Military Operation Centre (MOC)	• No strong transnational relations	• Military Operation Centre (MOC)	• Military Operation Centre (MOC)	• Military Operation Centre (MOC)	• Military Operation Centre (MOC)	• Military Operation Centre (MOC) • Personal relations to the MOC
Relations With Russia After 2018	No relations	No relations	Working relations through Daraa Central Committee	No relations	• Meetings with Russian officers • Nature of the relations is unknown	No relations	No relations
Incorporation By the Regime	Incorporated by Military Intelligence Directorate				Russian-backed 8th Brig. 5th Corps. Nominally part of the Syrian Army	Incorporated by General Security Directorate	Incorporated by Military Intelligence Directorate
Assassination Attempts	Several attempts	Killed during Syrian Army operation, March 2020 in Sanamayn	Several attempts	Several attempts	No	Several attempts	Detained for three months in December 2018 by the Air Force Intelligence Directorate

from foreign governments was a factor that empowered the new local leaders.

These characteristics were by no means unique to Daraa and its strongmen. Many other prominent rebel leaders across Syria were young, had emerged as a result of the conflict, and had forged strong ties with foreign actors. Some of them are still active in areas outside of government control in northern Syria. Others, who operated in the two-dozen or so rebel strongholds recaptured by government forces and their allies between 2016 and 2018, lost their role as powerbrokers. What makes Daraa unique is that some of the local powerbrokers remain in place today thanks to the particular way the state recaptured the south in 2018. This was made possible by Russia's efforts to bring about a negotiated return of Syrian government forces, making the deployment of Iranian and pro-Iran combatants in the border area much more difficult.

The multifaceted way that government forces regained control of the south resulted in a complicated map, roughly made up of three zones. The first included Busra al-Sham, Daraa al-Balad, and Tafas, as well as some regions surrounding them. In these places, Russia brokered agreements

170 A. TOKMAJYAN

limiting the government's return to its control over civilian institutions. Even today, the state has no security or military presence in these areas. In a second zone, in the northwestern rural areas of Daraa, the Syrian authorities returned with their security and military apparatus, though they have limited actual sway on the ground. That is because the Russian and government reconciliation tracks worked in tandem there, creating conditions that restrained the way government authority would be manifested. And in a third zone, which government forces recaptured without Russian involvement, they asserted firmer security and military control.[29]

By enabling some of the new powerbrokers to remain in Daraa, the settlement in the south allowed them to continue to play a role in local politics. This was true across Daraa Governorate, but was most clearly manifested in those zones where the state had no security or military presence. A prominent example of one such figure is the strongman in Tafas and its surrounding areas, Mohammed Murshid al-Baradan. During the military campaign in 2018, Baradan agreed to a Russian offer to reconcile with the government and became more important a player in southwest Daraa Governorate. Baradan is a native of Tafas and hails from a humble family of farmers in the city's largest clan.[30] He was merely 25 when the uprising began in 2011 and had no noticeable social status. He joined the protests from the first day and soon formed a small armed group named Mutaz Billah. His rise as a successful commander began after he built relations with local networks seen as affiliates of the Muslim Brotherhood. Through these channels, he received financial aid, military support, and advice.[31]

Baradan's rise and Mutaz Billah's transformation into one of the largest armed factions in southwestern Rural Daraa Governorate was made possible thanks to the backing of the MOC. As an activist from Tafas who lived through this period described it, "The MOC brought a whole new level of support to the rebels. If you had 500 men fighting for you, now it became 3,000–4,000. You had medium and heavy weaponry, monthly salaries, ammunition, warehouses of weapons, and so on."[32] At some point in 2014, 45–50 rebel groups had representatives in Amman to facilitate aid and report to donors, among other tasks.[33] This network of support sustained a large number of rebel leaders and enabled them to resist the Syrian military until assistance ended in late 2017, when US President Donald Trump ordered the suspension of the program.[34]

Three influential personalities gained prominence in Daraa al-Balad. One was a defector from the Syrian army, Colonel Abu Mundhir al-Duhni, who was a respected personality from a small family in Daraa city.[35] He was in his mid-forties at the onset of the uprising and became well-known in the south.[36] Duhni participated in negotiations with the Russians and has continued to do so with them and government representatives on local issues. However, since 2018 his influence has been limited to his native city.[37]

A second and more prominent figure was Adham al-Krad, whose reputation grew only during the uprising.[38] A multilingual engineer and a good public speaker, Krad returned to Syria in 2012 after having left his job in the United Arab Emirates when he was around 40. He formed the Katibet al-Handasa wa al-Sawarikh (the Engineering and Rocket Battalion), which deployed locally produced rockets. Krad also participated in negotiations with the Russians in summer 2018. After that he became even more prominent, not just in Daraa city but in the south in general.[39]

A third important figure is Adnan al-Masalmeh, a lawyer who is currently in his early sixties. He was a civilian official in the Daraa Provincial Council established by the opposition's Turkey-based interim government. Masalmeh gained prominence only after the return of government forces. Despite enjoying local support and respect, he does not have the same power as the military men nor did he ever secure foreign patronage.[40]

The strongman of Busra al-Sham, in southeast Daraa Governorate, is Ahmad al-Audeh. In 2011, Audeh set off on a remarkable transformation from a young English language teacher in his early thirties into the most prominent and ambitious rebel leader in the south. Young, bold, and a survivor, Audeh hails from a small family in Busra al-Sham with a history of migrating to the Gulf, a pattern prevalent in the eastern half of the governorate. This created diaspora networks that were crucial in attracting funding to Audeh at the beginning of the uprising from Syrian businessmen, some of them fellow townspeople.[41] This financing sometimes ran parallel to the support coming from the MOC. However, none of this was unique to Audeh. Krad, Duhni, and another prominent rebel leader, Bashar al-Zubi, who headed one of the largest armed groups in the south and left Syria after the government's military campaign in 2018, as well as others, had networks connecting them to states or private citizens outside Syria. But Audeh's case is perhaps the most noteworthy.

Audeh's first step toward prominence occurred in 2015 when he expelled all government forces from Busra al-Sham with the help of other rebel groups, although he alone gained fame and power from this success.[42] At that point, in addition to the MOC's backing, Audeh's extended family networks in the diaspora had reportedly connected him to foreign actors, especially the United Arab Emirates, which sustained his group, Quwwat Shabab al-Sunna (Forces of Sunni Youth).[43] In 2016, with Emirati support, Quwwat Shabab al-Sunna incorporated new factions and bought weapons sold on the black market by other rebels.[44]

Thought it initially opposed President Bashar al-Assad, the United Arab Emirates expressed support for the Russians' intervention in Syria in November 2015 and cooperated with them. Toward the end of 2019 it engaged in a more public rapprochement with the Syrian regime.[45] This allowed Audeh to become a crucial player in the military campaign of summer 2018.[46] He was quick to agree to Russia's plan for the south. Subsequently, he took charge of the Eighth Brigade of the Fifth Corps, which is nominally part of the Syrian Army but in reality serves as Russia's military wing in Daraa. Therefore, Audeh's success in repurposing his foreign relations, which placed him at the intersection of Russian and Emirati interests, enabled him to become the most influential powerbroker in the south. Audeh's trajectory illustrates the change in the nature of the political elite in Daraa. It shows, particularly, how new leaders emerged as the power of the Syrian state eroded during the conflict and amid growing involvement by foreign actors, which transformed center-periphery relations.

The Internationalization of Center-Periphery Relations

The transformation of the southern Syrian border area into a place of regional and international importance imposed a new context for interaction between the center and the periphery. After government forces recaptured the south in 2018, there began a process of renegotiation between a fragmented and weakened central authority and the new peripheral powerbrokers over the meaning of state authority and sovereignty in Daraa. This process was strongly influenced by regional dynamics and the delicate status quo after the military campaign.

The war in Syria shattered the instruments of central authority. Before 2011 there were multiple layers of authority managed from Damascus, each with its own latitude of action. However, today, in addition to these layers, there are also institutions that emerged after 2011 or that became more autonomous. These include security bodies, military units, and militias, which together have created a more complex landscape of state authority. Such institutions, while tied in various ways to the center, also grew closer to certain regional and international actors, such as Russia or

Iran. For instance, Iran has forged close relations with the Syrian Army's Fourth Armored Division and the Air Force Intelligence Directorate in Daraa, which are now perceived as being pro-Iranian forces in the south.[47] In Daraa, Moscow seems to have developed closer working relations with the Military Intelligence Directorate,[48] which historically was the most powerful intelligence agency in the south and neighboring Suwayda Governorate.

It is difficult to assess how much leverage Iran and Russia have over their local partners, though the likelihood is that the Syrian actors retain a margin of maneuver. For instance, the Fourth Armored Division, which is effectively led by Maher al-Assad, the president's brother, has tried to limit Iran's influence along the coast where most of the regime's Alawite base resides.[49] Nor should one assume that ties with foreign actors are immutable. Rather, the situation in the south today illustrates what the central authorities now represent in Deraa, namely, a disjointed whole that encompasses many local and regional interests.

This reality helped to create the special situation in Daraa, where the new local powerbrokers are redefining the scope of the state's territorial control. That is most clear in the three zones centered around Busra al-Sham, Tafas, and Daraa al-Balad where, according to the Russia-brokered agreement, the return of state authority was limited to civilian and service-providing institutions. Until today, the government has no direct security or military presence there.[50]

At the same time, within these zones the powerbrokers still have their own networks of former rebels, who on many occasions have been mobilized to challenge the Syrian military and security forces, without facing consequences for doing so. Ahmad al-Audeh is, undoubtedly, the leader who enjoys the strongest patronage from Russia. An incident in August 2019, when one of Audeh's men assaulted a pro-regime journalist after he entered Busra al-Sham, illustrates Audeh's leeway.[51] The journalist had published a Facebook post that was disrespectful of the late Abdul Baset al-Sarut, a onetime football player who had joined the rebels and become a symbol of the uprising. When the man behind the attack was asked whether he did not fear government retribution, he reportedly replied, "I know the regime wants revenge. I have received indirect threats. But I can go to Damascus [without problems] because I have Ahmad [Audeh] behind me."[52] Neither the perpetrator nor Audeh faced any reprisals.

Two incidents from Deraa Governorate, one in Sanamayn and another in Tafas, illustrate the impact of regional considerations on local dynamics.

In May 2020, military and security units close to Iran sought to escalate the situation in and around Tafas. This came after the authorities discovered the bodies of nine policemen in a town in Daraa's loosely controlled southwest. The perpetrator was a former rebel who sought to avenge the killing of his son and son-in-law by government security forces.[53] The incident became a pretext for the government to send substantial military reinforcements to the area and tighten its control. Many of the reinforcements were from military units considered close to Iran.[54] Tensions rose as former rebels who opposed their return vowed to fight.[55] Russia intervened, and after several rounds of negotiations between multiple regime representatives and local powerbrokers, the sides agreed to a slight increase in government forces while maintaining the equilibrium in place.[56]

In contrast, an earlier incident showed how local powerbrokers who did not have foreign, especially Russian, protection, and were not important for maintenance of the status quo, proved little match for government forces. In March 2020, government forces launched a brief military operation to impose their control over parts of Sanamayn city that were ruled by local militias with no transnational links.[57] The episode provoked mobilization against the regime's actions across Daraa Governorate.[58] These took a violent turn when gunmen exchanged fire with government military and security personnel, attacked their positions, and took hostages.[59] However, the Sanamayn operation ended with a swift victory by government forces and the evacuation of some of the local militiaman to rebel-held areas of northern Syria.

Damascus has been displeased with the way local powerbrokers have continued to challenge its authority.[60] Despite fragmentation among the regime's military and security forces, there are strong indications that it has pursued a policy of either eliminating or incorporating the new powerbrokers into the ruling system. Imad Abu Zuraiq, a former rebel who now has ties with the Military Intelligence Directorate, exemplifies the option of incorporation. After the military campaign in 2018, he fled to Jordan, only to return in late 2019 and settle his security issues thanks to the facilitation of Military Intelligence, which is seen as closer to Russia.[61] Abu Zuraiq runs a locally recruited militia in the border town of Nassib, made up mainly of former rebel fighters, and is involved in managing the informal economy near the crossing point with Jordan. This includes selling smuggled goods and levying taxes on passing cars, among other activities, and presumably sharing the profits with his Military Intelligence patrons.[62] Abu Zuraiq is not a notable or a respected personality, but through his network, he provides his patrons with an instrument of political control.[63]

Abu Zuraiq's case is not the only example of incorporation.[64] Othman Smer, a farmer in Inkhil turned rebel commander before becoming a regime client, provides another remarkable illustration of this. Smer, who is now in his sixties, remained far from public life before 2011. The uprising provided him with an opportunity to gain status in his town and to a lesser extent in rural areas of northwestern Daraa. His pragmatism, but also luck, enabled him to survive when most of his comrades, and several family members, were killed during the war.

Having established strong links to the regime well before the summer 2018 offensive, Smer and many of his former fighters settled their security issues upon the return of government forces to their city.[65] Today, his former networks are reportedly working on behalf of the General Intelligence Directorate, the most powerful agency in their region. This includes carrying out security operations. He retains ties with former rebels who also work for General Intelligence and carry out security operations for its benefit, including against former rebels.[66]

Even as it has sought to coopt onetime rebels, the regime has also pursued a strategy of elimination, targeting some strongmen in the south. One of its earliest victims was Alaa al-Zubani, a cleric turned rebel leader who was a second-tier commander mainly influential in his region of southwestern Daraa Governorate. After the military campaign, he settled his security affairs with the authorities and returned to his profession. Zubani had enemies among the pro-Tehran currents within the regime for preaching against Iran's expansion in the locality, making Iran the likely suspect in his assassination in February 2019.[67]

Since the return of government forces, 42 former rebel commanders have been killed by various sides, most of them second-rank commanders.[68] The most prominent among these is Adham al-Krad, who was assassinated on October 14, 2020, along with several comrades. Their car was attacked by gunmen near Sanamayn, a government stronghold where many of its security and military forces are stationed.[69] The location of the killing made it highly likely that pro-regime operatives were involved. Several people in Daraa who had defied government forces after their return in 2018 perceived this as a message to other former rebel commanders that they too would face retaliation at some stage.[70] Krad's killing

176 A. TOKMAJYAN

shook Daraa though it did not undermine the status quo, which remains a Russian priority. It also did not represent a direct challenge to Russia. Despite Krad's efforts to build stronger relations with Moscow, which included using personal networks he had built during the time he had studied in Russia, he did not enjoy Russian support.[71]

While the Assad regime may take every opportunity to eliminate those who have contested its authority, it seems to be wary about fundamentally upsetting the balance in the border region or targeting those implementing Russia's agenda. A collapse of the status quo could harm the regime's relations with Moscow. It would also very probably invite a very costly Israeli counterreaction. These dynamics may change, as very little can be taken for granted. However, one may confidently assert that for years to come Syria's central authorities, local powerbrokers, and their relationship will be affected by regional considerations.

CONCLUSION

The dynamics in Daraa show that some of the main instruments that had once enabled Hafez al-Assad to impose unprecedented control over Syria, including its faraway peripheries, are a thing of the past. The state is effectively fragmented, its institutions are weak and bankrupt, and its military and security order is being challenged constantly. The center also lacks strong informal local intermediaries to facilitate the state's domination over their communities. The old mechanism of authority, working through local notables, collapsed with the militarization of the Syrian uprising, while a new one has yet to be established.

The situation in Daraa also illustrates how the new political geography of the periphery—the strong influence of foreign actors, the presence of defiant local powerbrokers, and the status quo enabling the continuation of this situation—has imposed a new situation on the center: to accept compromised sovereignty in the south or risk an escalation that could prove very costly and may even threaten the regime's survival. In that sense, Daraa has helped to create a post-conflict reality in which Syria remains a playground for regional and international rivalries, even if, nominally, parts of the country are under the central government's control.

NOTES

1. Raymond A. Hinnebusch, "Syria Under the Ba'th: State Formation in a Fragmented Society," *Arab Studies Quarterly*, 4, No. 3 (1982): 187; for examples on how the Baath's rural politics weakened traditional social forces in society, see: Raymond A. Hinnebusch, "Local Politics in Syria: Organization and Mobilization in Four Village Cases," *Middle East Journal*, 30, no. 1 (1976), 1–24; Moshe Maoz notes that the first serious attempt to achieve national unity beyond tribal, sectarian, and ethnic divisions happened during the dictatorship of Adib Shishakli in the early 1950s. This process made "impressive progress ever since the Ba'th revolution of 1963." See Moshe Ma'oz, "Attempts at Creating a Political Community in Modern Syria," *Middle East Journal*, 26, no. 4 (1972), 398.
2. Patrick Seale, *Assad: The Struggle for The Middle East*, 4th edition (University of California Press, 1995), 338; Raymond A. Hinnebusch, "President and Party in Post-Ba'thist Syria From the Struggle for 'Reform' to Regime Deconstruction," in *Syria From Reform to Revolt: Political Economy and International Relations*, edited by Raymond A. Hinnebusch and Tina Zintl (Syracuse University Press, 2015), 25.
3. Patrick Seale, *Assad: The Struggle for The Middle East, Op. Cit.*, 85.
4. For a more detailed look at the post-2018 dynamics of the military campaign in the south, see Armenak Tokmajyan, "How Southern Syria Has Been Transformed Into a Regional Powder Keg," Carnegie Endowment for International Peace, July 14, 2020, https://carnegie-mec.org/2020/07/14/how-southern-syria-has-been-transformed-into-regional-powder-keg-pub-82202.
5. See "Popular Protest in North Africa and the Middle East (VII): The Syrian Regime's Slow-Motion Suicide," International Crisis Group, July 13, 2011, https://www.crisisgroup.org/middle-east-north-africa/eastern-mediterranean/syria/popular-protest-north-africa-and-middle-east-vii-syrian-regime-s-slow-motion-suicide, 12–13.
6. This approach could be understood as a "mechanism that stabilizes (patrimonial) regimes through an exchange relationship that provides political mobilization to the patron ... and material resources to the clients." See Birkholz, Sina, "Multi-layered Dependency: Understanding the Transnational Dimension of Favouritism in the Middle East," in *Clientelism and Patronage in the Middle East and North Africa*, edited by Laura Ruiz De Elvira et. al. (Routledge, 2018), 23. On how the regime of Hafiz al-Assad built patronage networks in the 1970s after coming to power, see, for example, Yahya M. Sadowski, "Patronage and the Ba'th: Corruption and Control in Contemporary Syria," *Arab Studies Quarterly* 9, No. 4, (1987): 449.

7. Author interview with the close relative of the notable who mediated the resolution, Syria (via Skype), May 28, 2020. The details of the story were cross-checked with three others sources—a resident from Inkhil who witnessed the event and a member from each of the two clans that were fighting.

8. Author interview with the son of a prominent notable, Syria, *Op. Cit.*

9. Author interview with a notable and former *mukhtar*, or local administrative official, from Daraa, Irbid, Jordan, December 15, 2019. The notable recalled an incident in Daraa during the 1990s involving several major clans that well-illustrates such dynamics. The family of the perpetrator disowned him after he had committed a horrendous crime, which in tribal culture means there wouldn't be a revenge killing for the shedding his blood. Then the mufti of Daraa, being from the clan of the perpetrator and having access to the central authorities, met with the then-president Hafez al-Assad and told him the perpetrator needed to be executed; otherwise, all of Daraa would flare up. Within a month, he was.

10. If a security official could not solve a problem, and it escalated and required intervention by the authorities in Damascus, he could lose his job. Author interview with a Baath Party "Active Member" (*'adu 'amel*) currently residing outside Syria (via Skype), May 23, 2020; author interview with a graduate in Islamic jurisprudence from Quneitra, Amman, Jordan, November 14, 2019.

11. Author interview with a son of a local notable from Inkhil, Amman, Jordan, December 19, 2019; author interview with a Syrian journalist from Daraa, Amman, Jordan, October 27, 2020.

12. Author interview with a notable from Busra al-Sham, Irbid, Jordan, March 14, 2020.

13. Author interview with a graduate of Islamic jurisprudence from Quneitra, *Op. Cit.*; author interview with a student of Islamic law from Daraa (via Skype), June 14, 2020.

14. Author interview with a student of Islamic law from Daraa, *Op. Cit.*

15. This tactic used by the state and the logic that it follows has been commonly cited by many interviewees. Author interview with a history teacher, Irbid, Jordan, December 15, 2019; author interview with a graduate of Islamic jurisprudence from Quneitra, *Op. Cit.*; author interview with a notable and former *mukhtar*, or local administrative official, from Daraa, *Op. Cit.*

16. Author interview with a notable from the Hariri clan from Daraa, Irbid, Jordan, December 14, 2019.

17. Mohammed Jamal Barout, "Al-'Aqed al-Akhir fi Tarikh Surya: Jadaliyyet al-Jumud wa al-Islah [The Past Decade in Syria: The Dialectics of Stagnation and Reform]," (Beirut: Arab Center for Research and Policy

Studies, 2012), 184; Hayyan Dukhan, "Tribes and Tribalism in the Syrian Uprising," *Syria Studies*, 6, no. 2 (2015), 7–8.

18. According to Mohammed Jamal Barout, the security forces collapsed when facing the first protest in Daraa on March 18, 2011. Atef Najib called in the special forces, who arrived with four helicopters and shot at protestors, causing the first victims of the uprising. Mohammed Jamal Barout, "Al-'Aqed al-Akhir fi Tarikh Surya," *Op. Cit.*, 187.

19. Author interview with a former Sanamayn resident, Beirut, Lebanon, April 26, 2018.

20. Author interview with the son of a prominent notable, Syria, *Op. Cit.*

21. For details, see Armenak Tokmajyan, "Politics of Rural Notables" in *Local Intermediaries in Post-2011 Syria: Transformation and Continuity*, edited by Kheder Khaddour and Kevin Mazur (Friedrich Ebert Stiftung, June 2019), http://library.fes.de/pdf-files/bueros/beirut/15547.pdf.

22. Author interview with a close relative of the notable involved, Amman, Jordan, December 19, 2019.

23. Jonathan Dupree, "Syria Update: The Southern Battlefronts," Institute for the Study of War, April 5, 2013, http://www.understandingwar.org/backgrounder/syria-update-southern-battlefronts.

24. "New Approach in Southern Syria," International Crisis Group, September 2, 2015, https://d2071andvip0wj.cloudfront.net/163-new-approach-in-southern-syria.pdf, 9.

25. For a map see: "Syria Conflict Map," Institute for United Conflict Analysts, August 12, 2015, http://www.mediafire.com/convkey/6a61/j86tau9of-w69137zg.jpg.

26. Author interview with a history teacher from Daraa, Irbid, Jordan, *Op. Cit.*; a similar view was expressed by a notable from the Khalidi clan interviewed by the author (via telephone), July 28, 2020.

27. Author interview with a young member of the Miqdad clan (via Skype), June 5, 2020.

28. The controversial arrest of prominent rebel commander Ahmad al-Nimeh by the jihadi faction Jabhat al-Nusra and the possible involvement of the Yarmouk Army, the largest faction that enjoyed support from Western and Arab countries, is a good example. See, for example, "I'tiqal 'al-N'ameh' Yakhlof Ihtiqanan fi Dar'a wa Ghadaban fi al-Urdun [The Arrest of Nimeh Causes Congestion in Daraa and Anger in Jordan]," Al-Jazeera, May 8, 2014, https://bit.ly/2YE17er.

29. For a more detailed look at the post-2018 military campaign dynamics, see Armenak Tokmajyan, "How Southern Syria Has Been Transformed Into a Regional Powder Keg," *Op. Cit.*; see also Humanitarian Access Team, "Southern Syria Reconciliation Agreement Update," January 2019, https://www.humanitarianaccessteam.org/reports/situation-reports/situation-report-southern-syria-reconciliation-agreement-update.

30. Author interview with an activist and journalist from Tafas who was inside Syria until 2018 (via Skype), July 28, 2020; author interview with a lawyer and activist from western parts of Daraa Governorate (via Skype), May 6, 2020.

31. Author interview with an activist and journalist from Tafas who was inside Syria until 2018 *Op. Cit.*; author interview with a journalist from Daraa who was inside Syria until 2018 (via Skype), July 17, 2020.

32. Author interview with a Syrian journalist from Daraa currently in Amman, Jordan (via Skype), June 26, 2020.

33. *Ibid.*

34. Evan Barrett, "Maintaining the U.S. CT Mission in Southern Syria," The Washington Institute for Near East Policy, August 2017, August 28, 2017, https://www.washingtoninstitute.org/policy-analysis/view/maintaining-the-u.s.-counterterrorism-mission-in-southern-syria.

35. Author interview with a former senior civilian public official from Daraa (via Skype), June 8, 2020.

36. Author interview with a Syrian journalist from Daraa currently in Amman, *Op. Cit.*; author interview with an activist and journalist from Tafas who was inside Syria until 2018, *Op. Cit.*

37. Author interview with a Syrian journalist from Daraa currently in Amman, Jordan, *Op. Cit.*

38. Author interview with a former senior civilian public official from Daraa, *Op. Cit.*

39. Author interview with a journalist from Daraa who was inside Syria up until 2018, *Op. Cit.*; author interview with a Syrian journalist from Daraa currently in Amman, Jordan, *Op. Cit.*

40. Author interview with a Syrian civil society leader, Irbid, Jordan, October 30–31, 2019.

41. Author interview with a journalist from Daraa who was inside Syria up until 2018, *Op. Cit.*; author interview with a young member of the Miqdad clan, *Op. Cit.*; author interview with a relative of Ahmad al-Audeh who asked that his location not be identified, March 14, 2020.

42. Author interview with an activist and journalist from Tafas who was inside Syria up until 2018, *Op. Cit.*

43. Author interview with a former senior civilian public official from Daraa, *Op. Cit.*; author interview with an activist and journalist from Tafas who was inside Syria up until 2018, *Op. Cit.*; author interview with a Daraa-born former senior state bureaucrat who worked in Damascus before 2011 and later defected and took part in negotiations with the Russians over the situation in the south of Syria in 2018, Jordan, March 13, 2020.

44. "Shahed … Indimaj 21 Fasilan Thawriyyan bi-Dar'a wa Tashkil (Quwat Shabab al-Sunna) [Watch … 21 Revolutionary Factions Merge in Daraa to

8 THE CENTER GIVES: SOUTHERN SYRIA AND THE RISE OF NEW... 181

Form (The Sunni Youth Forces)]," *Shabab Post*, August 22, 2016, https://bit.ly/31uftj4. In the video Ahmad al-Audeh is not present. Instead, a front man named Colonel Nassim Abu Arra declared the merger. Also, author interview with a Syrian journalist from Daraa currently in Amman, Jordan, *Op. Cit.*; author interview with a journalist from Daraa who was inside Syria up until 2018, *Op. Cit.*

45. Samuel Ramani, "Foreign Policy and Commercial Interests Drive Closer UAE-Syria Ties," Middle East Institute, January 21, 2020, https://www.mei.edu/publications/foreign-policy-and-commercial-interests-drive-closer-uae-syria-ties. See also, Samuel Ramani, "UAE and Russia Find Common Ground on Syria," The Arab Gulf States Institute in Washington, March 11, 2019, https://agsiw.org/uae-and-russia-find-common-ground-on-syria/

46. Author interview with a former senior civilian public official from Daraa, *Op. Cit.*; see also, "Mu'aridun Suriyyun lil 'Quds al-'Arabi': Na'ib Ra'is al-Hay'a al-'Ulya Wara Tajmid Jabahat Dar'a Bida'm Imarati [Syrian Opposition Figures to *Al-Quds al-'Arabi*: The Vice President of the Higher Committee Was Behind the Freezing of the Daraa Front, With Emirati Support]," *Al-Quds Al-'Arabi*, May 25, 2018, https://bit.ly/3fY0MZI.

47. Author interview with a Syrian journalist close to the Syrian regime, Beirut, Lebanon, March, 2020; author interview with a notable from Quneitra living in the western Rural Area of Daraa (via Skype), July 28, 2020. He said "We met with some officers from the Fourth Armored Division. The biggest and strongest part [of the division] is pro-Iranian, but not all. There are some who are not and we reached out to them."; See also, Kirill Semenov, "Russia, Iran in Tug of War Over Syria Military Reform," *Al-Monitor*, June 10, 2019, https://bit.ly/33z76nA; "Lessons from Syrian State's Return to Syria," International Crisis Group, 25 February 2019, https://d2071andvip0wj.cloudfront.net/196-lessons-from-syria_0.pdf, 14.

48. Author interview with a Daraa-born former senior state bureaucrat who defected and who had worked in Damascus before 2011, *Op. Cit.* He observed, "It is logical for Russia to have closer relations with Military Intelligence because its presence [in the south] took place through the Russian Military Police ... there is a direct channel between them." See also, "Ahali Dar'a Yarfa'un Qadayahom lil-Rus ... La Ijaba [The People of Daraa Report Their Issues to the Russians ... No Answer]," *Enab Baladi*, February 24, 2019, https://enabbaladi.net/archives/283570.

49. Author interview with a Syrian journalist close to the Syrian regime, Beirut, Lebanon, *Op. Cit.* Based on interviews, during the month of Ramadan, Iran received permission from the Syrian Ministry of Culture to organize festivals for children around Syria. The Fourth Armored Division pre-

182   A. TOKMAJYAN

vented one such event from taking place in Tartous, "fearing that this would have an [undesired cultural] influence on the Alawite community."

50. For a more detailed description, see Humanitarian Access Team, "Southern Syria Reconciliation Agreement Update," *Op. Cit.*

51. "Ba'da Isa'atihi Lil-Sarout ... Shubban Yabrahun Musawer Wakalet 'SANA' fi Rif Dar'a [After He Had Insulted Sarout ... Young Men Beat the Cameraman of the SANA News Agency in Rural Daraa]," Tajammu' Ahrar Hawran, August 25, 2019, https://www.horanfree.com/?p=4095

52. Author interview with two members of Tajammu' Ahrar Hawran, Irbid, Jordan, March 13, 2020.

53. Walid al-Nofal, "Maqtal Tis'et 'Anaser lil-Quwat al-Hukimiyyah fi Dar'a Yuhaded Bimarhala Hasima Jadida [The Killing of Nine Government Personnel in Daraa Threatens a New Consequential Phase]," *Syria Direct*, May 5, 2020, https://bit.ly/3i9isnk.

54. Armenak Tokmajyan, "A Gathering Storm in Syria's Volatile Southwest?" Carnegie Endowment for International Peace, May 19, 2020, https://carnegie-mec.org/diwan/81830.

55. Adham al-Krad, who was one of the strongest powerbrokers in Daraa Governorate, stated in a video that the people of Daraa didn't want war, but if they were forced into one, they would fight. Adham al-Krad, Facebook post, May 11, 2020, https://www.facebook.com/adham.alkarad.1/videos/580464219249582.

56. Author interview with a civil society leader currently residing in Irbid, Jordan (via Skype), June 1, 2020; author interview with a Syrian journalist from Daraa currently in Amman, *Op. Cit.*

57. "Al-Jihat al-Mukhtassa wa Quwat Hafz al-Nizam Tunhi Halet al-Falatan al-Amni fi al-Sanamayn" [The Concerned Parties and Law Enforcement Forces End the Lawlessness in Sanamayn], SANA, March 3, 2020, https://sana.sy/?p=1116936.

58. See, for example, "Muthaharaat fi Busra al-Sham bi Dar'a lil Tadamun ma' Idlib wa al-Sanamayn" [Protests in Busra al-Sham in Daraa in Solidarity with Idlib and Sanamayn], *Enab Baladi*, March 1, 2020, https://enab-baladi.net/archives/366976.

59. During the tensions in Sanamayn, the opposition arrested 54 regime personnel, who were later released. Author interview with a member of Tajammu' Ahrar Hawran, *Op. Cit.*; see also, Walid al-Nofal, "Clashes in Daraa Evoke Memories of the Start of the Syrian Revolution," *Syria Direct*, March 2, 2020, https://bit.ly/2XCN2xC.

60. Silva Razzouq, "Al-Zu'bi lil Watan: Al-Irhabi al-Subayhi Qaid al-Mulahaqa wa al-Dawleh Lan Tatruk al-Manatiq Ilaty Yastaghiluha al-Irhabiyoun fi Dar'a bi Hatha al-Shakl" [Al-Zu'bi to *Al-Watan*: The Terrorist Subayhi is Being Prosecuted and the State Will Not Allow the Areas Exploited by the

8 THE CENTER GIVES: SOUTHERN SYRIA AND THE RISE OF NEW... 183

Terrorists in Daraa to Remain in the Way That They Are], *Al-Watan*, May 7, 2020, https://www.alwatanonline.com/الزعبي-ل-الوطن-الإرهابي-الصيبي-ق/.

61. "'Amaliyyeh 'Amniyyeh lil-Nizam fi Dar'a Yaquduha Ahad Qadet al-Musalaha ... [A Regime Security Operation Led by One of the Reconciliation Leaders]," *Syria24*, May 18, 2019. https://bit.ly/2CKEGvz; author interview with an activist and journalist from Tafas who was inside Syria until 2018, *Op. Cit.*

62. *Ibid.*

63. Author interview with a relative of 'Abu Zuraiq who is also a former rebel and who asked that his location not be identified (via Skype), June 27, 2020.

64. Mustapha al-Masalima, known as Al-Kasm, has a similar profile as Imad Abu Zuraiq in the sense that he turned from being a rebel to an instrument of the regime. For more information see, "Dar'a: Muhawalat Ightiyal Mutakarira li Mustapha al-Masalima Alazi Tanaqala 'Ala Diff'atay al-Harb [Daraa: Repeated Attempts to Assassinate Mustapha al-Masalima Who Was Active on Both Sides of the War]," *Enab Baladi*, May 23, 2020, https://www.enabbaladi.net/archives/387086.

65. Author interview with a Syrian from Daraa with intimate knowledge of Smer and who chose to remain anonymous (via Skype), June 17, 2020.

66. Author interview with a resident of Inkhil, Syria (via Skype), June 20, 2020; author interview with a former resident of Inkhil currently living in Amman, Jordan (via Skype), June 26, 2020.

67. Author interview with a former Yadouda resident, in rural southwestern Daraa, currently residing in Amman, Jordan (via Skype), November 29, 2019; author interview with a Syrian journalist from Daraa currently in Amman, *Op. Cit.*

68. "Akhiruhom Adham Al-Krad ... Ightiyal 42 Qiyadiyan Sabiqan fi Quwat al-Mu'arada Bi-Dar'a Ba'd Tamuz 2018 [Adham Al-Krad Is the Latest Among Them ... Assassination of 42 Leaders from Daraa's Opposition Forces After July 2018]," *Enab Baladi*, October 15, 2020, https://www.enabbaladi.net/archives/423369.

69. "Ightiyal Qiyadi Mu'ared Barez fi Dar'a Khilal Tawajuhihi ila Dimashq [Assassination of a Prominent Opposition Leader in Daraa As He Was Heading to Damascus]," *Al-Sharq al-Awsat*, October 14, 2020, https://aawsat.com/home/article/2564776/اغتيال-قيادي-معارض-بارز-في-درعا-خلال-توجهه-إلى-دمشق.

70. Walid al-Nofal, "Bi'ajez 'al-Damen' al-Rusi aw Biridah: Ightiyalat Qiyadat al-Mu'arada al-Suriyeh fi Dar'a" [Because of the Shortcomings of Russia's Guarantees or With Its Consent: The Assassination of Syrian Opposition Leaders in Daraa], *Syria Direct*, October 18, 2020, https://syriadirect.org/ar/news/بعجز-الضامن-الروسي-أو-رضاه-تواصل-اغتي/.

71. Author interview with an activist and journalist from Tafas who knew Krad personally and who lived in Syria until 2018, *Op. Cit.*

CHAPTER 9

On the Edge: How Risks from Iraq Have Helped Form Kuwaiti Identity

Bader Al-Saif

Introduction

Border disputes have long characterized the countries of the Arabian Peninsula, thanks to the poorly defined boundaries drawn by foreign powers when they established protectorates there.[1] Whereas newly independent states sought advantageous boundary demarcations to project power, borders were later essential for enhancing security and economic gains while helping to refashion national identities.[2] Only one border conflict momentarily eliminated a state, namely, Iraqi's occupation of Kuwait between August 1990 and February 1991.[3]

Though Kuwait's concern with its northern border is primarily linked to the 1990–1991 occupation, its apprehensions predate that period.

Assistant Professor of History at Kuwait University, where his research focuses on the Gulf and the Arabian Peninsula.

B. Al-Saif (✉)
Kuwait University, Kuwait City, Kuwait
e-mail: bader.alsaif@ku.edu.kw

© The Author(s), under exclusive license to Springer Nature Switzerland AG 2023
M. Yahya (ed.), *How Border Peripheries are Changing the Nature of Arab States*, https://doi.org/10.1007/978-3-031-09187-2_9

185

186   B. AL-SAIF

Only six days after Kuwait became independent in June 1961, Iraq claimed it as Iraqi territory, provoking the country's first crisis.[4] The standoff was resolved in 1963 when Iraq reaffirmed an agreement on borders that had taken place in an exchange of letters with Kuwait in 1923 and 1932. However, Iraq's later invasion showed that Baghdad's territorial ambitions has not been laid to rest.[5]

In 1993, United Nations Security Council Resolution 833 confirmed a long-awaited border demarcation process—one that more tightly defined the delineations of 1923 and 1932—prompting Kuwait's former foreign minister to hail the border as "the best defined in the world."[6] However, the border has not been trouble free. There continues to be disagreement over a number of border issues, while much of the maritime boundary between Kuwait and Iraq remains undefined. These disputes are unlikely to lead to another occupation of Kuwait, but they have marred bilateral relations, posing a challenge to peace and stability.

This history has made the Kuwait-Iraq border, and bilateral relations in general, central to the evolution of Kuwait's national identity and policies.[7] Border relations have shaped Kuwaiti identity in three primary ways. First, because of the loss of sovereignty in 1990–1991, the Kuwaitis' collective sense of belonging to their country has only been reinforced. One way the ruling family has helped to reinforce this impetus is that in times of perceived threats, it has sought to widen its base of support in society. It has done so by reacting positively to popular demands for representation, primarily through the invigoration of a spirited Kuwaiti parliament that remains an anomaly in the Gulf.

A second way that threats from the northern border have impacted on the center is by broadening Kuwaiti national identity. This identity has moved beyond an embrace of the part, namely, the government's and society's tendency before the Iraqi invasion to focus on Kuwait City and its surroundings, to a consideration of the country as a whole, including sparsely populated areas bordering Iraq.[8]

Finally, Kuwait's sensitivity to border insecurity has advanced a third facet of the country's national identity. Because Kuwait's leaders have sought to neutralize outside threats against their vulnerable country, particularly from Iraq, while improving relations with Baghdad for the same purpose, Kuwait has promoted an image of itself as a benign political actor that comes to the aid of its neighbors.[9]

Building on such an approach, Kuwait should aspire to transform its border with Iraq from a place of friction to one that can incubate shared zones of opportunity.[10] The way to do so is for the two countries to more tightly link their security, economic, and cultural ties, transforming their border relationship. This would require that Kuwait and Iraq address the main issues of contention along their border, which in Kuwait's case are impacting the country's sense of self.

A Contentious Border and Kuwaiti Insecurities

The Kuwaiti-Iraqi border relationship continues to be marred by issues that have sustained mutual mistrust, heightening Kuwaiti insecurities with regard to its northern neighbor. These include security breaches, obstacles to cross-border trade and the free flow of individuals, and disagreement over maritime boundaries. However, there has also been progress on several fronts, including cooperation on upgrading Iraqi border crossings and talks over optimizing oil production in the joint oil fields located along the Iraqi-Kuwaiti border.

The Iraqi occupation of Kuwait was the culmination of decades of threats by successive Iraqi governments, which viewed Kuwait as a part of Iraq. Since February 1991, when the Iraqi army was expelled from Kuwaiti territory, the 240-kilometer Kuwaiti-Iraqi border has gone through two phases.[11] The first, between 1991 and 2003, was one of maximum risk during which Saddam Hussein remained in power. Even though Iraq accepted a ceasefire in 1991 and the United Nations' border demarcation in 1993, its behavior did not always reflect these understandings. Iraq violated the terms of the demilitarized border zone in 1993 and sought to intimidate Kuwait yet again in 1994 with a massive buildup of elite Republican Guard units near the border.[12] These actions led to US airstrikes against Iraq or US military reinforcements in Kuwait.[13] Due to the border demarcation, 250 Iraqi farmers living nearby had to evacuate when it became apparent that they had been living on the Kuwaiti side.[14] The United Nations Iraq-Kuwait Observation Mission managed border security, while the United Nations Iraq-Kuwait Boundary Demarcation Commission oversaw the reparations process in Security Council Resolution 899.[15] In turn, Kuwait paid Iraq $220 million through a UN fund to compensate the displaced farmers.[16]

The Baath regime's downfall in 2003 and its aftermath constituted the second phase in border relations after Kuwait's occupation. While the situation improved significantly, sporadic tensions persisted. This period was characterized by security breaches, concerns over cross-border mobility,

188   B. AL-SAIF

and continued disagreements over maritime boundaries. There was also the persistence of an Iraqi narrative, popular among parts of the population, that Kuwait had exploited its relationship with the United States and the United Nations during Iraq's isolation in the 1990s. It had done so to extract better borders and conditions for itself while restricting Iraq's access to the sea. This view was fueled by decades-old messaging in Iraqi education and media outlets. At the same time, Iraqi factions also engaged in criticism of Kuwait to score domestic political points, only compounding apprehensions there toward its former occupier.[17]

The mutual suspicions helped to drive border tensions during this second phase. Some of these were organic, reflecting the concerns of Iraqis living near the border, while others were orchestrated by political parties to advance their interests.[18] The first postwar skirmish took place in July 2005, two years after the Baath's downfall. Kuwait had built a metal barrier on its side of the border to enhance security, but hundreds of Iraqis living nearby, including shepherds, saw this as an infringement on their pastures. They tore down sections of the barrier, threw stones, and fired shots at Kuwaiti border guards. Part of the problem was a lack of effective communication explaining to Iraqis that the UN had rectified border irregularities.[19] Relations markedly improved subsequently, but this failed to prevent some Iraqi politicians from complaining about what they regarded as an unjust border settlement nor did it end breaches of border security.[20]

Tensions resurfaced on the tenth anniversary of the US-led invasion. In March 2013, individuals fired from Iraqi territory at a border maintenance team operating in Kuwait. This represented an escalation from 2005, when the target had been the border barrier. While eyewitnesses reported on what happened, neither Iraqi nor Kuwaiti official accounts mentioned the shooting, reflecting a desire to downplay the incident.[21] Such episodes were recurrent in 2012 and 2017 and included mass demonstrations by Iraqis near the border against perceived Kuwaiti control of Khor Abdullah, the waterway shared by Iraq and Kuwait.[22] Such incidents explained why Kuwait's threat perceptions with respect to Iraq remained high, regardless of what was actually behind the border disturbances.

A second point of contention between Kuwait and Iraq has been their disagreement over maintenance of the border's integrity and facilitation of the free flow of goods and people. Fulfillment of the border demarcation process embodied in Security Council Resolution 833 involved repairing border markers and updating maps according to the latest cartographical methods. That never happened under the Baath nor did a joint Iraqi committee formed to manage and improve the bilateral relationship greatly advance the process.[23]

The limited flow of goods and people between the two countries has also been a factor contributing to Kuwaiti uncertainty about Iraqi intentions. In 2014, Kuwait and Iraq signed a commercial treaty that became effective in 2016, but the volume of their trade still pales in comparison to Iraq's trade with Iran or Turkey.[24] This reflects Kuwait's dependency on hydrocarbons and its modest export capabilities as much as it underlines Iraq's stronger ties with Iran and its other neighbors. Part of the problem is connected to the fact that the two sides have failed to optimize cross-border transportation. In May 2019, Kuwait submitted a proposal to increase the flow of goods by electronically linking the two customs agencies and aligning their capabilities, as well as a draft treaty to create a free-trade zone.[25] However, by summer 2021 it had not yet received a response from the Iraqis. Similarly, bureaucratic obstacles pertaining to visas have hindered the flow of people across the border, including Iraqis traveling to Kuwait and Shiite pilgrims visiting holy sites in Iraq.[26] The two sides have negotiated to remove these impediments, but the results have been limited.

Contributing to the state of affairs on the border is the inadequacy of Iraq's only border crossing with Kuwait at Safwan.[27] This has translated into lower efficiency in terms of maintaining border security and permitting the smooth movement of goods and people. Safwan's long lines, inadequate storage capacity, and delays in lab tests for certain types of imports have made it more difficult for merchants and others to use the crossing in their commercial dealings with Iraq.[28]

Despite the limited movement on other fronts, Iraq did ask Kuwait in 2016 for assistance in upgrading Safwan. This underlined that despite the outstanding border problems between the two countries, there remained a willingness to cooperate on certain issues. Kuwait responded favorably to the Iraqi request. However, since September 2020, when Safwan was excluded from an Iraqi government list of border crossings that needed to be modernized, new doubts arose in Kuwait about whether Iraq was truly interested in improving relations. However, this could have been due simply to the Iraqi government's prioritization of less secure border crossings because of the country's instability.[29]

A desire to make headway has also been visible in the talks between Kuwait and Iraq over shared oil fields spread across their common border—Rumaila on the Iraqi side and Ratqa on the Kuwaiti side. Both states are looking for ways to optimize their oil production. They signed a memorandum of understanding (MOU) in March 2015 asking the British energy consultancy ERC Equipose to prepare a technical study outlining the best way to invest in the joint oil fields. Given the mutual benefits involved, both sides extended the MOU for two years in May 2019, allowing them to prepare a road map for cooperation in 2022.[30]

Such issues are less important, however, than the challenge of finalizing the demarcation of Kuwait's and Iraq's maritime boundaries. When the United Nations began to demarcate the land and sea borders between the two countries, it relied on previous Kuwaiti-Iraqi agreements, namely, correspondence from 1923 and 1932, as well as a memorandum from 1963 that reaffirmed the 1932 agreement. Yet the 1932 agreement did not complete the maritime demarcation, stopping at Point 162, which is located toward the southern end of Khor Abdullah, between Boubyan Island and the tip of Fao Peninsula, leaving much of the 190-kilometer maritime boundary undefined.[31] Agreement over what remained was left for bilateral discussions (Map 9.1).

Complicating matters was an unprecedented escalation that took place between August 2019 and March 2020, when Kuwait and Iraq submitted two letters of protest each to the UN. The Kuwaitis claimed the standoff began when the Iraqis surprised them with a letter sent to the international body. The letter stated that Kuwait was changing the status of maritime boundaries without consulting Iraq by building on Fisht al-Aych, a piece of land located beyond Point 162. The Kuwaitis wondered why Iraq had bypassed a joint committee established to address bilateral issues. Kuwait denied the Iraqi charges, noting it had informed Baghdad. Kuwait saw its action as a legitimate exercise of sovereignty, while Iraq said it would negatively impact future maritime boundary discussions.[32]

Senior officials in Kuwait's Foreign Ministry have attributed the standoff on the maritime boundary and other contentious border issues to several factors. First, a chaotic post-2003 situation in Iraq that has led to instability in the country and the emergence of multiple centers of power vying for control. This has weakened the decision-making process, affecting bilateral relations.

A second reason is the role that Iran plays in Iraqi politics. Iran is under US sanctions and seeks to maintain the preeminent role in Iraq that it built up following the overthrow of the Baath regime. Because Iraq remains Iran's main gateway to the outside, the Iranians want to ensure that

9 ON THE EDGE: HOW RISKS FROM IRAQ HAVE HELPED FORM KUWAITI... 191

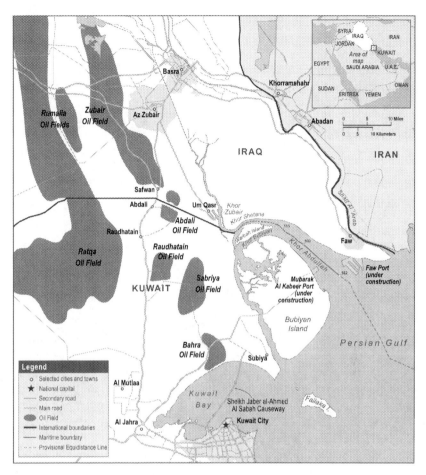

Map 9.1 Kuwait and Iraq's shared waterway

nothing will reduce their dominant position there, which has undermined Iraqi efforts to build a strong relationship with other neighbors such as Kuwait.

A third reason is that relations with Kuwait are not primarily run out of the Iraqi Foreign Ministry. Rather, since the last term of former prime minister Nouri al-Maliki, they have been managed by the prime minister's office.[33] Potentially, this can allow for bold breakthroughs or shield relations with Kuwait from domestic power plays. However, until now it has meant that the relationship has been halted at the prime minister's level, rather than advancing bureaucratically.

Finally, some Iraqi politicians have questioned Kuwait's intentions, undermining steps that they have described as being tantamount to Iraq giving up its "historical rights" to Kuwait.[34] These steps include the UN border demarcation process and an agreement signed in 2012 to ensure the safety of navigation in the Khor Abdullah waterway. Such rhetoric echoes that which preceded the Iraqi invasion of Kuwait, heightening worries in the country.

There are several possible paths for Kuwait and Iraq to come to an agreement over their maritime boundaries. The agreement over Khor Abdullah, like the ability to move forward on joint oil fields and the upgrade of the Safwan border crossing, has reaffirmed a willingness to cooperate and indicated that a return to the violence of the past is not probable today. Yet the complex nature of Iraqi-Kuwaiti border relations has not been limited to contentious border issues. It has also had a profound impact on fundamental outlooks in Kuwait.

Iraq and the Transformation of Kuwaiti National Identity

The Kuwait-Iraq border and Kuwaiti relations with Iraq in general have played a central role in shaping Kuwait's political system, identity, and policies. Iraq's early questioning of Kuwait's existence contributed significantly to producing the country's pluralistic political order. Tensions with Iraq have also influenced how Kuwait perceives itself spatially and figuratively, which is apparent in the way it is addressing the northern border today in the context of the country's national development plan. Finally, the Iraq factor has reinforced Kuwait's foreign and aid strategy. No understanding of how attitudes at the center are formed in Kuwait can be complete without grasping the impact of the periphery on them.

The effect of Iraqi threats against Kuwait, which predate Kuwaiti independence, has been particularly pronounced with regard to the development of Kuwaiti nationalism. King Ghazi of Iraq laid claim to Kuwait in 1938, ignoring the fact that the Al Sabah dynasty had been ruling the emirate since the mid-seventeenth century.[35] Those claims continued in subsequent decades. Days after Kuwaiti independence in 1961, Iraq again

9 ON THE EDGE: HOW RISKS FROM IRAQ HAVE HELPED FORM KUWAITI... 193

claimed Kuwait as its own, prompting Britain and some Arab states to come to its military assistance. Though Kuwait safeguarded its territory and independence, Iraq tapped into Cold War dynamics and succeeded in using Soviet backing to stall Kuwait's recognition at the United Nations for two years, until Baghdad agreed in 1963 to the 1932 border agreement that had been brokered by the British.[36]

The challenges to and momentary loss of the country's sovereignty prompted Kuwait to elaborate various facets of its identity and state policies. There emerged a national perception that Kuwait was a country under constant attack, so that the occupation of 1990–1991 was linked to earlier episodes of conflict between Kuwait and its neighbors—whether the Ottomans in the north before Iraq's creation in 1921 or tribal rivals from the Arabian Peninsula. The sense of collective threat, in turn, helped to consolidate an identity that centered around sacrifice, love of country, and national unity, as Kuwaitis from all backgrounds sought to serve Kuwait during its time of need during the Iraqi occupation.

After liberation, this homegrown solidarity was reinforced by giving an essential role to the legacy of occupation in the national consciousness. The consequences were integrated into educational curriculums, the narratives of those who had suffered or disappeared during the occupation were highlighted in media and other outlets, and museums and parks were established to commemorate the victims of occupation or episodes from the time of the Iraqi presence.[37]

Well before 1991 Iraq had inadvertently helped to provide the impetus for Kuwait's participatory political system.[38] The Iraqi threat after independence accelerated the Kuwaiti leadership's establishment of a system in which power was shared with an active parliament, whose authority was enshrined in the region's first constitution in 1962. The aim was to strengthen the country from within, reinforce national unity, and rally Kuwaitis behind their independent state in ways that could neutralize existential challenges. Moreover, a participatory political system had been a demand of Kuwaitis since the Shura Council of 1921 and the two councils of 1938–1939, the latter early attempts to include people in governance through rudimentary elected legislatures. This continued into the 1950s, especially during the rise of Arab nationalism.

Allowing a relatively free media and cultural environment was another example of how Kuwait maintained an open system. Known as a leading regional cultural hub since the mid-twentieth century, Kuwait promoted theater and the arts, tolerated vibrant newspapers, and published leading pan-Arab magazines such as *Al-Arabi*.[39] This served three goals: it responded to an organic process long in the making that echoed and advanced Kuwait's history of consensual politics; it ensured a domestic consensus to better parry regional threats; and it helped to establish an Arab following for Kuwaiti cultural and media expression in a way that could elicit support in times of need. The pluralistic media environment served as an additional means of bolstering a participatory political system.[40]

If the sense of insecurity emanating from Iraq helped shape a more open system, this was not always true in Kuwaiti politics. When the threat from Iraq receded in the late 1970s, the government suspended several clauses of the constitution, disabling parliament and emptying the political system of its democratic advantages.[41] Domestic factors played a role, with parliamentarians pushing for expanded rights and implementation of the constitution, which provoked pushback from the ruling family and its allies who sought to protect their privileges. But the impact of the Iraqi invasion on decision-making at the center was decisive, as evidenced by the return to parliamentary life in 1992. Kuwait's leadership needed to show the international community that its intervention on Kuwait's behalf was justified because of the country's open political and cultural system. More importantly, given the continuing Iraqi threats after that, a more representative order guaranteed popular buy-in as a safety valve to bolster the system's legitimacy and Kuwaiti sovereignty, as it had during the early 1960s.

A second consequence of how the northern border has affected Kuwaiti decision-making and identity-building is the shift that Iraq induced in Kuwait's view of itself. While the country's national focus had long been centered on the hub of Kuwait City, the heart of Kuwait's political and economic life, the Iraqi occupation brought home that the country's leaders could no longer afford to ignore the border areas from which the danger to its sovereignty had emanated.

In practical terms, the rising importance of the periphery was reflected in Kuwaiti policies and culture. Given that the northern border had become a source of potential danger, it made sense to populate the area, integrate it better with the center, and create a more holistic Kuwaiti identity, one that encompassed both the center and the periphery, urban areas and desert landscapes, and acknowledged the country's tribal and sectarian diversity. As examples of this understanding, farms in the border area of Abdali have become increasingly available for long-term leasing and purchase, when this had been less common previously. This allows Kuwaitis to better connect with lands once deemed to be on the fringes of the country and compensate for Kuwait's deficiency in grazing and agriculture by promoting its greener parts.

There has also been a rising trend of naming businesses, ships, and literary works after northern areas and islands.[42] This has helped to better anchor border areas in the national consciousness. Such an outlook has been most noticeable in the country's national development plan, Kuwait Vision 2035. The late emir, Sabah al-Ahmad Al Sabah, and his late son Nasser Sabah al-Ahmad, a former first deputy prime minister, supported the plan. Its primary aim is to build up and increase the population of the north. The vision statement highlights dimensions of Kuwaiti identity and the image that the country is seeking to project of itself:

> In the 2030s, Kuwait should once again be a preeminent player in the Gulf region. It should be the main international trade, energy and services' hub for the Northern Gulf, serving as gateway to a vast and prosperous northern hinterland. Its strength should be based on its uniquely open, tolerant and diverse society, a strong and well-diversified economy led by the private sector, well-prepared people, and the best possible infrastructure links to the countries around it.[43]

Missing from the statement is the rationale behind developing the northern region. Populating the north and initiating projects there would optimize the use of Kuwaiti land that has long been the subject of dispute with Iraq. It could also create an economic zone that benefits both Iraq and Kuwait, putting to rest Iraqi requests to lease Kuwait's northern islands, which the Iraqis had made prior to 1990.[44] This would enhance Kuwaiti security and bolster the reimagined national identity that includes all segments of society.[45] Therefore, grounding this vision in lands once deemed to be peripheral and risky due to their proximity to Iraq has transformed the view of the periphery into a place of opportunity for Kuwait's growth and economic development. It has also led to investing resources in a string of projects in the north after the announcement of Kuwait Vision 2035 in 2010 and its relaunch for marketing purposes in 2017 as "New Kuwait."

A sample of these projects includes the Al-Mutlaa residential city, the largest housing project ever in Kuwait, which is supposed to lodge 400,000 residents and should be completed in 2023.[46] It will be located only 93 kilometers from the Iraqi border and will serve as an anchor for the remainder of the northern projects and a focal point for the population of the north.

A second project tying together the center and the north is the recently completed $3 billion Sheikh Jaber al-Ahmad Al Sabah Causeway, the fourth longest bridge in the world. The causeway shortens the distance between Kuwait City and the border and will link to a third project in the north, namely, Silk City, which has yet to be built.[47] Silk City is an economic border zone that has been described as Kuwait's future "international trade and financial hub ... its largest marine front project." The project will cover some 250 square kilometers and has an estimated budget of $86 billion.[48]

A fourth project under construction is the massive Mubarak al-Kabir Port on the undeveloped northern island of Boubyan, once claimed by Iraq. The port is an ambitious $3.3 billion project overlooking Khor Abdullah waterway.[49] The project was launched in 2011, and the ambition is to build 24 harbors there. The port is supposed to service Iraq, which has limited access to the sea, and the rest of the northern Gulf region, and will house a free-trade zone and offer rail capacity. However, the project has stirred controversy given its proximity to Iraq and the fact that the Iraqis are building the larger $6 billion Fao Port across from the Mubarak al-Kabir Port, in what promises to be another source of friction and competition between the two states.[50] There is a growing belief in Iraq that Kuwait Vision 2035 is meant to squeeze the Iraqi economy by establishing alternative trade and investment routes in and through Kuwait.[51]

Kuwaiti Foreign Ministry officials, in turn, have responded that Kuwait has sought to cooperate with Iraq in order to better coordinate the work of the two ports. It has provided the environmental impact study of its port to the Iraqi authorities and registered it at the United Nations, while it is still waiting for the same from Iraq for the Fao Port.[52] This is an important step for the integrity of the shared waterway, especially since Fao Port is intended to be larger than Mubarak al-Kabir Port and is being built in shallower waters, which will require massive funding and maintenance costs.[53] As a sign of goodwill, Kuwait canceled one of the harbors it planned to build close to the Iraqi side.[54] Yet the possibility of cooperation is tied to an agreement over the maritime boundary. If this is left unresolved, it may lead to a new crisis between the two countries.

Kuwait needs to exert more efforts to demonstrate the benefit of its northern projects to Iraq, or else the mutually apprehensive attitude will

9 ON THE EDGE: HOW RISKS FROM IRAQ HAVE HELPED FORM KUWAITI...   197

continue. Without Iraq's understanding of what the northern projects entail, or its involvement and buy-in, the value of these projects for Kuwait's security and the stability of border relations will be lessened. Kuwait Vision 2035 proclaims that its attendant projects are aimed at fostering a spirit of openness, tolerance, and entrepreneurship. Yet they also serve other objectives, including reducing tensions and developing the contested areas along the Kuwait-Iraq border. Kuwait's management of its relationship with Iraq and the reinforcement of its national identity have come together through its national development plan.[55] However, the north's development is not the only way the Kuwaiti state has dealt with Iraq, nor is it the only manifestation of Kuwait's evolving national identity.

Indeed, a third way border issues have impacted on Kuwait's identity is that they have led its leaders to project an image of a country both peaceful and altruistic. This has allowed Kuwait to anchor its security in conciliatory policies and Arab mediation efforts that have created goodwill among other states. The result has been an activist Kuwaiti policy of addressing the needs of Arab countries through aid organs established in the 1960s, which include the Kuwait Fund for Arab Economic Development.[56] Kuwait has also traditionally sought to portray itself as a responsible Arab actor by formulating policies that advance pan-Arab causes. There is pragmatism in this position, as being at the center of regional initiatives allows the country to more easily fend off potentially antagonistic Iraqi behavior.

Border skirmishes with Iraq continued in the 1970s and 1980s, yet the Iraqis still benefited from Kuwaiti economic aid and loans for development projects. They also benefited from Kuwait financing for their war effort against Iran in 1980–1988. Kuwait regarded post-2003 Iraq as ideal for enhancing its benevolent image and reducing tensions with its northern neighbor, especially as several of its initiatives were directed at areas or towns in southern Iraq. This included, among others, humanitarian aid worth $2 billion, pledged in Madrid at the International Donors Conference for the Reconstruction of Iraq in October 2003; $200 million in 2015 and $176 million in 2016 for educational, health, infrastructure, and humanitarian purposes; and $100 million to the Iraqi health sector in 2017, along with the regular delivery of medical aid and food baskets.[57] In September 2014, Kuwait's efforts in Iraq and elsewhere were recognized by the UN, when it named the country a humanitarian center and its then ruler a humanitarian leader.[58]

These efforts placed Kuwait at the forefront of Arab states helping Iraq, to the extent that the general secretary of Iraq's cabinet announced in February 2018 that "Kuwaiti aid to Iraq equals that given by all Arab states."[59] This was before Kuwait proposed to Iraq that it host, with the World Bank, the Kuwait International Conference for the Reconstruction of Iraq, in February 2018.[60] The conference was expanded to include the United Nations and European Union as cochairs. Seventy-four states and over 2000 companies pledged $32 billion for projects and credit facilities in Iraq.[61] Of the total amount, Kuwait pledged $2 billion—$1 billion in direct investment and $1 billion in loans.[62]

In addition to such support, Kuwait has built hospitals, schools, and a residential city in Iraq.[63] Of special significance is the Umm Qasr residential city proposed as a sign of goodwill when Kuwait asked Iraq to relocate farmers living close to the border after the border's demarcation. Iraq agreed and the project was completed in spring 2021.[64]

Despite such efforts, Kuwait has a long way to go before resolving underlying tensions with Iraq and changing antagonistic Iraqi attitudes toward the country. Kuwait may have garnered allies in the Iraqi political establishment, but it has not effectively persuaded the mass of the population or overturned the negative opinion of some members of parliament who continue to use criticism of Kuwait as a card in their domestic political disputes. That is why Kuwait needs to diversify its tactics by highlighting its projects in Iraq through Iraqi media outlets, pursuing outreach among various Iraqi factions and Iraqis in general, and engaging in educational projects that overturn negative views of Kuwait.

However, until now, instead of diversifying its soft-power approaches, Kuwait's foreign policy overtures have focused on the provision of aid and have remained at the state-to-state level. In 2015, Kuwait accepted an Iraqi request for a two-year delay in paying reparations for its occupation.[65] Kuwait has also supported Iraq's removal from the authority of Chapter VII of the UN Charter, even though it has not yet fulfilled the conditions for doing so. Iraq needed to complete all reparation payments and return property and the remains of Kuwaitis abducted during the occupation to no longer be subjected to sanctions or be seen as a threat to international security.[66] Kuwait was also keen to facilitate a deal in September 2019 between the Gulf Cooperation Council and Iraq to connect the GCC's electricity grid with Iraq's to meet the country's electricity needs.[67] Kuwait's keenness in having Iraq rejoin the Arab fold after years of isolation also became evident when, in 2012, the emir of Kuwait at the time, Sabah al-Ahmad Al Sabah, was the first Gulf leader to visit Iraq and was among the first to recognize the new regime.[68]

Kuwait's relations with Iraq have ebbed and flowed. Unresolved tensions over border-related issues call for a more proactive approach between the two countries. Not only would Kuwait and Iraq gain by exchanging more often and transparently on issues of mutual concern; they could also benefit by pursuing common security, economic, and cultural interests. This can only come about through a networked border, one that would transform the current border from a rigid gateway to a flexible enabler of cooperation.

A networked border entails more than normal bilateral border relations and involves proactive interaction to search for multifaceted ways to enhance the mutual prosperity of states sharing a border. In Kuwait's and Iraq's case such interdependency will not evolve overnight but requires hard work and communication to acknowledge the fears and aspirations of each side. This, in turn, will lead to increased collaboration over a variety of matters. Connecting Iraq to the GCC electricity grid or Kuwait's upgrading of the Iraqi border crossing are examples of the kind of cross-border actions that can benefit both sides, even if there is room for collaborative actions that are far wider in scope.

Increased trade is a major example of this. Several policies could expand the collaboration between Kuwait and Iraq. Swiftly acting upon the Kuwaiti proposal to establish a free-trade zone would be a major step forward. Joint management of the border oil fields is a second measure that Kuwait and Iraq could adopt. Discussions have been smooth when it comes to developing a roadmap in this direction. Taking this further by moving toward shared production would benefit both sides. This stands in stark contrast to viewing these oil fields as a source of tension, as was the case in the period just prior to the 1990 crisis.

Treating the northern Gulf area as a mutually beneficial shared space could be a third pillar of a networked border. It could also lead to much-needed cooperation in maritime trade and security. Some policymakers from both sides have viewed the construction of the other country's port on the Khor Abdullah waterway with suspicion. But Fao and Mubarak Ports need not define a zero-sum relationship. Developing synergies between the ports is much more advisable than engaging in competition that may lead to losses for both ports. Given the existence of shallow waters in Khor Abdullah and the need for regular joint maintenance, integrating some of the two ports' operations makes sense. Ferry services, for instance, could connect the two ports and streamline certain import-export processes, thereby increasing the appeal of both ports to a wider client base. By increasing the stability of the Iraqi-Kuwaiti relationship, such an approach could also accelerate the stalled delimitation of the remaining maritime border.

To increase public support for the idea of a networked border, policy-makers on both sides need to involve average citizens and work toward shifting public perceptions of threat toward cooperation. This, in turn, would encourage initiatives that enhance the border relationship. That may include, for instance, easing the movement of people and advancing joint cultural and educational projects that lure the young, who form the bulk of the population in both countries. Such projects may involve joint theater and drama productions, student exchanges, scholarly working groups, and coauthored curriculums covering sensitive periods in the two countries' history. A networked border will produce mutual benefits and strengthen positive elements of Kuwait's and Iraq's national identity, as well as embolden the countries to adopt farsighted policies.

CONCLUSION: TOWARD A JOINT IDENTITY AND A NETWORKED BORDER

No understanding of Kuwait is complete without considering the impact of borders on the country's national identity and its decision-making. In particular, the Iraq-Kuwait border and bilateral relationship have affected a host of issues, both in the past and present, that have helped define Kuwait's understanding of itself and its formulation of policies. The border with Iraq has been central for Kuwait's leaders. It has helped to mid-wife the country's political system, to integrate the periphery into the state by prompting development of the northern regions, and to shape Kuwait's foreign policy—based on generating regional and international goodwill as a way of limiting tensions with Iraq while also ensuring that countries would align with Kuwait when it was under threat.

Such steps have tended to be reactive, however, a response to the uncertainties inherent in Kuwait's complicated relationship with Iraq. For both countries to gain more from their border, what is needed is a willingness to take the initiative and together imagine innovative ways of exploiting border relations for their mutual profit. Kuwait believes that acting proactively in the northern border area is a matter of national security, while Iraq sees improved ties with its southern neighbor as contributing to reviving an economy that has suffered from years of domestic instability and corruption.

Successfully achieving this requires buy-in from citizens on both sides of the border. Kuwait and Iraq, by integrating their people into efforts to reinforce border cooperation, have a golden opportunity to reshape and upgrade their relations in a sustainable fashion. It took over a decade for Kuwait and Iraq to move away from the legacy of the 1990–1991 occupation; but true normalization and the potential for mutual benefits and prosperity will not occur until the two countries are able to replace that memory with mechanisms of cooperation that can alter the character of their relationship.

NOTES

1. Yoel Guzansky, "Lines Drawn in the Sand: Territorial Disputes and GCC Unity," *The Middle East Journal* 70, no. 4 (Autumn 2016): 543-559; Harry Brown, "The Iraq-Kuwait Boundary Dispute: Historical Background and the UN Decisions of 1992 and 1993," *Boundary and Security Bulletin* 2, no. 3 (1994): 66–80. The boundary brokered by the British when delineating lands between Kuwait and Iraq in the 1932 correspondence is one clear example of a vague boundary. When the British advisor to Iraq, Edmonds, was questioned about the meaning of "a point just south of the latitude of Safwan," he responded with a vague "one mile south of the southernmost tree south of Safwan," which disappeared after the marking by that tree was removed and more trees were planted in that area. See Brown 67–69 for these excerpts of the correspondence. In the 1940s, the British suggested another boundary marker tied to the customs post in Safwan, but that too brought with it differing interpretations.

2. Gwenn Okruhlik and Patrick J. Conge, "The Politics of Border Disputes: On the Arabian Peninsula," *International Journal* 54, no. 2 (Spring 1999): 230–248.

3. Frauke Heard-Bey, "Conflict Resolution and Regional Cooperation: The Role of the Gulf Cooperation Council 1970-2002," *Middle Eastern Studies* 42, no. 2 (March 2006): 199–222.

4. Robert Lowe, "Iraq-Kuwait," in *Border and Territorial Disputes of the World*, 4th edition, edited by Peter Calvert (London: John Harper Publishers, 2004), 470–476. See 470–471 for this reference.

5. Ibid., 471. See also Maymuna Al-Sabah, *Al-Kuwait fi dhill al-Himaya al-Britaniyya: al-Qarn al-'Ishrin* [Kuwait under British Protection: The Twentieth Century], third edition (Kuwait: Matabi' al-Watan, 2000).

202 B. AL-SAIF

6. "Iraq-Kuwait border is one of the best defined in the world—Sheikh," press release, KUNA, August 6, 2005, https://www.kuna.net.kw/ArticlePrintPage.aspx?id=1574622&language=en. For the complete text of UNSC 833 and other related UN resolutions, see Congressional Research Service, *Iraq-Kuwait: United Nations Security Council Resolutions Texts – 1992-2002* (Washington, D.C.: Library of Congress, 2003).
7. Daniel Meier, "Introduction to the Special Issue: Bordering the Middle East," *Geopolitics* 23, no. 3 (2018): 495–405. See page 497 for the "dialectic relationship" between the two.
8. Claire Beaugrand refers to a "spatial imaginary" to explain this phenomenon. She notes that state identity formation was restricted to the city center, while tribal and Islamist voices later on pushed for an expanded identity that went beyond the hub. I add to that idea by showing that the state picked up on this thanks to the tensions with Iraq and moved to an embrace of the whole of Kuwait in its national identity reformulation post-liberation. See Claire Beaugrand, "Borders and Spatial Imaginaries in the Kuwaiti Identity," *Geopolitics* 23, no. 3 (2018): 544–564.
9. "Kuwait's "Exemplary Humanitarian Leadership" has Saved Thousands of Lives, Secretary-General Says at Ceremony Recognizing the Amir of Kuwait," press release, UN, September 9, 2014, https://www.un.org/press/en/2014/sgsm16132.doc.htm; Mara Leichtman, "History and Expansion of Kuwait's Foreign Assistance Policies," Stimson Center, Policy Brief no. 11, August 2017; "Kuwait is Universal Humanitarian Center," press release, Ministry of Awqaf and Islamic Affairs, State of Kuwait, accessed August 25, 2020, http://islam.gov.kw/Pages/en/MeetingsDetails.aspx?meetId=245.
10. Author interview with Mohammed Abulhasan, advisor to the emir of Kuwait and former minister and ambassador to the UN, August 25, 2020. Abulhasan raises the joint identity idea. See Meier, 501, for literature on networked borders. Meier frames it as the most advanced border type after borderlines and borderlands.
11. The most common distance to which sources refer is 240 kilometers, while some speak of 254 kilometers. It may depend on whether parts of maritime boundaries are factored in or not since the latter have not been delimited yet.
12. Art Pine, "US, Iraq Move More Troops Toward Kuwait," *Los Angeles Times*, October 9, 1994, https://www.latimes.com/archives/la-xpm-1994-10-09-mn-48375-story.html; Alfred Prados, "Iraq: Post-War Challenges and US Responses, 1991–98" (Washington, DC: Congressional Research Service, 1999). Iraq mobilized two Republican Guard divisions totaling 64,000 soldiers by the border. Operation Vigilant Warrior was the

9 ON THE EDGE: HOW RISKS FROM IRAQ HAVE HELPED FORM KUWAITI...   203

title the United States gave to its 1994 deployment to counter Saddam Hussein's provocation.

13. Ibid.

14. See page five of Jasem Karam, "The Boundary Dispute between Kuwait and Iraq: an Endless Dilemma," *Digest of Middle East Studies* 14, no. 1 (2005): 1-11; Brown, 8; Hussein Hassouna, "The Kuwait-Iraq Border Problem," in *Iran, Iraq, and the Arab Gulf States*, edited by Joseph Kechichian (NY: Palgrave, 2001), 237–261. Different sources relay different numbers. For example, this piece speaks about 95 Iraqi farms as opposed to 40 farms and 206 residential houses.

15. Repertoire of the Practice of the Security Council, "The Situation Between Iraq and Kuwait," United Nations, https://www.un.org/en/sc/repertoire/93-95/Chapter%208/MIDDLE%20EAST/93-95_8-23-IRAQ%20AND%20KUWAIT.pdf. Pages 969–970 detail the background of UNSC 899 including the process Kuwait will follow to pay Iraqi private citizens compensations for lands and assets that are now under Kuwaiti jurisdiction.

16. J.T. Nguyen, "UN Security Council allows compensation to Iraqi farmers," UPI, March 4, 1994, https://www.upi.com/Archives/1994/03/04/UN-Security-Council-allows-compensation-to-Iraqi-farmers/9845762757200/. It is unclear whether the Iraqi regime distributed these funds to the farmers. The report speaks of Kuwait allowing the farmers to remain until they collect the season's crops.

17. Author interview with Harith Hassan, senior fellow at the Malcolm H. Kerr Carnegie Middle East Center (via WhatsApp call), September 11, 2020; and author interview with Iraqi official at the Ministry of Foreign Affairs (via WhatsApp call), September 25, 2020; Krista Wiegand, *Ending Territorial Disputes: Strategies of Bargaining, Coercive Diplomacy and Settlement* (Athens, GA: University of Georgia Press, 2011), 42–43. Wiegand details how territorial disputes benefit domestic causes or get used as bargaining leverage for other demands such as economic support and better aid conditions. Kuwaiti popular opinion has also held to a narrative of mistrust toward the former Iraqi "occupiers," with some people not distinguishing between Saddam Hussein's regime and Iraqis in general.

18. Author interview with senior Kuwait Ministry of Foreign Affairs officials, Kuwait, September 17 and 20, 2020. Officials requested anonymity as a precondition to speaking freely about the topic. The officials believe certain protests are orchestrated, based on their comparison to previous protests and the coordinated media attention the protests received. Author interview with Waleed al-Nisef, editor-in-chief of *Al-Qabas* newspaper, Kuwait, September 16, 2020.

204   B. AL-SAIF

19. Colin Freeman, "Iraqis Hit Back Over Kuwait Border Grab," *Sunday Telegraph*, July 31, 2005, https://www.telegraph.co.uk/news/world-news/middleeast/iraq/1495219/Iraqis-hit-back-over-Kuwaits-border-grab.html

20. Lillian Frost, "The Iraq-Kuwait Border Issue: A Step in the Right Direction or More Empty Rhetoric?" Stimson, January 7, 2011, https://www.stimson.org/2011/iraq-kuwait-border-issue-step-right-direction-or-more-empty-rhetoric/. The article notes that in "July 2010 … the Iraqi representative to the Arab League, Qays Al-Azzawi, made statements rejecting the UN's demarcation of the Iraq-Kuwait border" prompting Kuwait's protest. Notable Iraqi current and former members of parliament who consistently object to the current Kuwait-Iraq border include Alia Nassif, Aziz Ugaili, Wael Abdul Latif, or current and former officials like Hadi al-Ameri and Mohamed Jaber. For an internal Iraqi discussion on this issue, see "Crisis of Khawr Abd Allah: National Interests or Political Gains," Rawabet Center, February 3, 2017, http://rawabetcenter.com/en/?p=1615.

21. "Gunfire breaks out along Iraq-Kuwait border," Reuters, March 11, 2013, https://www.reuters.com/article/us-kuwait-iraq-border/gunfire-breaks-out-along-iraq-kuwait-border-idUSBRE92A0VS20130311.

22. Nazli Tarzi, "This Land is Ours: Iraqi-Kuwait Tensions Rise in Waterway Row," *Middle East Eye*, February 9, 2017, https://www.middleeasteye.net/news/land-ours-iraqi-kuwait-tensions-rise-waterway-row; Habib Toumi, "Kuwait Moves Security Forces Near Borders with Iraq," *Gulf News*, February 11, 2017, https://gulfnews.com/world/gulf/kuwait/kuwait-moves-security-forces-near-borders-with-iraq-1.1976548.

23. The issue resurfaced in all higher committee meetings, whether between 2014 and 2016 or 2019 per the minutes of meeting agreed by both sides and that detail their proceedings. The minutes respectfully put the onus on the Iraqi side whose official agreement to the process subsequently outlined by the UN remains pending. Kuwait expressed its approval on November 30, 2016, to the plan drawn up jointly by the UN and the Kuwait and Iraq delegations. Kuwait submitted its portion of the fund allocated for the task ($725,000) and is waiting for Iraqis to approve the process. Other than the minutes of meeting, an Iraqi official I interviewed admits to the internal challenges and delays faced by Iraq that keeps it from addressing the border issue with Kuwait. Author interview with Kuwait Foreign Ministry Iraq desk officers, September 20, 2020, quoting one of the desk officers who requested anonymity; Author interview with Mohammed Abulhasan, advisor to the emir of Kuwait and former minister and ambassador to the United Nations, August 25, 2020.

9 ON THE EDGE: HOW RISKS FROM IRAQ HAVE HELPED FORM KUWAITI...   205

24. Trading Economics, "Kuwait Exports to Iraq," Trading Economics, October 2020, https://tradingeconomics.com/kuwait/exports/iraq#:~:text=Kuwait%20exports%20to%20Iraq%20was,updated%20on%20October%20of%202020. Kuwaiti exports to Iraq in 2018 were worth $623.85 million with vehicles occupying the lion's share, while Iran exported to Iraq in five months (March to August) of 2020 alone around $2.4 billion. See Tasnim News Agency, "Iran's Exports to Iraq On Rise: Official," press release, Tasnim News Agency, August 31, 2020, https://www.tasnimnews.com/en/news/2020/08/31/2338641/iran-s-exports-to-iraq-on-rise-official. In 2017, Iran exports to Iraq were $6.43 billion, "Iran exports to Iraq," *Trading Economics*, October 2020, https://tradingeconomics.com/iran/exports/iraq#:~:text=Iran%20exports%20to%20Iraq%20was,COMTRADE%20database%20on%20international%20trade. Turkish exports to Iraq were at $8.35 billion in 2018, "Turkey Exports to Iraq," *Trading Economics*, October 2020, https://tradingeconomics.com/turkey/exports/iraq.

25. Minutes of Meeting, Kuwait-Iraq Seventh Higher Joint Committee, Kuwait, May 11–12, 2019, p. 15.

26. Minutes of Meeting, Iraq-Kuwait Sixth Higher Joint Committee, Baghdad, December 27–28, 2016, item 19, p. 10; Author interview with Kuwait Foreign Ministry Iraq desk officers, September 20, 2020, and author interview with senior officials at the ministry, September 17, 2020. There is a difference in opinion over coordinating the entry of pilgrims between a collective visa scheme (Iraq) versus individual visas (Kuwait). This contrasts with Kuwait's open access policy with its Gulf Cooperation Council neighbors. The officials with whom I spoke cite Kuwait's reluctance toward such an opening given the legacy of the occupation and the chaotic security situation in Iraq. That said, there are 9000 Iraqis living in Kuwait according to the Iraq desk officers.

27. Author interview with Kuwait Foreign Ministry Iraq desk officers, September 20, 2020, referencing feedback received from visitors on status of Safwan.

28. Ibid.; Minutes of Meeting, Kuwait-Iraq Fifth Higher Joint Committee, Kuwait City, December 21-22, 2015, items 7 and 10, pages 7–10. There was another border crossing by Umm Qasr for US military use.

29. Michael Knights, "Kadhimi's Rolling Reshuffle (Part 2): Protecting Iraq's Economic Institutions and Borders," The Washington Institute, Policy Watch 3378, September 15, 2020. In September 2020, Prime Minister Mustapha al-Kadhimi replaced directors of Umm Qasr Port and assigned protection of that border crossing to the army and upgraded the systems of the border crossings with Iran and Syria.

206   B. AL-SAIF

30. Minutes of Meeting, 2019, p. 14; Minutes of Meeting, 2016, item 4, p. 4; Minutes of Meeting, 2015, item 4, p. 4; "Kuwait, Iraq Ink Contracts to Consider Shared Oilfields," press release, KUNA, August 2, 2019, https://www.kuna.net.kw/ArticleDetails.aspx?id=2812092&language=en.

31. Omar Sultan and Nawal Ghazal, "Preview on the Demarcation Process of the Maritime Boundary Between Iraq and Kuwait by Using GIS and Satellite Image," *Iraqi Journal of Science* 60, no. 1 (2019): 178–188. Numbers cited are from Sultan and Ghazal, 178. It is unclear if this is the distance from Point 162 onwards or the whole maritime border. When I shared this number with Kuwait's Foreign Ministry, they noted that the exact distance left cannot be determined because each state has a claim in mind and it needs to go through negotiations.

32. "Letter dated 7 August 2019 from the Permanent Mission of Iraq to the United Nations addressed to the President of the Security Council," Security Council, distributed 9 August 2019, https://undocs.org/en/S/2019/642; "Letter dated 20 August 2019 from the Permanent Representative of Kuwait to the United Nations addressed to the President of the Security Council," Security Council, August 20, 2019, https://undocs.org/en/S/2019/672; "Identical letters dated 20 January 2020 from the Permanent Representative of Iraq to the United Nations addressed to the Secretary-General and the President of the Security Council," distributed January 21, 2020, Security Council, https://undocs.org/en/S/2020/55; "Identical letters dated 9 March 2020 from the Permanent Representative of Kuwait to the United Nations addressed to the Secretary-General and the President of the Security Council," Security Council, March 12, 2020, https://undocs.org/en/S/2020/190. The letters entered into a lengthy discussion on the proper adjectives to describe the referred to land—whether it is an island (Iraq) or a "naturally occurring area of land that is above water on low tide" (Kuwait). The letters notably diverge to vent about other issues, whether Kuwait raising Iraq's lack of transparency concerning its construction of Fao Port by Khor Abdullah or its environmental impact or Iraq flagging Kuwait's "fait accompli" strategy questioning its push for maritime boundary discussions while its maritime boundaries with Iran have not been determined yet.

33. Author interview with senior officials at the Kuwaiti Foreign Ministry, September 17, 2020. Unlike what the officials noted, Kuwait also enjoys a good standing with several Shiite groups.

34. Peter Sluglett, "The Resilience of a Frontier: Ottoman and Iraqi Claims to Kuwait, 1871–1990," *The International History Review* 24, no. 4 (Dec 2002): 783–816; Jim Horner, "The Iraq-Kuwait Border Dispute," *Journal of Borderland Studies* 7, No. 1 (1992): 1–18; Richard Muir, "The

Iraq-Kuwait Border Dispute: Still a Factor for Instability?" *Asian Affairs* 35, no. 2 (2004): 147–161.

35. Stephen Hemsley Longrigg, "Iraq's 'claim' to Kuwait," *Journal of the Royal Central Asian Society* 48, no. 3–4 (1961): 309–311; Peter Sluglett, "The Resilience of a Frontier: Ottoman and Iraqi Claims to Kuwait, 1871–1990," *The International History Review* 24, no. 4 (Dec. 2002): 783–816. Much literature has come out debunking this argument. The rule of the Al Sabah was conventionally known to start in the mid-eighteenth century (1752), but recent evidence has moved that date up to the mid-seventeenth century with a 1613 entry into Kuwait and with rule given to Al Sabah by consensus later in the century. See Abdullah Al-Hajeri, *Tarikh al-Kuwait: al-Imara wal Dawla* [*The History of Kuwait: The Emirate and the State*] (Kuwait: self-published, 2017), 116–120.

36. For the minutes of the meeting that details the proceedings leading to the USSR veto, see "Application for Membership Kuwait," November 30, 1961, United Nations Library, https://undocs.org/en/S/PV.985.

37. Kuwait Martyrs Office, Amiri Diwan, accessed September 22, 2020, http://new.martyr.com.kw/?lang=en; Al-Qurain Martyrs Museum, "Homepage," Qurain Martyrs Museum, accessed September 22, 2020, https://www.atlasobscura.com/places/al-qurain-martyrs-museum; "Kuwait's Women Martyrs," KUNA, August 1, 2017, https://www.kuna.net.kw/ArticleDetails.aspx?id=2626867&language=en; *Al Shaheed* [Martyrs] Park, "About the Park," *Al Shaheed* Park, accessed September 22, 2020, http://www.alshaheedpark.com/about/; "Kuwait to Honor Oil, Education martyrs With a new Memorial," KUNA, May 3, 2015, https://www.kuna.net.kw/ArticlePrintPage.aspx?id=2439298&language =en; "Education Ministry's Official Calls for Commemorating Kuwait Liberation Martyrs," KUNA, November 2, 2015, https://www.kuna.net. kw/ArticleDetails.aspx?id=2469067&language=en

38. Michael Herb, *The Wages of Oil: Parliaments and Economic Development in Kuwait and the UAE* (Ithaca: Cornell University Press): p. 2 for the quotation and more on the topic on pages 63–66. Scholars who reiterate this view include Ghanim al-Najjar, *Madkhal lil-Tattawur al-Siyasi fi al-Kuwait* [Introduction to Political Development in Kuwait] (Kuwait: Dar Qurtas, 2000); Shafeeq Ghabra, "*Al-Mu'assasat wa al-Tanmiya al-Siyasiyya al-'Arabiyya: Halat al-Kuwait* [Arab Political Institutions and Development: The Case of Kuwait]," *Al-Mustaqbal al-Arabi* 229 (1998): 30–45.

39. Sultan Sooud al-Qassemi, "Toward Abstraction: The Case of Kuwait in the 1960s," in *Taking Shape: Abstraction from the Arab World, 1950s–1980s* (Munich: Hirmer Verlag, Grey Art Gallery NYU, 2020), 107–115; Najla al-Rostamani, "Al Arabi magazine rises to new heights," *Gulf News*, March 15, 2002, https://gulfnews.com/uae/al-arabi-magazine-rises-to-new-

208   B. AL-SAIF

heights-1.380990; "Counting Down Writers, Artists, and Poets of Kuwait's Golden Era," Archisys Global, accessed November 1, 2021, https://archisysglobal.com/blog-post/counting-down-writers-artists-and-poets-of-kuwaits-golden-era/.

40. Kuwait invited and sponsored Arab intellectuals and artists in the process, such as Palestinian cartoonist Naji al-Ali and Egyptian actors and intellectuals such as Zaki Tulaimat and Ahmad Zaki, to name a few. Kuwait's media and cultural scene was a nexus of local and regional voices, further underscoring the impact of Arab nationalism and notable Arab cultural centers on Kuwait.

41. Ghanim Alnajjar, "The Challenges Facing Kuwaiti Democracy," *Middle East Journal* 54, no. 2 (Spring 2000): 242–258.

42. Muir, "The Iraq-Kuwait Border Dispute: Still a Factor for Instability?" p. 157.

43. *Ru'yat al-Kuwait 2035 Mullakhas Tanfidhi* [Vision Kuwait 2035 Executive Summary] (Kuwait: Government of Kuwait, 2010): 27; Tony Blair Associates, "Vision Kuwait 2030 Final Report," 41 (unpublished report).

44. Horner, "The Iraq-Kuwait Border Dispute," 10–11.

45. Ibid., 27.

46. New Kuwait, "Projects Follow-up," New Kuwait, accessed September 25, 2020, http://www.newkuwait.gov.kw/followup.aspx. The size of the city and its absorption of 400,000 residents is significant when one realizes that the current number of Kuwaitis is 1.3 million. These projects and the vision as a whole are not without challenges. See Sophie Olver-Ellis, "Building the New Kuwait: Vision 2035 and the Challenge of Diversification," LSE Middle East Center, Paper Series 30, January 2020.

47. "Kuwait's Sheikh Jaber al-Ahmad al-Sabah Causeway opens," *Road Structures*, August 27, 2019, https://www.worldhighways.com/wh10/feature/kuwaits-sheikh-jaber-al-ahmad-al-sabah-causeway-opens.

48. Yasser Mahgoub, "Kuwait Silk City," *World Architecture*, August 19, 2009, https://worldarchitecture.org/architecture-projects/fhnf/kuwait_silk_city-project-pages.html; "The Silk City Project Puts Kuwait on Global Investment Map," KUNA, July 11, 2018, https://www.kuna.net.kw/ArticleDetails.aspx?id=2736653&language=en.

49. Different reports offer different budgets for the port, which could be due to rising costs and change orders in later years. For the $3.3 billion figure, see "Major Projects," New Kuwait government portal, accessed April 4, 2021, https://www.newkuwait.gov.kw/r2.aspx.

50. Azhar Al-Rubaie, "Death of Daewoo Director in Iraq's Al Faw Sparks Criminal Probe," The *National*, October 9, 2020, https://www.the-nationalnews.com/world/mena/death-of-daewoo-director-in-iraq-s-al-faw-sparks-criminal-probe-1.1091068; "Mubarak Al-Kabeer Port to Play

Key Role in International Trade—Official," press release, KUNA, November 30, 2019, https://www.kuna.net.kw/ArticleDetails.aspx?id=2838859&language =en; Salam Sarhan, "Iraqi, Kuwaiti ports: From Competition to Partnership," *Arab Weekly*, October 3, 2019, https://thearabweekly. com/iraqi-kuwaiti-ports-competition-partnership; Oxford Business Group, "Kuwait's Seaport Project Boosts Transport Connectivity and Strengthens Partnership," Oxford Business Group—Transport, accessed September 25, 2020, https://oxfordbusinessgroup.com/analysis/ ground-major-seaport-project-boosts-connectivity-and-strengthens-partnerships. For the USD 6 billion figure for Al Faw Port, see "Al Faw – Rice Bowl Rationale?," Port Strategy, February 17, 2020, https://www. portstrategy.com/news101/world/middle-east/ al-faw-rice-bowl-rationale.

51. *"Al-Kadhimi yattahim al-Kuwait bi-tahdid al-wadh' al-Iraqi min khilal muhawalataha bina' Mina Mubarak"* [Kadhimi Accuses Kuwait of Threatening Iraq Through its Attempt to Build Mubarak Port], *Noon News*, September 16, 2020, http://www.non14.net/public/127896. Kadhimi did not mention Kuwait by name but did attack those who stood in the way of building Fao Port, which many saw as a reference to Kuwait. He made this statement while an Iraqi delegation was in Kuwait conducting its follow-up meetings. Aref Mohammad, "Tale of Two Ports Strains Iraq-Kuwait Ties," Reuters, June 29, 2011, https://www.reuters.com/ article/iraq-kuwait-ports/feature-tale-of-two-ports-strains-iraq-kuwait-ties-idUKLDE75O03H20110629. A former minister I interviewed mentioned an exchange he had with a now former Iraqi minister of transport who expressed his opposition to Mubarak Port by promising to pitch a tent in Fao until the latter was built—a way of underlining how important the Iraqi port was for him. This shows the extent of dissatisfaction harbored by some Iraqi politicians toward the Kuwaiti port.

52. Author interview with senior officials at the Kuwaiti Foreign Ministry, September 17, 2020; "Letter dated 7 August 2019 from the Permanent Mission of Iraq to the United Nations addressed to the President of the Security Council," Security Council, distributed August 9, 2019, https:// undocs.org/en/S/2019/642; "Letter dated 20 August 2019 from the Permanent Representative of Kuwait to the United Nations addressed to the President of the Security Council," Security Council, August 20, 2019, https://undocs.org/en/S/2019/672; "Identical letters dated 20 January 2020 from the Permanent Representative of Iraq to the United Nations addressed to the Secretary-General and the President of the Security Council," distributed January 21, 2020, Security Council, https:// undocs.org/en/S/2020/55; "Identical letters dated 9 March 2020 from

210 B. AL-SAIF

the Permanent Representative of Kuwait to the United Nations addressed to the Secretary-General and the President of the Security Council," Security Council, March 12, 2020, https://undocs.org/pdf?symbol=en/S/2020/190.StudyGroup

53. Fao Port is going through various problems that reflect Iraq's endemic corruption and bureaucracy challenges. The port has been standstill because of this. See Azhar al-Rubaie, "Iraq's al-Faw port project's endless delays," *Al-Monitor*, August 18, 2020, https://www.al-monitor.com/pulse/originals/2020/08/iraq-basra-fao-port-persian-gulf.html; Al-Rubaie, "Death of Daewoo Director," The *National*, October 9, 2020, https://www.thenationalnews.com/world/mena/death-of-daewoo-director-in-iraq-s-al-faw-sparks-criminal-probe-1.1091068.

54. This goodwill gesture was mentioned by a senior government official in an interview with the author. It was first announced in 2012 by then-public works minister Fadhel Safar. See Mervat Abduldayim, "*Safar: Istaghnayna 'an al-marhala al-rabi'a fi mina Mubarak* [Safar: [Kuwait] dropped the fourth phase of Mubarak Port," *Al-Watan*, July 5, 2012, http://alwatan.kuwait.tt/articledetails.aspx?id=206191&yearquarter=20123.

55. The state is moving ahead with its northern projects. Its latest government plan indicates ten priority areas that include "the development of the northern zone (islands and Silk City)." See Government Plan, PowerPoint presentation (Kuwait: Government of Kuwait, January 2020): 15.

56. Kuwait Fund for Arab Economic Development, "Partners in Development," Kuwait Fund for Arab Economic Development, accessed September 10, 2020, https://www.kuwait-fund.org/en/web/kfund/home.

57. "Amir heads to Iraq to Strengthen Relations," *Arab Times*, June 18, 2019, https://www.arabtimesonline.com/news/amir-heads-to-iraq-to-strengthen-relations/; "Kuwait Dispatches 15 Tons of Medical Aid to Iraq," Relief Web, January 27, 2017, https://reliefweb.int/report/iraq/kuwait-dispatches-15-tons-medical-aid-iraq; Mara Leichtman, "History and Expansion of Kuwait's Foreign Assistance Policies," Stimson Center, Policy Brief no. 11, August 2017.

58. "Kuwait's 'Exemplary Humanitarian Leadership' has Saved Thousands of Lives, Secretary-General Says at Ceremony Recognizing the Amir of Kuwait," press release, UN, September 9, 2014, https://www.un.org/press/en/2014/sgsm16132.doc.htm; Mara Leichtman, "History and Expansion of Kuwait's Foreign Assistance Policies," Stimson Center, Policy Brief no. 11, August 2017. Kuwait's proactive aid policy stretches back in time to encompass various states and occupies a sizable portion of its GDP (over 1.5 percent target in the development plan and 2.1 percent reported in 2014). See Hessa Alojayan, "Kuwait's Economic Toolkit:

Foreign Aid and the Kuwait Investment Authority," LSE Blogs, November 13, 2015, https://blogs.lse.ac.uk/mec/2015/11/13/kuwaits-economic-toolkit-foreign-aid-the-kuwait-investment-authority/. Kuwait's humanitarian aid to Syria alone and since the eruption of war is $1.9 billion, per Minutes of Meeting, 2019, 8.

59. Alaa Al-Huwaijel, "Kuwait Aid to Iraq Equals Whole Given by All Arab States—Official," press release, Kuwait News Agency, February 4, 2018, https://www.kuna.net.kw/ArticleDetails.aspx?id=2687965&language=en

60. Minutes of Meeting, 2015, 2; Kuwait International Conference for the Reconstruction of Iraq, "About the Summit," Kuwait International Conference for the Reconstruction of Iraq, accessed October 6, 2020, https://kicri.gov.kw/en/.

61. "Kuwait summit promises $30 billion in Iraq reconstruction aid," *DW*, February 14, 2018, https://www.dw.com/en/kuwait-summit-promises-30-billion-in-iraq-reconstruction-aid/a-42586658; "Iraq looks to private sector for post-IS reconstruction," *The New Arab*, February 10, 2018, https://english.alaraby.co.uk/english/news/2018/2/10/iraq-looks-to-private-sector-for-post-is-reconstruction.

62. "Kuwait Pledges $2 billion for Iraq's Reconstruction," *Arabian Business*, February 14, 2018, https://www.arabianbusiness.com/politics-economics/389908-kuwait-pledges-2-billion-for-iraqs-reconstruction. Several Iraqis I interviewed highlight that these are pledges from which they have not benefited yet, while donors claim that the pledges require action from the Iraqi side for them to materialize.

63. These projects were managed by the Kuwait Fund for Economic Development. They include a hospital project for Basra in 2005 ($70 million); 18 schools ($50 million) in 2007; a city in Umm Qasr ($80 million); and support for areas damaged by the so-called Islamic State group ($100 million) in 2017. See Kuwait Fund, "Homepage," https://www.kuwait-fund.org/en/web/kfund/home. "Technical Assistance, Loans, and Aid for the Republic of Iraq - Internal Memos," Kuwait Fund for Arab Economic Development. More recently, Kuwait offered Iraq aid to combat the novel coronavirus pandemic.

64. Author interview with Abdullah al-Musaibeeh, Regional Manager for Arab Countries, Operations Department, Kuwait Fund for Arab Economic Development, September 24, 2020, and June 7, 2021. The project is ready for delivery, and the delay is from Iraq's side related to connecting the complex with electricity. As an example of the challenge of multiple decision-makers in Iraq, the contract to build this complex was signed by 12 persons from Iraq, while 1 person represented the Kuwaiti side, according to Musaibeeh. Per an internal Kuwait Fund memo, the city is laid over

212   B. AL-SAIF

328,750 square meters and consists of 228 two-floor houses (300 square meters), schools, a health clinic, a police station, a mosque, and a mall, along with all infrastructure development work.

65. "Kuwait Approves Iraq War Reparations Payment Delay to 2017," Associated Press, October 28, 2015, https://apnews.com/article/0b990 5da3e4846f2b11ca4853d61efea.

66. "UN recommends bringing Iraq closer to ending 1990s sanctions," Reuters, June 19, 2013, https://www.reuters.com/article/us-iraq-kuwait-un-idUSBRE95I00L20130619. On March 31, 2021, Kuwait's finance minister reported that Iraq has paid back $38.9 billion over 27 years with $2,099,788.324 remaining and expected to be finalized by summer 2022 if the oil price remained at $60 a barrel, at least since the reparations were tied to Iraq's sale of oil. See Fahaad al-Shammari, "*Wazir al-maliya: milyara dollar akhir mustahaqqat al-Kuwait 'ala al-Iraq*" [Finance Minister: $2 billion Are the Last Installments Owed by Iraq to Kuwait], *Al-Qabas*, March 31, 2021, https://alqabas.com/article/5843835-%D9%88%D8%B2%D9%8A%D8%B1-%D8%A7%D9%84%D9%85%D8%A7%D9%84%D9%8A%D8%A9-%D9%81%D9%8A-%D8%B1%D8%AF-%D8%B9%D9%84%D9%89-%D8%B3%D8%A4%D8%A7%D9%84-%D8%A8%D8%B1%D9%84%D9%85%D8%A7%D9%86%D9%8A-%D9%85%D9%84%D9%8A%D8%A7%D8%B1%D8%A7-%D8%AF%D9%88%D9%84%D8%A7%D8%B1-%D8%A2%D8%AE%D8%B1-%D9%85%D8%B3%D8%AA%D8%AD%D9%82%D8%A7%D8%AA-%D8%A7%D9%84%D9%83%D9%88%D9%8A%D8%AA-%D8%B9%D9%84%D9%89-%D8%A7%D9%84%D8%B9%D8%B1%D8%A7%D9%82.

67. Antonino Occhiuto, "What Can Iraq Gain from Kuwait and Saudi Arabia," Italian Institute for International Political Studies, September 4, 2020, https://www.ispionline.it/en/pubblicazione/what-can-iraq-gain-kuwait-and-saudi-arabia-27259. This has been delayed to mid-2022 due to the pandemic and need to complete required infrastructure. "Key GCC-Iraq Electricity Interconnection Delayed to Mid-2022," *Middle East Economic Digest*, February 5, 2021, https://www.mees.com/2021/2/5/power-water/key-gcc-iraq-electricity-interconnection-delayed-to-mid-2022/bce37680-67b8-11eb-9feb-8f773d134d6e.

68. "Sheikh Sabah in Baghdad: Summit Brings Back Cordiality Between Iraq, Kuwait," *Middle East Online*, March 29, 2012, https://middle-east-online.com/en/sheikh-sabah-baghdad-summit-brings-back-cordiality-between-iraq-kuwait.

INDEX[1]

A
Akkar, 63–77
Alawite, 63–65, 68, 71, 74
Algerian War of Independence
    (1954–1962), 18
Al-Kef, 18
Al-Ouenza, 21, 23, 24, 33n2, 38n60
Al-Qaeda in the Arabian Peninsula
    (AQAP), 132, 142, 143, 146,
    147, 151
Al Qaeda in the Islamic Maghreb
    (AQIM), 28, 29
Arabian Peninsula, 133, 147
Arabs, 107, 110, 116
Arab state, 2–4, 9
Assad's Syria, 107

B
Baath, 85, 90–92, 161, 164,
    178n10, 187–190

B (col 2)
Baba Amr, 107, 121, 122
Bakkaria, 23, 36n42
Ben Guerdane, 48, 51, 52, 55
Beylik, 18
Bir El Ater, 21, 23, 33n2, 37n45
Border, 63, 64, 67–74, 85–99
Border demarcation process, 186,
    188, 192
Border issues, 186, 190, 192, 197
Borderland, 17, 23, 26–30, 32, 33,
    36n43, 37n46, 106, 107, 109,
    113, 115, 117–119, 121, 123
Border regions, 1–8
Border security, 187–189
Bourguiba regime, 41
Busra al-Sham, 169, 171, 173

C
Center-periphery relations, 115
Centralization, 98, 99

---

[1] Note: Page numbers followed by 'n' refer to notes.

© The Author(s), under exclusive license to Springer Nature
Switzerland AG 2023
M. Yahya (ed.), *How Border Peripheries are Changing the Nature of
Arab States*, https://doi.org/10.1007/978-3-031-09187-2

213

214 INDEX

Citizenship, 66, 67
Conflict, 3, 5, 6, 9, 10, 87, 94, 97, 98
Crossborder relations, 68

D
Daraa, 121, 159–167, 169–176
Daraa al-Balad, 166, 169, 170, 173
Development, 2–5, 9
Diesel, 20, 21, 34n13, 35n29

E
Economic development, 195, 197
El-Kouif, 23, 38n60

F
Fakhfakh, 48–51
Fiscal crisis, 47
Fuel, 19–21, 34n13, 35n22, 35n28

G
Gasoline, 19–26, 28, 30, 34n12,
    34n13, 34n18, 38n62
Governance, 1, 2, 4, 5, 7, 8, 10, 106,
    107, 109, 110, 113, 115,
    117–120, 122
Government, 64, 72–74, 76, 77

H
Hadramawt, 131–133,
    135–140, 142–151
Hadramawt Tribes Alliance (HTA),
    139, 140, 144, 149, 150
Hadrami Elite Forces (HEF), 143,
    147, 148
Hasakah, 106, 109, 114, 115
Haydra, 23
Houthis, 132, 137, 140, 142,
    144–147, 150

Hybrid governance, 106, 110, 118

I
Identity, 87–90, 93, 98, 99
Illicit networks, 3
Informal economy, 39–41, 44–46,
    48, 51–53
Informal networks, 160–162
Informal ties, 117, 119
Inkhil, 162, 163, 165, 175
Intercommunal relations, 65, 71, 72
Iran, 189, 190, 197
Iraq, 186–190, 192–199
Islamic State, 86, 88, 89, 92–94,
    96–99, 114

J
Jaramana, 107, 110–113, 119, 120
Jihadis, 28–30

K
Kasserine, 18, 21, 23, 24, 37n44
Khedma, 23
Kurdistan, 86, 87, 94, 96
Kurds, 109, 110, 116
Kuwait, 185–199

L
Lebanon, 63–70, 72–77
Local notables, 105, 108, 113, 115,
    118, 119

M
Marginalization, 64, 67, 68
Maritime boundary, 186–188,
    190, 196
M'Daourouche, 21, 33n2
Military, 18, 29–32, 37n53, 38n63

INDEX 215

Military Operations Center (MOC), 166, 170
Militias, 9, 10, 11
Muslim Brotherhood, 160, 170

N
National Dialogue Conference (NDC), 132, 139, 140, 142
National identity, 186, 195, 197, 200
National Liberation Front (FLN/ NLF), 18, 33n4, 135, 136
Nefta, 18
Nonstate actors, 5, 6
Notables, 160, 162–167, 175

O
Oil fields, 189, 190, 192, 199

P
Peripheral areas, 106, 108, 110, 117, 118, 123
Peripheral groups, 87, 95
Peripheral regions, 39, 40, 46, 47, 54
Periphery, 159–161, 166, 172, 176, 192, 194, 195
Popular Front for the Liberation of the Arabian Gulf (PFLOAG), 136
Powerbrokers, 159–161, 163, 165–167, 172–174, 176
Projects, 195–198, 200

Q
Qa'im, 87, 89, 90, 92, 93, 96
Qamishli, 109, 113, 115, 116, 121

R
Regime, 105–123
Russia, 160, 161, 166, 169–174

S
Safwan, 189, 192
Sahel, 41, 52
Saied, Qaïs, 40, 52, 54
Sanamayn, 164, 173–175
Sectarian relations, 65, 72
Security services, 106, 107, 115, 116, 118, 119, 123
Sfax, 41, 43, 52
Sinjar, 85–87, 90, 93–95
Smugglers, 9, 10
Smuggling, 17–24, 26–33, 40, 43–46, 48–50, 52, 64, 66–73, 75–77
Sovereignty, 5–7, 18, 19, 26, 27
Statelessness, 67
Subsidies, 19–22, 34n17, 35n22
Sufi, 133, 143, 148
Sunni, 63–65, 67, 68, 71, 73–75
Syria, 63–65, 67–72, 74–77
Syriacs, 116
Syrian conflict, 64, 66–70, 72, 74, 75, 77
Syrian regime, 68, 71, 73–76

T
Tafas, 169, 170, 173
Tahrib, 23
Tal, 107, 116, 118
Tébessa, 23, 33n2
Territory, 106, 108, 113, 120, 121
Thala, 18
Tijara, 23
Trade, 40, 42–44, 46–48, 51–53, 55, 187, 189, 195, 196, 199

W
Wadi Khaled, 67, 74

Y
Yazidi, 85–87, 90, 93–95, 99